Date Due

BRODART, INC.   Cat. No. 23 233   Printed in U.S.A.

Holy Theatre

Holy Theatre

Ritual and the Avant Garde

CHRISTOPHER INNES

CAMBRIDGE UNIVERSITY PRESS

Cambridge
London   New York   New Rochelle
Melbourne   Sydney

Published by the Press Syndicate of the University of Cambridge
The Pitt Building, Trumpington Street, Cambridge CB2 1RP
32 East 57th Street, New York, NY 10022, USA
296 Beaconsfield Parade, Middle Park, Melbourne 3206, Australia

First published 1981

Printed in the United States of America
Typeset by the Composing Room of Michigan, Inc., Grand Rapids, Michigan
Printed and bound by Vail-Ballou Press, Inc., Binghamton, New York

British Library Cataloguing in Publication Data
Innes, Christopher D
Holy theatre.
1. Drama – History
I. Title
809.2   PN1721   80-41505
ISBN 0 521 22542 6

Contents

Illustrations

Acknowledgments

I SHOULD LIKE to thank the following individuals and institutions for providing illustrative material and for permission to reproduce the various sketches and photographs: Akademie der Künste (West Berlin), Chris J. Arthurs, Agence de Presse Photographique Bernand, Zoë Dominic, Adolf u. Luisa Haeuser-Stiftung, Stadt u. Universitäts-Bibliothek Frankfurt am Main, Ted Hughes, Lindsay Kemp, Lipnitzki-Viollet, Theatermuseum des Institutes für Theaterwissenschaft der Universität Köln, Museum of the Performing Arts, New York Public Library at Lincoln Center, Theatre Museum Collection Victoria and Albert Museum, Max Waldman. The Cambridge University Press has made every attempt to seek permission from the copyright owners of illustrations nos. 1, 4, 28.

I also wish to express my deep appreciation to those who helped me to define the avant garde line of development that I have called 'Holy Theatre' by responding to my questions and providing information: in particular Roger Blin, Richard Schechner, Charles Marowitz, Lindsay Kemp, members of Jean-Louis Barrault's company at the Gare d'Orsay and Karin Bamborough of the National Theatre. In addition I would like to thank Edward Bond for persuading me that, despite similarities in a play like *Early Morning,* his work had no place in this study. My thanks are also due to York University for the research fellowship that allowed me to complete the writing of this book, to Marion Jaeckel for bibliographical assistance, to Ann Saddlemyer for her helpful criticism and to my wife for her unflagging encouragement.

C.I.

Toronto 1979

1   *The politics of primitivism*

Themes and definitions

The starting-point of this enquiry was a simple question. Why were self-styled 'theatre laboratories' or 'centres for international theatre research' producing work that was mythic and ritualistic? An avant garde concentrating on the archaic seems incongruous, even if it is clearly superficial to associate modernity solely with Georges Antheil's 'aeroplane sonata', Corrado Govoni's 'poesie elettriche' or Enrico Prampolini's 'theatre of mechanics'. And yet artists who could hardly be thought of as reactionary or escapist, and critics too, had indeed turned to an ideal of primitive man, whose natural relationship to a mystical and timeless world was claimed with at times embarrassing innocence to be a viable alternative to contemporary civilisation. At the same time it was obviously too simplistic to dismiss this as the recurrence of romantic primitivism that Philip Rahv had described as motivated by a desire to escape from 'the powerhouse' of history, to abrogate 'progress' by a retreat into mythomania, the darker side of which has been only too recently and horrifyingly illuminated by the Jonestown episode of 'revolutionary suicide'. For what looked from one angle like an anti-artistic cult of irrationality and inarticulacy had produced some of the most striking moments in modern drama.

What immediately became obvious was that the question applied to more than any single artistic grouping, with just about the only critical term that could embrace all being 'avant garde'. Unfortunately 'avant garde' needs redefinition, since it has become a ubiquitous label, eclectically applied to any type of art that is anti-traditional in form or incomprehensible. For Marxist critics like Georg Lukács it is synonymous with decadence, a cultural symptom of a particular social condition; for apologists it is the defining imperative in all art of our time, and 'the modern genius is essentially avant-gardistic'.[1]

When coined in the nineteenth century, the term described politically radical artists who believed they were prefiguring social change by revolutionising aesthetics, and it is significant that Bakunin titled the short-lived anarchist journal he published in Switzerland in 1878 *L'Avant-Garde*. The movement we are dealing with is still characterised by a radical political posture and some of its members even describe themselves as anarchists or quote Bakunin. But the military metaphor now seems misleading. True, the avant garde may see themselves as shock troops (taking the shock only too literally as 'shocking' since the surface rationale for much of their work seems little more than *épater les bourgeois*), and they may like to compare themselves to a vanguard whose vision is a transition to some revolutionary future and therefore equally as hostile to artistic tradition, sometimes including the immediately preceding avant garde movement, as to contemporary civilisation. Yet to the observer they appear more like conscientious objectors who have side-stepped into a no-man's-land outside the historical boundaries of the social battlefield.

Consequently the avant garde is usually seen as a whole in terms of what they are against – the rejection of institutions and established artistic conventions or the antagonism towards the public (though the latter is more evident in visual art and poetry than in the theatre which demands an audience) – while any positive programme tends to be dismissed as the exclusive property of isolated and even mutually antagonistic sub-groups. So modern art appears fragmented and sectarian, defined as much by manifestoes as imaginative work and representing the amorphous complexity of post-industrial society in a multiplicity of dynamic but unstable movements focussed on philosophic abstractions. Hence the use of '-isms' to describe them: symbolism, futurism, expressionism, formalism, surrealism.

In fact it could be argued that this apparent fragmentation of modern art, like the view of society itself as fragmented, has gained popular currency precisely because it contradicts contemporary realities, serving as an implicit defence of individualism in an increasingly monolithic era of mass-communications and cultural standardisation. Beneath this misleading emphasis on diversity there is a clearly identifiable unity of purpose and interest (at least in the theatre) which has all the characteristics of a coherent trend, since its principles can be shown to be shared quite independent of direct influence.[2] At the same time one can trace all the network of cross-fertilisation that normally defines a single artistic movement, signalled equally by the continuing interest in a single precursor (Alfred Jarry) or shared vocabulary (for instance 'theatre laboratory'), as by cooperation and imitation.[3] For contemporaries what is central was often obscured by the rhetoric of manifestoes claiming uniqueness for different aspects of the general movement. But from today's perspective shared concerns stand out clearly because they recur. And this recurrence is even more significant since, although it is obviously a response to the ethics of the age, it by no means reflects popularly accepted ideas or the dominant ideological assumptions.

Beneath variations in style and theme there appears a dominant interest in the irrational and primitive, which has two basic and complementary facets: the exploration of dream states or the instinctive and subconscious levels of the psyche, and the quasi-religious focus on myth and magic, the experimentation with ritual and the ritualistic patterning of performance. These form a leitmotif that also finds expression in other related arts, particularly modern dance or early film; and the twin aspects are integrated both by the dubious Jungian concept that all figures of myth are contained in the unconscious as expressions of psychological archetypes, and by the idea that symbolic or mythopoeic thinking precedes language and discursive reason, revealing fundamental aspects of reality that are unknowable by any other means.[4] They are also united as variations of the same aim: to return to man's 'roots' – whether in the psyche or pre-history – which is reflected on a stylistic level by the return to 'original' forms of drama, Dionysian ritual and the mysteries at Eleusis, tribal drama from New Guinea and archaic survivals like the Balinese dance. And it is in light of these qualities that the term coined by Antonin Artaud is so apt: 'the Holy Theatre'. In fact the hallmark of avant garde drama is an aspiration to transcendence, to the spiritual in its widest sense. At the same time, along with anti-materialism and radical politics, Christianity is frequently rejected as the official organ of the social establishment, with the result that the 'holiness' of this theatre is unrecognisable by conventional religious standards or, where the links with religion are closest, is sacrilegious.

This idealisation of the primitive and elemental in theatre, together with the rediscovery and adapting of remote or archaic models, is of course an extension of the medievalism and orientalism of nineteenth-century romanticism. It parallels the borrowings from African sculpture or pre-Columbian Indian artifacts in the visual arts, and like the romantics the avant garde could be characterised (in Friedrich Schlegel's phrase) as 'retrospective prophets'. But as the wide-spread use of a term like 'theatre laboratory' indicates, this is far more than a cult of the superficially exotic and barbaric, since it goes hand in hand with rigorous aesthetic experimentation designed to

advance the technical and scientific progress of the art itself by exploring fundamental questions: 'The questions are: What is a theatre?
What is a play? What is an actor? What is a spectator? What is the
relation between them all? What conditions serve this best?'[5]

In attempting to reconcile these contradictory drives this enquiry
expanded into almost all the theatrical movements that have succes-
sively been labelled as avant garde. But if the intention had been a general survey this study would have included many more names, since it
rapidly became clear that what was revealed could well be counted, in
Matthew Arnold's phrase, as one of the master-currents in the literature of our epoch. However a bird's-eye view tends to be bird-brained
too, and groups like Joe Chaikin's Open Theatre or the Café La Mama
have been omitted because covering their work would only illuminate
elements already discussed with reference to others. Minor figures
ranging from Maurice Béjart to Jorge Lavelli have also been excluded,
as have those whose work, however interesting, is on the fringes of
the movement, like Jérome Savary or Luca Ronconi; while a wide-
ranging movement like expressionism in Germany has been analysed
in the work of a bare few but representative figures. The aim has been
to analyse general principles in specific examples, with the hope that
once the pattern was seen the same qualities, their flaws and advan-
tages, would then become obvious to any one looking at all the others
that have not been mentioned.

A wider problem, of course, has been where to draw the boundaries. In one sense, if ritual is taken to have its roots in social activity,
all theatre could be described as ritualistic. And unfortunately such
syllogistic thinking is far too commonly accepted, so that terms like
'ritual' have become almost meaningless as critical clichés describing
anything and everything non-naturalistic. But this itself is partly because the influence of the avant garde movement is so pervasive. On
one hand it can be traced in an official institution like Vilar's Théâtre
National Populaire, which also searched for 'ceremonial subjects' that
would establish a communion between actors and spectators comparable to the mass-enthusiasm evoked by medieval mysteries. On the
other hand there are rock festivals, where the rhythms and
psychedelic lights urge a similar surrender to the instinctive id that in
the right conditions resembles a Dionysiac revel. The only solution
was to limit the study to the major contours of the movement; to be
provocative rather than encyclopaedic. Consequently although the
primary focus is on the way anthropological descriptions of primitive
or savage rites have influenced the theatre, the obverse – the analysis

of 'ritual' role playing in conventional behaviour patterns by such sociologists as Goffman, which is reflected in plays like Harold Pinter's – has not been included. Similarly, established critical categories have at times been broken up or only one aspect of a playwright's work considered, since this master-current concerns, as it were, only one of the main polarisations in the dramatic field: tragedy. Not the conventional Aristotelian concept of tragedy superimposed on contemporary material, but an entirely new form comparable only in outline. One that has sprung up unrecognised in response to specifically modern, not Greek or Renaissance needs, and evolved almost unconsciously, in strong contrast to those all too deliberate nineteenth-century attempts to create tragedy by imitating past models or following academic prescriptions. Thus only the 'ecstatic' side of expressionism has been discussed, not the satiric or despairing, though both shared the same stylistic traits, and were practised at times by the same artists. Though 'avant garde' is a label that frequently refers to a style, or rather to the determined absence of 'style', we are concerned here more with issues of substance, so this does not pretend to be a study of the avant garde as a whole – which has shown an equal aptitude for comedy or history plays (also in new and untraditional shapes) as for tragedy.

The line of development we are following is broadly that of imagistic and quasi-religious plays or psychodramas: plays which represent archetypes or dreams and use ritualistic structures, substitute visual symbols and sound patterns for verbal communication, or rely on extreme audience participation in an attempt to evoke subliminal responses and tap the subconscious. Of course some of these elements can also be found in what are essentially quite different kinds of plays, and even in drama which is fundamentally antagonistic to this avant garde primitivism. Mythology has held a perennial fascination for major twentieth-century writers from James Joyce and Yeats to Tennessee Williams – so much so that this ought perhaps to make us question our automatic clichés about the agnostic age. But the treatment of myth by more conventional playwrights provides not so much a comparison with the avant garde as a way of defining it by contrast, since in most contemporary traditional drama myth is either used for eminently rational, even anti-mythic ends, or we have the unfortunate but overwhelming impression that the author does not believe in his own material. For Anouilh and Hauptmann myth serves simply as allegorical disguise, allowing the oblique treatment of contemporary themes under a dictatorship that approved 'Classics'

(*Antigone*, 1944/*The House of Atreus*, 1940–4). For Brecht the same Antigone material was useful as a known example from literary history, which could be applied as a distancing frame to underline general issues in a contemporary situation. For Sartre, Giraudoux or Gide myth becomes a concrete example to illustrate essentially abstract and anti-religious intellectual statements, and its value is explicitly as a method of giving philosophic generalisation to a specific dramatic action, since, as Gide noted in his *Journal* for 1932, the interest is in the conflict of ideas, not tragedy. T. S. Eliot indeed used myths to represent the spiritual side of existence, using classical stories as a subliminal structure beneath a surface of drawing-room comedy. But the problem of integrating the two levels proved insurmountable. When mythical figures were given concrete shape, like the Eumenides in *The Family Reunion* (1939), they appeared farcical because of their incongruity in a contemporary naturalistic setting; and his subsequent plays gradually diminished any direct reference to the mythical sub-strata, along with the overt poetic effect of the verse dialogue, to the point where, as he himself admitted, both became invisible. This failure was perhaps inherent in Eliot's essentially intellectual approach. Despite his belief in their universality and the modern tone of his plays, he in fact used myths as an overt anachronism in imposing them as 'a way of controlling, of ordering, of giving a shape and significance' to an apparently incomprehensible present. Quite apart from the dubious rationality of such a process, which is more likely to obscure the real patterns and motives of contemporary history, the process of explaining one thing in terms of something else depends on a complete separation of the two metaphoric poles. So what actually becomes valuable is not the myth *per se* but the fact that it is alien, and inevitably that made it seem artificial. But Eliot at least took his myths seriously, whatever the flaws in his use of them as controlling images. More typical is Anouilh's approach, applying irony to the Sophoclean story through his characterisation of the chorus as an authorial *deus ex machina*, whose comments stress literary artifice and effectively demythologise the tragedy. Alternatively in O'Neill's ponderous *Mourning Becomes Electra* (1932) or Williams' melodramatic *Orpheus Descending* (1957) myth is transformed via vulgarised Freud into psychoanalysis, simultaneously giving interior depth and symbolic inflation to modern characters. Fate becomes subconscious repressions or compulsions, but the link with archetypes destroys the individuality required by the psychology, since the motivation for their actions is external, and what they do is solely determined by the fact that their Greek prototypes did that.

These adaptations of myth are a far cry from avant garde theatre, although the Freudian has a slight resemblance to the exploration of dream states and the subconscious. But Yeats and Cocteau, both of whom have avant garde connections through their respective association with the symbolists and the surrealists, reflect some of the essential elements, though in a form which is literary, even classical, and which lacks any sense of anarchistic protest. Some of Yeats' comments seem to echo exactly the same concerns – 'I have always felt that my work is not drama but the ritual of a lost faith'; 'drama which would give direct expression to reverie, to the speech of the soul with itself'[6] – while his borrowing from Nōh drama is comparable, as is his concept that myth embodies universal and timeless experience in an intensified form. Yet in practice the effect of his work is very different. He uses incantation, but this is primarily to 'call up' a scene 'to the eye of the mind', an appeal to the conscious imagination and not to the subconscious. The poetry is directed to the aesthetic sense rather than liberating irrational energies in the listeners. Ritualised movement is used to create atmosphere, and his central image of the dance that gives physical expression to an invisible spiritual essence tends to stasis. The turning gyre reaches a point of perfect balance 'all whirling at an end, and unity of being perfectly attained'; and even though the rhythm is designed to create a trance effect at the moment when the increasing tempo reaches a crescendo of motionless silence, as at the point of the kiss in his version of *Salome*, *The King of the Great Clocktower* (1935), this is purely passive. Even his stress on the direct communication of spiritual states in a symbolic dance is misleading, since the true result of the stasis and the slow, puppet-like movement underlining the symbolic quality of the figures is to create the gulf of distance that art, for Yeats, must 'hold against a pushing world' and to de-emphasise the physical qualities of drama, allowing the restoration of 'the ancient sovereignty of words'.[7] By contrast avant garde theatre is characterised by the merging of audience and action, by a rejection of language or verbal logic as a primary means of communication; and where the aim is to induce trance states these are active and tend toward convulsion.

In Cocteau's work there is a similar stress on myth and ritualistic incantation, and here it is allied with an attempt to create a physical language for the stage, indeed cast in a variety of typically avant garde forms. He worked with Picasso, Honegger, Diaghilev and

Stravinsky, artists who contributed to the development of a subliminal and mythic approach; and he experimented with masks, the separation of dialogue and action, or the use of verbal rhythms and tones
to communicate, independent of logical meanings. In *The Wedding on
the Eiffel Tower* (*Les Mariés de la Tour Eiffel*, performed by the Swedish
ballet in 1921) silent actors danced the action, while the conscious
thoughts of the characters were reduced to mechanical superficiality
in the mouths of the two human gramophones who spoke all their
words. His adaptation of Sophocles' *Oedipus Rex* (1927) was in Latin,
a language chosen deliberately for its incomprehensibility as well
as its associations with religious ritual, so that the musical qualities of speech formed an 'opera-oratorio' without any interference
from grammatical sense, and again gestures and movements were
highly stylised, since the roles were danced by the Ballets Russes.
Similarly *Roméo et Juliette* (1924) was a 'pretext for a choreographic
production in five acts and twenty-three tableaux', and a hallucinatory effect, strongly emphasising rhythms of movement, was gained
by setting actors in black against a black background, throwing dis-
embodied hands and heads into high relief. Alternatively *The
Double-Headed Eagle* (*L'Aigle à deux têtes*, 1946) experimented with musical structure, interweaving two separately stated thematic motifs in
imitation of a fugue. But at the same time there is almost always a
tendency to undercut and even ridicule these typically avant garde
elements. Cocteau's perennial theme is the nature of poetic inspiration, and this transforms his mythical material into an analysis of the
mythmaking capacities of the artistic temperament, and even (in a
play like *Les Monstres sacrés*, 1940) to dismiss this as the self-
destructive egoism of mythomaniacs. And this ambiguity carries over
onto the technical level, as in *The Wedding on the Eiffel Tower*, where
the 'human phonographs' are intended to have the function both of
'the classic chorus' and of the music-hall *compère* and *commère*, and
the characters were 'built up, enlarged by every device of artifice to a
resemblance of epic proportions'. Not surprisingly, although Cocteau
claimed the play to be 'the plastic expression and embodiment' of
pure poetry, it was received simply as farcical parody. His well-
known definition of a physical theatre, where scenic structures replace the indirect and intellectualised verbal images of traditional
drama, in some ways anticipates Artaud:

I am attempting to substitute a 'poetry of the theatre' for 'poetry in the
theatre.' Poetry in the theatre is a delicate lace, impossible to see at any
distance. Poetry of the theatre should be a coarse lace, a lace of ropes, a ship

at sea. *Les Mariés* can have the frightening appearance of a drop of poetry seen under a microscope. The scenes are linked like the words of a poem.[8]

But as his metaphor indicates, the result in his plays is purely lyrical spectacle, pictorially pleasing and in no sense either tragic or the expression of a coherent artistic approach.[9]

In short, what the examples of Yeats and Cocteau demonstrate is that the use of typically avant garde techniques does not by itself qualify a dramatist for the movement – that the mainstream of the avant garde is not simply defined by shared stylistic qualities, though these may be what is most immediately obvious: rather, that the avant garde is essentially a philosophical grouping. Whatever the dramatic achievements of Yeats and Cocteau, the essential quality of their work and its aesthetic attitude is alien to the anarchic primitivism of the avant garde. Ultimately they are concerned with the traditionally poetic even with neo-classical forms of harmony that implicitly serve to preserve the *status quo*, while the avant garde search is for ways of tapping the sources of poetic instinct for politically radical aims.

Bakunin versus Bali

The identifying signature of avant garde art, all the way back to Bakunin and his anarchist journal *L'Avant-Garde* in 1878, has been an unremitting hostility to contemporary civilisation. And its most obvious aspect has been negative: the rejection of social organisation and artistic conventions, aesthetic values and materialistic ideals, the bourgeoisie, syntactical structure and logic. But, in theatre at least, this nihilism has taken two positive and highly productive forms, apparently contradictory but actually complementary. On the one hand there is the transformation of the theatre into a laboratory for exploring fundamental questions about the nature of performance and the relationship between actor and audience. On the other, primitivism in various shapes: the exploitation of irrationality, the exploration of dream states, the borrowing of archaic dramatic models, mythological material or tribal rituals. What unites the scientific with the quasi-mythical is that stripping down drama to the naked actor on a bare stage also ultimately leads to an interior focus on the psyche and to experiments with subliminal or direct physical communication. Both are returning to the 'roots' of theatre, whether in its primitive origins or by divesting it of scenic or illusionistic 'accretions', as much as to the psychological or prehistoric 'roots' of man.

This atavism itself is a symptom of the avant garde hostility to modern society and all the artistic forms that reflect its assumptions. The point of borrowing from African sculpture or Balinese dance is that because it is primitive it embodies an alien value scale, just as the point of exalting the unconscious and emotional side of human nature is intended to provide an antidote to a civilisation that almost exclusively emphasises the rational and intellectual. The conviction that bourgeois society destroys the artistic individual led expressionists like Toller, surrealists like Breton or absurdists like Adamov to join the communists. Quite rightly, however, their real motives were questioned by the more logical of their fellow party workers, since in the totalitarian state they were committed to their artistic approach would be impossible, as the suicide of Mayakovsky had already demonstrated – and it was exactly the same conviction that also led Artaud to describe the 'social suicide' of Van Gogh as a prototype for the modern artist and to define an incoherent scream of protest as the official theme of the avant garde. From another angle Artaud's statement might seem completely apolitical, just as primitivism could be seen simply as escapism, or the value put on the subconscious as a retreat from reality. Indeed the misconception that ritualistic, mythical theatre and political theatre are mutually exclusive opposites – epitomised in the Tynan/Ionesco controversy (*The Observer*, 1958) – is far too commonly accepted. Perhaps this is because at its extreme the avant garde repudiation of society either harks back to a 'mystic in the state of savagery' stance (as Claudel tellingly described Rimbaud) or alternatively expresses itself obliquely in a movement towards abstraction which, in defining itself as 'anti-theatre', rejects thematic meanings, logical structures and anything that might be identified as an ideological position or 'message'. This tends to be justified – misleadingly and paradoxically – as 'theatre of pure form' (Witkiewicz, 1921) or drama 'that cannot serve any other kind of truth but its own' and therefore has the sole function of revealing 'the fundamental laws of [dramatic] construction' (Ionesco, *The Observer*, 1958). On one level such claims are an attempt to align the stage with advances in other art forms. As the expressionist director Jessner put it: 'Just as there is a pure (absolute) music and a pure (absolute) painting, we must have pure theatre.'[10] But emphasising stylistic exploration at the expense of statement does not really rule out commitment, despite avant garde statements dismissing any drama that is 'fixated on politics' by insisting that the most advanced phenomena are neither literary nor political, but formal. If the middle of the twentieth century is going to be remembered, it will be for the ensembles of the Living Theatre, the Open Theatre, Café la Mama and Grotowski, whose common factor is a physical, unnaturalistic theatre-language, spiritually revolutionary and standing in opposition to . . . psychological realism, Aristotelian time structure.[11]

Leaving aside the incorrect assertion that ideological commitment rules out stylistic advances, which is clearly contradicted by the work of ideological artists like Bertolt Brecht or Peter Weiss, what is significant is the stress on spiritual revolution. In the conventional Marxist view, Brecht's *Man is Man* being a representative example, man's nature is determined by environmental conditions, and therefore social change must precede any alteration in consciousness. The avant garde reverses the process, seeing a fundamental change in human nature as the prerequisite for social alteration. 'Our craft is the possibility of changing ourselves, and thus changing society', and 'the ambition to make theatre into ritual is nothing other than a wish to make performance efficacious, to use [theatrical] events to change people'.[12]

Naturally in light of this political intention, the most appropriate – and in fact the most frequently used – ritual forms were the 'rites of passage', analysed by anthropologists like Van Gennep as early as 1908. The basic pattern here is the separation of participants from their previous environment, frequently through sensory deprivation and disorientation; an action that symbolises a change in their nature, and their physical integration into a new group. And recognition of this type of ritual is the key to understanding the treatment of the audience in Grotowski's 'paratheatrical' projects or the Living Theatre.

This borrowing of ritual forms to manipulate the audience is what distinguishes avant garde aims most clearly from social or politically committed drama. Both kinds of theatre may repudiate existing social conditions and work for change. But commitment uses logical structures, whether 'dialectical' as in Brecht or the conventional cause-and-effect of Bernard Shaw, since its aim is to promote a future programme (class revolution/eugenics) through a conscious awareness of specific issues. Shaw's desire for 'a pit of philosophers' is as typical as Brecht's attempts to instill the 'smoking-observing' attitude of 'experts' in his audience, and emotional responses are secondary, evoked only as a technique of positive reinforcement for the intellectual message. The essence of a rite of passage, by contrast, is that it requires physical and emotional involvement in a present action, and seeks to change the nature of the participants directly by irrational, often highly disturbing means: 'In philosophical terms, initiation is equivalent to a basic change in existential condition; the novice emerges from his ordeal endowed with a totally different being from that which he possessed before his initiation; he has become *another.*'[13]

This may seem an unrealistic expectation for the modern theatre with an audience who are not only self-aware but aware of the make-believe and pretence inherent in stage performance. Yet, on one hand, in the political sphere images are all too often taken for reality, and the concept of a ceremonial action changing one's existential nature is the basis of the major surviving rituals of our secularised society. Baptism literally gives anonymous babies a spiritual and social identity, a name and a place in the group; marriage transforms two individuals into 'one flesh' legally as well as figuratively; the funeral service marks the transition from mortal clay to an unknown spiritual state. On the other hand there are still existing models in certain primitive cultures which offer a graphic demonstration of tantalising possibilities by not only presenting ritual in what is clearly a form of theatre, but by apparently inducing a change in the participants that is not merely symbolic but actual. The best-documented example is the Balinese dance drama, and it is no coincidence that this was the model Artaud chose for his ideal theatre after seeing a single performance by a Balinese troupe in 1931. Although there is no record of the details of that performance, if it corresponded to Margaret Mead's pathbreaking anthropological film of *Trance and Dance in Bali*, shot only six years later, it epitomised many of the qualities that the expressionists and surrealists had been working towards, but in an authentic mythic and ritual form. As such it was a logical extension of the experimentation that Artaud had already begun in his Théâtre Alfred Jarry.

The film records the dramatised re-enaction of a myth. Masked actors represent supernatural beings, a hieratically stylised dragon and a nightmarish but grotesquely human witch, whose conflict symbolises a quintessential spiritual conflict – the protective deity, which is the principle of life itself, against chaos, night and death in the form of the plague (the image that Artaud took to define the ideal effect of his theatre). This clash of symbols is the centre of the drama, and the two symbolic forces are the only characters with prescribed speeches.

1(a) Balinese Maiden's Chorus: formalised postures & archaic gestures.

1(b) Balinese dancers in different degrees of trance, tension & invulnerability. Note the force needed to bend the kris and the use of incense.

But the focus of the performance is on the choruses of warriors and maidens, who stand for the human population. They are unmasked, wear traditional folk dress rather than 'costumes', and their dances have been elaborated during the annual repetition of the spectacle until these form the theatrical action, while the original sacred play is reduced to a thematic prologue defining the issues at stake. The climax of their dance is psychological rather than dramatic. It is marked by a shift from acted-out pretence to actuality at the point where the dancers enter a state of trance and turn the swords, with which they had unsuccessfully (in dramatic terms) attempted to attack the witch, against their own breasts. So although unable to kill death itself in the symbol of the witch, they achieve victory by the dominance of spirit over body in proving their flesh (in reality) invulnerable to the razor-sharp sword points they thrust and stab against themselves.

Artaud was correct in describing all the elements of the Balinese performance he witnessed as 'calculated': 'Nothing is left to chance or personal initiative... everything is thus regulated and impersonal; not a movement of the muscles, not the rolling of an eye but seem to belong to a kind of reflective mathematics which controls everything and by means of which everything happens.'[14] But he was quite wrong in attributing this to 'the absolute preponderance of the director (*metteur en scène*) whose creative power *eliminates words*'.[15] Each step in the dance, bend of the torso, toss of the hair or flex of the fingers, like the flattening of individuality in the dancers' facial rigidity, are as fixed by custom and prescribed by immemorial tradition as the sequence of events in the mythical history. Postures and formalised hand attitudes found in the dancing figures of twelfth-century Hindu–Javanese religious monuments are still retained with amazing precision, and these are clearly archaic survivals not consciously adopted forms. Apart from shading the eyes with the hand, fingers curled back and body drooping to indicate despair, or first and second fingers pointing at the end of a rigidly extended arm to embody anger, few of the gestures have dramatic meaning. On one level, like the hypnotic monotone musical accompaniment with its strongly stressed rhythms, all the stylised movements of the dance can be seen as techniques designed to induce the trance which is the justification for the performance. As anthropologists noted, the length of a performance and the number of times sequences of movement are repeated or elaborated in different permutations are determined by the difficulty the dancers find in entering a trance, and by the intensity of what can only be called mass self-hypnosis.[16] Another aspect that observers have commented on is the contagious nature of this delirium. Once one dancer achieves it others succumb almost immediately, and Margaret Mead's film records the instance of an elderly woman in the audience being unwillingly but irresistibly sucked into the trance state, in spite of her earlier declaration that she would not participate.

For Artaud the conjunction of trance and fixed, depersonalised gestures expressed 'the automatism of the liberated unconscious'.[17] Certainly if we are to believe our eyes this type of communicative delirium is real and in no way pretended. Indeed the final event in this particular Balinese performance was a ceremony of exorcism. The dancers apparently could not return to their 'right minds' without the aid of a priest. This in fact is a common element in much primitive drama. The actor becomes 'possessed' by the spirit he impersonates and has to be 'released' from his role by a member of the audience who removes his headdress, his make-up or his mask so that he reverts to his everyday face underneath, or by a priest who burns incense under his nose. Clearly this type of performance draws on areas of the mind that our intellectual western tradition represses or ignores, and – quite apart from discrediting the rationalistic nineteenth-century definition of myth as a fictitous narrative, since those re-enacting a myth have no conscious control over their actions once they have fully entered their 'role' and so do not function as 'storytellers' in any usual sense – its psychological effectiveness made it a natural model for the avant garde.

There are other ways too in which the Balinese model was significant. Like all early dramatic forms, it is closely linked with religion. In addition to its ritual context, being preceded by the ceremonial purification of the dancers as well as followed by exorcism, the type of performance documented by the film was performed in temple precincts on a religious festival – an aspect that Artaud was able to ignore since the performance he attended was in the artificial setting of a colonial exhibition. Hence his assertion that this was a 'purely popular' rather than sacred theatre, which reflected his own opposition to socially ratified religion (and particularly Christianity). More to the point, being an immediately transferrable technique, was a particular use of language. What little dialogue the Balinese spectacle contained was in an archaic tongue that apparently neither performers, audience nor even priests understood. It thus became an incantation, while the only other vocal communication was on the level of pure sound, expressive of general emotional states; and the meaning was carried on a physical level through attitudes which, while not directly allegorical, had an intrinsically symbolic effect through their highly formalised codification.[18] These aspects gave Artaud a working example of the 'concrete language, intended for the senses and independent of speech', which has been such an influential concept in avant garde theatre.

As a re-enactment of myth, however, the Balinese dance represents only one aspect of primitive drama. The other primary form, traditionally dismissed as superstition and only recently recognised as a valid object for analysis through the work of anthropologists, is the shamanistic performance. This typically contains the same rhythmic use of music and a similar stylised level of mime, but the performer is a single expert (the shaman) in contrast to the Balinese model where all members of the social group participate; and it relies more on illusion for its effect, being usually conducted in a darkened space and frequently involving sleight-of-hand or ventriloquism. The basis of the performance is the same; a self-induced trance in which the physical and spiritual worlds are assumed to interpenetrate. But here the functional focus is on the spectator, not the actor. In one general pattern of shamanistic séance the witchdoctor goes into a trance by a sick man's bedside, mimes a journey to the spirit world and a struggle to rescue the invalid's soul, which is assumed to have been stolen by demons and only has to be returned to restore physical health. Obviously in this faith-healing process it is the level of belief that can be generated which is the healing agent, and in a description of a typical performance

the Shaman went further and further into a state of ecstasy, and finally, throwing the drum into the hands of his assistant . . . began the shamanistic dance – a pantomime illustrating how the khargi [spirit guide], accompanied by the group of spirits, rushed on his dangerous journey fulfilling the Shaman's commands . . . Under the hypnotic influence of the shamanistic ecstasy, those present often fell into a state of mystical hallucination, feeling themselves active participants in the Shaman's performance.[19]

Avant garde drama generally shares this kind of quasi-mystical therapeutic aim, whether in the expressionist form of emotional inspiration that supposedly 'transfigured' the spectators so that they 'rose up New Men'; or in Artaud's 'exorcism', which was intended both to strip away the constraints of civilisation, restoring the natural relationship to the spiritual universe, and to purge the audience of violence by indulging them (against all psychiatric principles) in im-

ages of 'gratuitous crime' and cruelty; or in Grotowski's 'paratheatrical' projects and the Living Theatre's political psychotherapy, where
both these approaches are combined.

The attempt to reproduce the effects of ritual theatre helps to explain avant garde elements that might otherwise seem puzzling, such
as the apparent incompatibility of stressing emotional authenticity
and using stylised movement or unnatural gesture to express it. It is
also the attempt to reproduce the primitive focus on spiritual transcendence and the cathartic effect of intense participation that is responsible for the development of those aspects that qualify their work
as a modern form of tragedy. At the same time the aesthetic and
rhetorical nature of ritual action is inherently theatrical, and has
helped to disguise some of the philosophical problems in this return
to 'roots'.

But all this did not happen at once. Initially the avant garde concentrated on adapting symbolic structures from the familiar Christian
tradition or attempting to reproduce dream states. It was really only
in the 'theatre laboratories' of the sixties that models from outside
the European cultural heritage were applied in anything more than a
superficial way, or that ritual was consciously explored in terms of its
reciprocal effect on the actor and onlooker. Nevertheless the principles of these later experiments were already formulated by the
symbolists and expressionists.

Symbolism and Alfred Jarry

From the first this atavistic trend in avant garde drama was very much a child of its time, reflecting a general intellectual climate that had been produced by literary trends earlier in the nineteenth century. The seeds can be found in the late romantic fascination for the 'night-side of nature', out of which came two related positions, both equally antagonistic to the rationalistic and factual documentation of naturalism. One is well represented by Rimbaud's notorious claim that 'One must be a visionary... The poet makes himself a visionary through a long, immense and reasoned derangement of the senses.' The other can be characterised by the symbolist stress on 'suggestive indefiniteness of vague and therefore spiritual effect' (Poe).

In the theatre, the most noticeable effect of symbolist theories was an undramatic progression into abstraction and stasis, a withdrawal from the audience epitomised by the number of plays that followed Maeterlinck's *Pelléas and Mélisande* (1892) in being performed behind gauzes.[1] But certain aspects of their work do anticipate later productive developments. Thematically a great many symbolist plays expressed a religious revival, whether in the traditional terms of Edmond Harancourt's updated mystery play, *La Passion* (performed on Good Friday 1890, in Holy Week 1891 and at Easter 1892), or in the esoteric and occult Babylonian spectacles of Joséphin Péladan's Théâtre de la Rose Croix. Technically their more interesting devices were the attempt to find symbolic 'correspondences' between colours and sounds which led to multi-level, synaesthetic productions, the emphasis on expressive tone and pitch in speaking, rather than on the sense of what was said, and the development of mime to portray psychological states in immediate, physical terms, instead of describing these in dialogue.

The aim was to reach a deeper level of reality than deceptive surface appearances – to embody the inner nature of archetypal man in concrete symbols, in contrast to the naturalistic depiction of

socially defined individuals. The key figure here was Maurice Maeterlinck, whose plays produced at the Théâtre d'Art set the standards
for symbolist theatre. Already in his first play, *The Wicked Princess*
(*La Princesse maligne*, 1889), Maeterlinck concentrated on the atmospheric evocation of subliminal images, using details of the
setting – which were typically indistinct and impressionistic: rust-
ling leaves, moonlit reflections in water, shadows on a wall – solely
for their symoblic value, rather than as representations of a social
context to authenticate the dramatic situation. External reality had
become a psychic projection of the characters. This was the hallmark of symbolist drama, and it reached its fullest expression in
the cavern scene of *Pelléas and Mélisande*. Here Golaud, having caught
Pelléas caressing Mélisande's long blonde tresses, leads him into the
subterranean vaults beneath the castle, and it is immediately clear
that this is a descent into the abysses of the subconscious mind. The
characters are revealed as elements of the psyche, the castle itself as
the intellect, and the relative valuation of conscious versus subconscious is typical. The apparently massive, impregnable edifice of
rationalism is seen as precariously perched on unstable foundations,
an artificial construction beneath which are dark caverns filled with
stagnant pools where 'strange lizards' live. Representing the house of
intellect as a castle stresses its defensive, repressive aspect, but belief
in its permanence can only be maintained by a deliberate refusal to
see what it covers. As Golaud says, implicitly attacking nineteenth-
century rationalistic attitudes:

There are hidden workings here which no one suspects, and the whole castle
will be engulfed one of these nights if we don't watch out. But what can one
do? There's no one who wants to come down here.[2]

This negative value placed on rational structures of thought was
what led the symbolists to attempt to find direct, as opposed to discursive ways of communicating: a language, at once sensual and subliminal – and it is this linking of apparent opposites that has become a
basic characteristic of all avant garde drama, leading directly to Artaud's ideal of 'directly affecting the organism' of the spectator by
creating a 'concrete language, intended for the senses and independent of speech', which would give a 'physical knowledge of images'
in a manner comparable to acupuncture.[3] At first, however, it simply
meant a change of emphasis. The traditional elements of stage production were retained, but the expressive quality of the visual was
emphasised over the verbal. This is not to be confused with the type

of spectacle that dominated the conventional nineteenth-century theatre: a detailed, three-dimensional living picture in a proscenium frame. Instead the setting was reduced to single objects, which would evoke the whole scene by their symbolic resonances, and pure colours chosen for their emotive, not representational value. Following this line, Maeterlinck worked towards a 'theatre of silence', implicitly dismissing the discussion basis of Pineroesque or Ibsenite problem plays. Words (in an argument that strikingly anticipates Samuel Beckett) automatically substitute habitual reactions for existential awareness; verbalising emotion deprives it of authenticity; and 'static drama' replaces external conflict, which by definition is superficial. By the 1920s a school of silence was building on these ideas in plays where characters only speak past each other in overlapping monologues while the action is located and developed on a wordless, sub-textual level that bears little relationship to the direction of the spoken dialogue (Jean-Jacques Bernard). As a result the psychological incomprehensibility of the figures becomes a claim to authenticity: 'We have progressed beyond the explanatory drama... Let the characters speak for themselves, their inconsistencies and illogicalities express their essential humanity. We [authors] have no better claim than anyone else to be able to explain them' (Denys Amiel, 1923). This was a principle that Harold Pinter was later to repeat almost word for word, and the premise that 'the more acute the experience the less articulate the expression' is typical.[4] On another level Maeterlinck's ideal of musically structured gesture and movement, intuitively expressing the nuances of internal states in plastic form, was equally significant; and its influence can be seen in the high development of mime in French theatre, represented by the art of Decroux, Barrault and Marceau.

For critics at the turn of the century the mime artist automatically presented 'a hieratic image of life'. His silence, which led to stylised, exaggerated gestures and the transformation of his face into a mask, gained resonance from its distance to the everyday – and, precisely because 'mute and representing symbols, gave a more powerful impression of [psychological] reality and consequently generated a much more intense emotional field than conventional actors with their vocal imitations'.[5] A natural extension of this interest led the symbolists to explore the possibilities of puppet theatre, which until then had been associated primarily with crude and popular entertainment. Gordon Craig's vision of the ideal actor as an 'übermarionette' was paralleled by Maeterlinck's belief that puppets would be the most suitable performers for his early plays, or by Lugné-Poe's original intention of founding his Théâtre de l'Oeuvre as a puppet theatre. Indeed there is a natural symbolist aspect to marionettes. Their abstraction of the human form represents emotions on a general level, and simplifies a sequence of actions to its essentials. Individual experience never obtrudes, as it inevitably does to some extent with an actor's personality. The particular value of this is that a puppet stands in the same relationship to reality as a national flag does to a nation, so that the complete vision reaches full expression in the spectator's mind and not on the stage – subjectively realised instead of being presented as something objective, external – and in the typical symbolist view 'impersonal puppets, beings of wood and cardboard, possess a pure and mysterious life. Their aspect of truth catches us unawares, disquiets. Their elemental gestures contain the complete expression of human feelings.'[6]

Elements of symbolist staging have become an accepted part of the modern theatre's technical repertoire, and even the theory of 'correspondences' was taken up by the expressionists, as in Kandinsky's scenario *The Yellow Sound* (1909). But most of the general concepts of symbolist drama have dated badly because their viewpoint was basically conventional. Their choice of subject matter tended toward traditional legend and artificial medievalism, while the religious aspect of their work remained within the socially accepted limits of catholicism and their attempts to explore the subconscious appear facile in the light of Freud and Jung. Yet out of this context comes one of the key works of modern drama which has had a decisive influence on avant garde theatre, Alfred Jarry's *Ubu* trilogy, and it is no accident that *Ubu roi* (1896) was originally conceived as a puppet play and first performed by Lugné-Poe's Théâtre de l'Oeuvre, where the same year Jarry had played the role of the Old Man of the Mountains in Lugné-Poe's symbolist production of *Peer Gynt*. At the same time the more obvious superficial aspects of the play, the scatological obscenity, the deliberate crudeness of dialogue and presentation, the grotesque farce, all make a statement that is fundamentally opposed to symbolist principles, as W. B. Yeats, whose French was too limited to understand any of Jarry's deeper intentions, was quick to see:

I go to the first performance of Alfred Jarry's *Ubu roi* . . . and [my friend] explains to me what is happening on the stage. The players are supposed to be dolls, toys, marionettes, and now they are all hopping like wooden frogs, and I can see for myself that the chief personage, who is some kind of King, carries for Sceptre a brush of the kind that we use to clean a [water] closet.

Feeling bound to support the most spirited party, we have shouted for the play, but that night at the Hotel Corneille I am very sad... I say 'After Stéphane Mallarmé, after Paul Verlaine, after Gustav Moreau, after Puvis de Chavannes, after our own verse, after all our subtle colours and nervous rhythm, after the faint mixed tints of Conder, what more is possible? After us the Savage God.'[7]

The uproar at that first performance was so violent after Gémier uttered Ubu's first word, the infamous 'merdre', that the action was brought to a complete halt; and it continued throughout, with catcalls and vociferous arguments between rioting factions in the audience making the dialogue almost entirely inaudible.[8] It is therefore hardly surprising that the initial reactions to the play concentrated on those elements designed to insult the audience's sensibilities: the flouting of moral taboos, the anarchic attack on social institutions or the provocative parody of all the turn-of-the-century thematic and stylistic expectations of serious drama. What primarily came across was the deliberate childishness of plot and characterisation. On this level the monstrous figure of Ubu seems to sum up Jarry's intentions, a grotesquely ugly embodiment of our most despicable instincts, whose involvement in any situation reveals his own amoral and anti-social qualities in all the participants, exposing the rapacity, avarice, self-serving treachery and ingratitude, conceit, cowardice and simple greed that he epitomises to be at the root of all human activities, and particularly those that are conventionally valued as honourable, heroic, altruistic, patriotic, idealistic or in any way socially respected. Thus Ubu reduces kingship to gorging oneself on sausages and wearing an immense hat, economic competition to a kicking, struggling race, social reform to slaughter motivated solely by envious cupidity, battle royal to boastful brawling, or religious faith to fearful superstition manipulated by the unscrupulous for their own benefit. In other words, a figure symbolising all that bourgeois morality condemns is claimed to be representative of the real basis of bourgeois society, which then stands condemned by its own principles.

To attack society on the basis of hypocrisy, even when it aroused vehement indignation on the part of 'right-minded' critics, as with *A Doll's House* or *Ghosts* or Strindberg's naturalistic dramas, was intellectually acceptable. But here the style of presentation undermined the satiric commentary. The characters, 'depersonalised' by masks and grotesque costumes or represented by life-size dressmaker's dummies (there were forty of these, outnumbering the actors), lacked any of the psychological depth associated with serious drama. Their motivations are inconsistent, their inner natures openly expressed in the simplest terms – so removing any suspicion that they might have a three-dimensional core of individuality. And their lines were delivered in an artificial singsong voice with exaggerated articulation. Similarly, instead of a setting which either documented a specific social environment naturalistically, or even served as a symbolic projection of emotional states, Jarry's scene, with its centrepiece of a marble fireplace incongruously set in a landscape where tropical foliage arbitrarily mixed with arctic snow, was explicitly 'supposed to represent Nowhere'. This had a poetry of its own, related both to a primitive like Gaugin and to the later surrealists, but the overall effect hardly corresponded to conventional notions of the poetic. The execution was crude, like Ubu's mask which was obviously cardboard, or the costumes which were deliberately 'shoddy'. The plot is equally paltry. Ubu leads a palace revolution, murders the King of Poland, who is too stupid to take even elementary precautions, and all the royal family except the queen and Bougrelas, the crown prince. The queen promptly dies of 'misfortunes' and the ghost of the dead king demands that Bougrelas avenge him, while Ubu works his way through the population, starting with the aristocracy and moving down through judges and financiers, massacring everyone and expropriating their money. His henchman and co-conspirator, thrown into prison for demanding the reward Ubu had promised him, escapes to Russia and persuades the Tsar to declare war on Ubu, who by now is slaughtering even the peasants for their petty cash. While Ubu marches off fearfully to meet the Russian invasion, his equally replusive wife tries to rob him of the accumulated treasure he has buried in the palace, is driven out by Bougrelas at the head of a popular revolt and flees to Ubu, who has been defeated by the Tsar and attacked by a bear. She pretends to be a supernatural apparition, the archangel Gabriel, to frighten him into forgiving her for stealing his loot, and in the ensuing marital quarrel she is saved from being torn to pieces only by the entry of the pursuing Bougrelas. Knocking down their attackers with the dead bear, the Ubus take to their heels and set sail for France.

In his epigraph to the play Jarry refers to Shakespeare, singled out undoubtedly because the romantics had elevated him to practically divine status as the proponent of heroic individualism, and the action is clearly a farrago of Shakespearean situations: the bloody murder of a good king and the flight of his son from *Macbeth*, the father's ghost and Fortinbras leading a revolt against the palace from *Hamlet*, Buck-

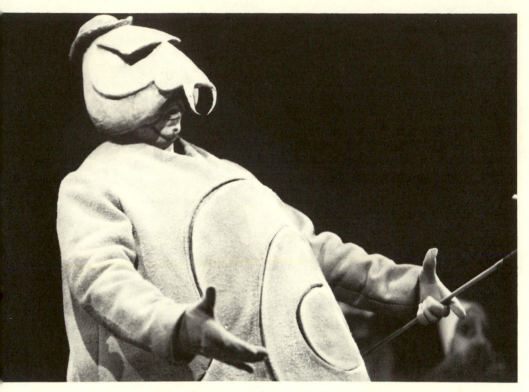

2 Ubu. Grotesque masks & symbolism – satire that surpasses its object.

ingham whose reward for helping a usurper is refused from *Richard III* and the bear from *The Winter's Tale*. At first sight this seems no more than frivolity, literary parody without a point. But it ties in with Jarry's rejection of art as 'a stuffed crocodile' and gains thematic relevance in the context of his exploration of 'the power of the base appetites',[9] since Shakespeare can be seen as representing the ideals of western culture which are thus shown to be fake. If *Ubu roi* undermines the very concept of man's nobility by treating as ludicrous the images that were held up to every schoolboy as models of human as well as dramatic excellence (remembering that Jarry was still at school when he wrote the first version of the play), reducing heroic actions to burlesque and fine sentiments to pastiche, the other plays in the trilogy attack equally basic aspects of 'civilised man'. *Ubu Cuckolded* (*Ubu cocu*, unpublished until 1944) dismisses the moral nature of the individual, with Ubu flushing the toilet on the shapeless figure of his conscience, which he carries around in a suitcase and only consults to discover if the innocent are helpless enough to be victimised without personal danger; while *Ubu Enchained* (*Ubu enchaîné*, published in 1900 but unperformed until 1937) discredits the notion of individuality *per se*. Here it is the national motto of 'liberty, equality, fraternity' itself that is under attack with 'free men' being drilled in 'blind and un-wavering indiscipline', demonstrating their liberty by such consistent disobedience that they can be controlled by simply being ordered to do the opposite of what is required. Individualism is presented as such rigid conformity that paradoxically the only possibility of asserting free will, which by definition must be the opposite of orthodoxy, lies in fol-lowing orders, and Ubu decides to become a slave. He progressively 'promotes' himself to lower and lower forms of servitude, from a domineering servant to a serf who can be whipped, from a gaoler to a galley-slave. Finally, since the whole population emulates him, storming the prisons to win the deepest dungeons for themselves, stealing his fetters and rushing to the Turkish galleys in a wild com-petition for the most absolute form of 'freedom', Ubu is left with no one to act as his master or gaoler, and determines that 'from now on I shall be the slave of my Strumpot', or base instincts and physical appetites, which is indeed the point at which liberty (to indulge one's desires) and slavery (to one's 'lower' nature) become inseparable.

This attack on the fundamental concepts of western civilisation is ac-companied by the satiric denigration of everything bourgeois, ranging from snobbery and artistic salons to rent-collection and academic pedantry. But the satire is curiously unfocussed, and the constant de-scent into nonsense undermines any conventionally serious point Jarry might be making. The nihilism is so anarchic that it discredits itself – and the surprising thing is that recent commentators, like the critics in that first audience who at least had the justification that the uproar prevented any of the play's subtler aspects from coming across, continue to see the primary intention of *Ubu roi* in purely negative protest and shock effect.[10] If this were its real value, Artaud would hardly have named his theatre after Jarry.

As Jarry's friend Apollinaire pointed out, his satire 'operates upon reality in such a way that it totally destroys its object and rises com-pletely above it', becoming a form of poetic vision in which the com-prehensiveness of the negation itself becomes creative.[11] The *Ubu* plays in fact are exercises in Jarry's theory of 'pataphysics', a 'science of imaginary solutions'. This bears much the same relationship to science, the rational way of analysing and describing the world, as Jarry's anti-theatre does to conventional drama. Its premise is that what we perceive as our world is no more than a mental construct, and that therefore there is no true distinction between perception and hallucination. What has the status of reality is simply whatever exerts the most powerful hold on the imagination, and in Jarry's view the accepted laws of physics, being based on observed norms, are 'correlations of . . . accidental data which, reduced to the status of unexceptional exceptions, possess no longer even the virtue of originality'. Obviously these are imaginatively inferior to 'the laws governing exceptions', and pataphysics deals with the particular instead of the general. It also works on the principle of the identity of opposites, defines external form as essence in a true symbolist way, and so becomes a way of describing 'a universe which can be – and perhaps should be – envisaged in the place of the traditional one'.[12] It is in this sense that the staging for *Ubu roi* should be understood, a contradictory synthesis of incongruities, liberating the imagination by the unusual juxtaposition of everyday objects and simultaneously offering an alternative universe in which anything is possible:

Just as a play can be set in Eternity by, say, letting people fire revolvers in the year one thousand or thereabouts, so you will see doors opening onto snow-covered plains under blue skies, mantelpieces with clocks on them swinging open to turn into doorways, and palm trees flourishing at the foot of beds so that little elephants perching on book shelves can graze on them . . . A set which is supposed to represent Nowhere . . . and the action takes place in Poland, a country so legendary, so dismembered that it is well qualified to be this particular Nowhere, or, in terms of a putative Franco-Greek etymology, a distantly interrogative somewhere.[13]

However, Jarry's intention is not simply to present his audience with a surrogate reality, but to force each spectator to imagine his own; and all the elements in this comedy of total warfare, quite apart from their thematic significance, can be seen as hallucinatory techniques. Beneath the crudely insulting and childishly simple surface is a sophisticated manipulation of vision. The inversion of norms, exaggeration and oversimplification undermine our everyday frame of reference, as do the fusion of the inflated and prosaic or the tone of grandiose banality. The scatological obscenity and gratuitous violence are shock effects to make normal reactions seem obsessive or inappropriate. Thus try as we may to apply socially approved feelings to Jarry's mass demolition of characters, who are literally chopped to mincemeat, torn to pieces, stuffed into sewers, impaled or exploded, we can only find the violence and death funny. Such extreme and wholesale slaughter discredits or deadens conventional responses –

particularly if there is no relation between cause and effect, as when one character is chopped in two and both halves continue to function as before, or another's hair is set on fire and his only comment is 'what a night, I've got hair ache'. Similarly, the distortions of perspective in the setting overload the audience's capacity to rationalise the picture presented to them, as does the syllogistic logic demonstrating the identity of opposites (which is particularly obvious in *Ubu Enchained*) or the transformations and multiplications of characters (like Achras and Rebontier in *Ubu Cuckolded* who have a crocodile and monkey as their doubles, while the crocodile, whistling like a steam engine, is defined as a snake).

Where Rimbaud had advocated a 'reasoned derangement of the senses' for the poet, Jarry applies it to the audience, and one of his lighter, non-dramatic essays on 'The surface area of God'[14] provides a clear example of his working method. Logical thought patterns form the wall which must be breached before any level of visionary experience can be evoked, so the weight of satiric humour is brought to bear against the structures of rationalism themselves. Here the rational tools for analysing the physical world – geometry, algebraic equations, symbolic logic – are used to define the dimensions of an abstract symbol, and the resulting confusion of categories has a curious double effect. The scientific approach, with its careful mathematical framework of premise, postulate, demonstration, corollary and definition is made to appear ludicrous, empty pedantry. Paradoxically it also gives an impression of solidity and intellectual coherence to an imaginary construct. In a similar way the conclusion that 'God is the tangential point between zero and infinity' both presents a thesis that a theologian might accept and (punningly) denies the very existence of God. It is precisely the 'reasoned' nature of this 'derangement' which makes it so effective, and the same paradoxical irrationality characterises Jarry's plays. Habitual assumptions about reality and socially learned responses are called into question, cutting the ground from under our mental feet. At the same time our imagination is challenged, both by the extravagance of the dramatic world and by the self-parodying theatricality of the presentation, where single characters stand for a whole army, but puppet qualities and unnatural voices exaggerate their symbolic nature into artificiality, or where placards announce changes of scene, but without any of the unobtrusiveness of Shakespearean staging, being carried in by a man in full evening dress who trots across the stage on the points of his toes to underline the irrelevance of specifying place in a setting that is

'Nowhere'. As Jarry put it in the epigraph to *Ubu Enchained*: 'We shall not have succeeded in demolishing everything unless we demolish the ruins as well. But the only way I can see of doing that is to use them to put up a lot of fine, well-designed buildings.'[15] The 'ruins' stand for traditional concepts, the nationalisms and rationalisms of post-industrial society, and these can only be effectively abolished by re-structuring the bricks into alternate visions. Hence the extra letter in Ubu's notorious opening expletive, which gives an example of Jarry's method in miniature. Transforming 'merde' into 'merdre' makes the familiar strange, the scatologically shocking becomes simultaneously hallucinatory, and (in one of Jarry's typical puns) a fundamental aspect of reality is subtly distorted to challenge and liberate the spectator's imagination.

Jarry's approach is too confused, his techniques, drawn from *grand guignol* puppet theatre, symbolist abstraction and Shakespeare, too diversified for the full impact of his drama to be realised. On the one hand his intention is satiric protest, confronting the public 'like the exaggerating mirror in the stories of Madame Leprince de Beaumont, in which the depraved saw themselves with dragons' bodies, or bulls' horns, or whatever corresponded to their particular vice'. On the other he is trying to create 'an ABSTRACT theatre', with masks replacing the psychological portrayal of an individual by 'the effigy of the CHARACTER' and 'universal gesture' achieving 'essential expression'.[16] The contradictions are too extreme. Ubu is not only an anti-social force capable of devastating the bourgeois *Weltanschauung*, a wish-fulfilment figure destructive to the point of self-destruction – hence Jarry's own identification with his character, signing himself 'Ubu' and speaking in a Ubuesque 'special voice' that reduced the semantic content of his words to nonsense by giving equal weight to each syllable. Ubu also epitomises the qualities of the bourgeoisie, whom Jarry despised. Negative and positive elements are superimposed, self-cancelling. As a result his plays had little immediate effect. After the initial shock, Jarry's work rapidly became accepted as 'art'. He was taken up by Ambroise Vollard, the impressario of symbolist and post-impressionist painting, who popularised Jarry along with Cézanne, Chagall and Odilon Redon as well as Bonnard and Rouault, both of whom illustrated the 'further adventures' of Père Ubu that Vollard wrote; and when Gémier played the role again in 1908 it was 'before a completely calm, one might almost say indifferent audience... neither amused, nor scandalised, nor surprised'.[17] The performance was prefaced by an academic lecture appraising

Jarry's literary significance, the effect was judged to be 'very spiritual' and Gémier planned to found a 'Théâtre Ubu', creating new plays around Jarry's characters. The most dispiriting thing for an artist who aims to *épater les bourgeois* is the capacity of society to absorb irritants, like an oyster seeing dirt thrown into the works only as a potential pearl, and by the 1920s the academic industry had made Jarry's anarchism harmlessly respectable with pedantic essays such as 'Brahma and Ubu, or the historical spirit'.[18] But his true significance lies in the appeal to the irrational and (through the elements of deliberate naivety and the primitive, child's convention in stage presentation) pre-social level of the mind, which was picked up by Artaud and by the 'College of Pataphysics', founded in 1948 and including Eugène Ionesco, Boris Vian and René Clair among its members.

August Strindberg

By the turn of the century another anti-naturalistic movement was taking shape, which shared many of the symbolist premises and in particular the concept of the world as a dynamic projection of the human mind, while avoiding both the Maeterlinckian retreat into lyrical, indefinite stasis and Jarry's extreme of satiric irrationalism. The initial impetus came from Strindberg, whose most influential work after his 'inferno' period of psychological crisis was largely autobiographical and attempted to transcribe subjective experience directly into stage terms.

The key plays were *To Damascus* (1898–1904), *A Dream Play* (1902) and *The Ghost Sonata* (1907), although Strindberg's subjective involvement was strong even in his early naturalistic drama, and already by 1888 in the preface to *Miss Julie* one can see him breaking out of the naturalist format. Here the concept of the individualised character, determined by hereditary attributes and environmental influences, is already in the opening stages of dispersal. People are presented as 'conglomerations of past and present stages of civilization', a fragmentary patchwork of contradictory and transient elements, and referred to as 'souls' not self-aware personalities. The minor figures are already thought of as 'abstract... without individuality', the setting is designed to produce 'unfamiliar perspectives' and the principles of composition are defined by musical analogy instead of as patterns of cause and effect: 'the dialogue wanders, gathering in the opening scenes material which is later picked up, worked over, repeated, expounded and developed like the theme in a

musical composition'.[19] Here Strindberg could still give such elements a naturalistic rationale, but they point straight to the new dramatic form that he developed in *To Damascus* with its unitary characterisation and contrapuntal structure. These qualities can be clearly
seen in the first part of this monumental trilogy of spiritual exploration, the tone of which echoes an early letter of Strindberg's, where
he confesses:

> It seems to me that I am walking about in my sleep, as though fiction and life
> were blended . . . Through much writing my life has become a shadow of life.
> I no longer seem to be treading on earth but rather to be hovering without
> weight in an atmosphere not of air but of darkness . . . all concepts of right,
> wrong, true, false, disappear; and whatever happens, no matter how unusual
> it is, strikes me as quite fitting.[20]

This is repeated in the opening scene by the clearly autobiographical
central figure of the Unknown (or the Stranger), an author who also
doubts whether his life has any more reality than his own writings.
On the surface the dramatic conflict is presented as a Promethean
challenge to God, with the Unknown defying the 'Invisible One',
daring 'unseen powers' to strike him down with a bolt of lightning,
and working to free mankind from 'suffering'. But the sufferings are
in fact psychological repressions and the human beings to be saved,
as well as those characters who represent the 'unseen powers' he
struggles against, are all projections of his own mind. The Lady, for
instance, on one level clearly modelled on Strindberg's wives (Frieda
Uhl in parts I and II, Harriet Bosse in part III), not only represent all
women, the quintessential female – for Strindberg at once redemptive
and destructive of the male spirit, and christened 'Eve' by the Unknown – she is also an integral part of his own psyche. She appears
each time in answer to an unspoken 'call', responding to a subconscious wish of the Unknown who sees her as 'impersonal, nameless';
and the Mother, whom he acknowledges to be only echoing his own
thoughts, tells him that he has made her in his own image. If there is
any solution in the drama it is in this recognition by the Unknown
that his antagonist is an aspect of himself. Other characters clearly
represent alternate or auxiliary egos. Like the Unknown, on his forehead the Beggar carries the scar of a blow from his brother's axe, simultaneously Cain and Abel. Both of them fit the description of a wanted
criminal and, when pallbearers describe the Dead Man in the coffin
they are carrying, he too resembles the Unknown. Finally, in the
central scene, all the figures are refracted yet again in an asylum
where the Unknown recognises the Beggar, the Lady and the Mother

in different lunatics, and himself in the figure of a megalomaniac who believes himself to be Caesar. In this world of self-reflections any extension is merely a regression into more and more distorted mirror images, from the Beggar's appearance, which is 'very strange', to the inmates of the asylum, now at several removes from the 'reality' of the central ego, and therefore presented as spectres, whose faces are death's-heads with waxen skin and crumbling features. As a mental universe, the world of the play is self-enclosed, and there can be no escape from this terrifying vision. The deformation of the figures represents the guilt of the Unknown, the psychological effect of breaking 'the Commandments.' But these nightmares also occur because the Unknown is 'bankrupt' having 'lost the power to create',[21] and – significantly – the solution therefore lies in the will, the ability to transform this internal world through the poetic imagination:

This is life... I feel myself swell and stretch, rarefy, become boundless; I am everywhere, in the sea which is my blood, in the mountains which are my skeleton, in the trees, in the flowers. And my head reaches to heaven. I look out over the Universe which is, I feel the strength of the Creator within me, for I am the Creator. I should like to take this globe into my hand and knead it into something completer, more lasting, more beautiful. I should like to see all creation happy...[22]

As a 'deliverer' therefore the Unknown has to free himself, and the God he wrestles with is his conscious intellect which represses and restrains, so that in the title image of Saul of Tarsus the spiritual illumination on the road to Damascus brings him to terms with the creative elements of his psyche that his rational mind had denied. Hence what he has learned by the end of the trilogy is to marry 'thesis, assent; antithesis, dissent' in the affirmative Hegelian synthesis of 'Don't say: Either – Or. Say: Both – And', uniting not only opposed attitudes to life but the different parts of a divided personality. In Hegelian terms each synthesis is the formation of a fresh thesis, repeating the pattern of antithesis and synthesis on a higher level, and it is in this sense that the Unknown is said to 'rise from the dead, having renounced your old name'.[23] He has become the expressionist New Man. 'Like a little new-born child', however, his baptism will still consecrate him to a saga of suffering on this higher spiritual plane of existence.

Conventional plot construction based on a linear sequence of cause and effect, in which the characters are independent entities while the conflict rises out of mutually exclusive personal motivations and can be resolved only in terms of action, is clearly inappropriate to this type of thematic pattern and internalised characterisation. Instead Strindberg developed what has been called a 'polyphonic form' for *To Damascus*. The structure in part 1 is geometrical, rather than being built up out of rising climaxes as in a conventional dramatic action. It begins and ends on the same street corner, moving inward through different levels of memory and hallucination to the 'fever' vision of the ninth scene in the asylum, then repeating the same sequence of eight scenes in reverse order to return the Unknown to the everyday awareness of ordinary experience. Within this formal progression and inversion, associative links determine the transition from one stage to another, not causality, while varying degrees of intensity are created by repetitions. Phrases recur: 'life's fool', 'my liberator / I the liberator', 'the changeling'. Concepts resurface continually: Bluebeard's castle, the mill grinding souls, the Curse of Deuteronomy. Mendelssohn's 'Funeral March' follows the Unknown everywhere: theme and variation. This enables Strindberg to break out of the conventional framework of time, which here becomes a measure of subjective experience, expanding and contracting, so that the last scene in which the Unknown receives money by post follows on directly from the first scene where he is waiting for the post office to open. It also allows symbolic relationships to be substituted for temporal sequences.

It seems to have become almost obligatory to identify *To Damascus* as the source of much that is experimental in modern theatre. Yet although poets on the path of self-discovery, 'strangers' even, and the division of scenes into seven steps on a road to Calvary (following the pattern that Strindberg outlined in the Mother's advice to 'plant a cross at every station, but stop at the seventh. You don't have to suffer fourteen, like Him')[24] are among the platitudes of German expressionist drama, this is not precisely accurate. Strindberg admired Maeterlinck, and some of the play's dream effects can be traced back to his work. But quite apart from that, it strains the credulity to see how *To Damascus* could have had much direct influence, given its stage history (or rather lack of it). Not surprisingly when one takes the 250-page length with its forty-five speaking parts plus additional Shadows, Sisters of Mercy, Musicians, Monks, Venus Worshippers, Witnesses and Whores into account, the trilogy has never been staged in its entirety, and even the first and most easily performable part has had relatively few productions, only reaching the English stage for example in 1937. In fact *To Damascus* must be seen as a seriously flawed work. The symbolism is obvious and overexplicit, therefore limiting connotations instead of acting as a nexus for meanings. There is an uneasy mixture of purely personal references and universal imagery. The characters are not so much paradigmatic as unconvincing abstractions, and their dialogue is too often leaden with stilted and sententious phrasing. In short the general stylistic effect is one of pretentious imprecision while, as Eric Bentley has put it, the thematic tone is 'unconvincing religiosity'. It is rather *A Dream Play*, given striking productions in Germany by the expressionist director Rudolph Bernauer (1916) and by Max Reinhardt (1921), and in France by Antonin Artaud (1928), or *The Ghost Sonata*, which Artaud also worked on, that were directly influential.

In these plays the same qualities that made *To Damascus* so innova-

3 Scene design for *To Damascus*. Stations of the Cross & the subconscious world.

tive recur, but in progressively subtler and better-integrated forms. In writing *A Dream Play* Strindberg's ideas were modified by *The Philosophy of the Unconscious* by Eduard von Hartmann, a forerunner of Freud whose *Interpretation of Dreams*, though apparently unknown to Strindberg, had been published the year before in 1901; and the structure is far closer to the workings of the subconscious mind than the mathematically balanced, schematic patterning of the earlier play with its intellectualised correspondence to the Stations of the Cross. There is the same fluidity of scene, but the transitions are motivated by the action and occur in response to the characters' desires or fears, rather than simply representing the central figure's states of mind in visual terms, as in the earlier play with its schematic stage directions like:

The scene grows dark. A medley of décors ensues – a landscape, a palace and a room descend and come forward, while the characters and furniture disappear. At length the STRANGER, who has been standing as though paralysed and asleep, also vanishes and out of the confusion emerges a prison cell...[25]

There is an equivalent development in the way repetition and variation are used. Only one phrase 'Alas for mankind...' is reiterated, and its simplicity as well as its frequency gives it the emotive focus of a leitmotif. Instead of abstract concepts recurring, physical objects are reused from scene to scene; the doorkeeper's shawl or the secret door, which expand in meaning with each change in their function or shape and take on continually new symbolic connotations, like the castle that grows, blooms and bursts into flames. And although scenes are again repeated and inverted, there is no sense of an artificial and superimposed geometry. The Fairhaven/Foulstrand reversal has an internal logic, based on the identity of opposites, with misery being the common denominator. Similarly the repetition of the scene outside the theatre, with the Officer waiting hopelessly for the singer he loves, is justified by the emotive force of the characters' desires, not by an abstract pattern, and becomes a way of embodying one of the major themes:

POET: I think I have seen this before...
            Perhaps I dreamed it?
            ... Or wrote it.
DAUGHTER: Then you know what poetry is.
POET: Then I know what dreaming is.
DAUGHTER: I feel we stood somewhere else and spoke these words.
POET: Then you can soon work out what reality is.
DAUGHTER: Or dreaming.
POET: Or poetry.[26]

The only other scene repeated serves a comparable framing function to the street corner in *To Damascus*, except that here the return to the opening measures a decisive change in perception, with the forest of gigantic and colourful hollyhocks on the backcloth being transformed into a wall of enquiring and agonised human faces by the illumination of the burning castle, while flowers spring from the manure and the chrysanthemum-bud blooms in a symbol of spiritual transcendence. Again this return is designed to create a double time, in which the action of the play seems to take place in a limbo of the mind and therefore outside temporal or spatial laws, since the final tableau follows straight on the opening lines, where the chrysanthemum is described as already beginning to unfold:

DAUGHTER: Won't it flower soon? We're past midsummer.
GLAZIER: Don't you see the flower up there?[27]

Unlike *To Damascus*, where this underlines the essentially rational image of a circle, here the effect is elliptical, a hallucinatory foreshortening designed to follow our experience of dreams.

Together with this structural evolution goes a corresponding development in characterisation. Instead of a single central figure standing like a rock of psychological reality in a swamp of illusion, with all the other characters existing only as distorted or projected derivatives, in *A Dream Play* all the characters move on the same imaginative plane. The Officer, the Advocate and the Poet are not just all reflections of their author, but equal alternatives. Unlike the Lady, Agnes is not presented as an image created by the male psyche. Rather, her independence from the author's representatives is stressed by the prologue, added after the play was written, which gives her divine status as Indra's Daughter. No one character dominates, and consequently the play seems to have more general relevance. In place of the earlier play's analysis of a single psyche, however representative its spiritual states are assumed to be, the theme becomes an exploration of the human condition: again an aspect underlined in the prologue with

INDRA'S VOICE: Descend and see, and hear, and then return,
                and tell me, child, if their complaints
                and wailings are well-founded.[28]

In this way the symbolic figures are given a certain objective validity, replacing the unbridled subjectivity of *To Damascus* with a concept akin to Heidegger's definition of man as '*Existenz*', in which the essential level of being is what all individuals share in common though each apprehends it in a unique way.[29]

The extent to which Strindberg's ability to depict the workings of the subconscious has progressed in *A Dream Play* is indicated by the well-known 'Author's note', which is frequently referred to as a concise synopsis of his stylistic aims:

In this dream play the author has, as in his former dream play, TO DAMASCUS, attempted to imitate the inconsequent yet transparently logical shape of a dream. Everything can happen, everything is possible and probable. Time and place do not exist; on an insignificant basis of reality the imagination spins, weaving new patterns; a mixture of memories, experiences, free fancies, incongruities and improvisations. The characters split, double, multiply, evaporate, condense, disperse, assemble. But one consciousness rules over them all, that of the dreamer; for him there are no secrets, no illogicalities, no scruples, no laws. He neither acquits nor condemns, but merely relates...

The approach described here, with its echoes of Strindberg's letter of 1887 referring to his inability to distinguish life from imagination and his automatic acceptance of whatever presented itself to his mind, however unusual or immoral by conscious standards, is clearly derived from his personal dream experiences. As an outline of the way autobiographical elements have been transmuted into symbols through the prism of subliminal contrasts and connections in the play, this is accurate enough; and it illuminates the principles of intensification and condensation on which the 'new patterns' (by implication superior to the logical perceptions of the waking world) have been created. But it is not simply a straight transcription of Strindberg's working method here, although it could indeed be applied directly to his previous play. This becomes clear as soon as one asks who the dreamer is and sees that, unlike *To Damascus*, there is no dominating 'consciousness' in the play itself. The 'Author's note', in fact, has more relevance to the theme of *A Dream Play* than its form. As the Daughter reveals, repeating the entry in Strindberg's diary for the day when he finished writing the play, it is 'the divine primal force', a spiritual essence divided between all men, that is assumed to have created the vision. Life itself is therefore an illusory dream in which men, as physical entities, are no more than phantoms; and as the final image of fire and flower clearly affirms, 'death really is the awakening'.[30] One of the draft titles, *Prisoners*, referred overtly to the idea of mankind as spirits locked in bodies, serving the life sentence of a materialistic definition of existence. The secret of the door is the 'nothingness' to which, as the opposite of physical 'being', the spiritual nature of man aspires, and suffering becomes the catalyst that liberates the spirit by making daily life unendurable – a remarkable transformation in which the suffering and humiliations, that Strindberg had earlier raged against as meaningless, and totally evil, become positive values.

At the same time, unlike Rimbaud or the surrealists, for whom the function of poetry is to transcribe the subconscious, since dreams are revelations of reality *per se*, Strindberg's prefatory note explicitly states that what *A Dream Play* reproduces is the structure of dreaming but not the actual content of a dream. His theme presupposes that dreams are false (the dream of life being unreal), although the dream state (an awareness that life is a dream) is true perception. What Strindberg in fact seems to be attempting is the creation of a myth. The story of the daughter of a god, whose descent to earth and involvement in all possible variations of imperfect human love reveals the spiritual meaning of existence, corresponds closely to Eliade's definition of myth as a 'primordial revelation, exemplary model' that 'gives meaning and value to life' by narrating 'how . . . a reality came into existence'.[31] In light of this, Strindberg's use of the dream form to present a myth has additional significance in anticipating the association between dreams and myths noted by Otto Rank in *The Myth of the Birth of the Hero* (1909) and picked up by Jung, who saw myths as embodying the collective dreams of the tribe.[32]

German expressionism

As might be expected, staging is a major problem in Strindberg's dream plays. They demanded technical resources that did not exist at the beginning of the century, and even Strindberg's own Intimate Theatre never produced *A Dream Play*, although the original intention in founding it was to provide suitable performance conditions for precisely this, following what Strindberg felt was the failure of the play's first production six months earlier (April 1907). To achieve his intended effect of '*Förvandlingsbilder*' or slow dissolves from one scene to the next, Strindberg had recommended the use of a magic lantern. But the light could not be focussed sufficiently and the back-projections had to be abandoned. His alternative proposal, a curious return to the traditional staging of the eighteenth-century court theatres with fixed perspective wings, on which a flat, stylised mixture of landscape and architectural detail was depicted, and with scene changes indicated by unrolling a sequence of different backdrops, was equally unsatisfactory. Although this was obviously meant to be symbolically representational, rather than illusionistic, providing bare suggestions as a catalyst for the active imagination of the spectator, it turned out to be limiting instead of liberating. 'The whole performance became "a phenomenon of materialisation" instead of the intended dematerialisation'[33] – a problem that equally affected Reinhardt's 1921 production, which presented the tableau of suffering human faces by rows of real actors, clothed in black and with whitened, staring features. Strindberg himself moved away from any attempt to realise his vision in physical terms. His proposals to August Falck, the director of the Intimate Theatre, reveal symbolist influence – neutral drapes taking on different nuances of colour from the lighting to reflect changing moods, with simple 'allegorical' objects to evoke imaginative echoes for the location of each scene: sea shells for Fingal's Cave, signal flags for Foulstrand, a number-board for songs representing the church – and his thoughts on his 'chamber plays' show him working towards a theatre of the mind, independent of the stage or physical representation:

if Shakespeare's highly sophisticated contemporaries could do without scenery, we too should be able to imagine walls and trees . . . everything is make-believe on the stage.
The poet's vision is profaned through the written word; the written drama is profane in a definite way when it is materialised through performance.[34]

It is this concept of a theatre of the mind, in which the stage ceases to be a physical representation of the world and becomes a projection of myth or the author's inner self, that struck the German expressionists with such force. Elsewhere in Europe Strindberg's main impact seems to have been as an example of drama in revolt. The obsessional qualities in his work were valued primarily as a form of subversive anarchy, irrationality being anti-social, and when Lugné-Poe produced *The Ghost Sonata* he stressed 'this stifling atmosphere of agony and madness'.[35] Since conservative critics rejected Strindberg as 'one of the most execrated and execrable writers of our time' whose 'work is nothing but a series of pamphlets against religion, the monarchy, science',[36] productions of his plays became a natural focus for avant garde rejections of society. It was certainly in this spirit that Artaud, who (like Jarry) had begun his career as an actor under Lugné-Poe, staged *A Dream Play*. When his surrealist ex-colleagues disrupted the one and only performance, his defence – in a speech from the stage that only added to the uproar by alienating his Swedish supporters who had financed this production – was to claim that 'Strindberg is a renegade, just like Jarry, like Lautréamont, like Breton, like me. We are presenting this play because it vomits on its fatherland, on all nations, on society.'[37] By contrast, in Germany Strindberg's drama was more easily accepted – between 1913 and 1915 there were more than 1,000 performances of twenty-four of his plays in sixty-two cities – partly perhaps because dramatists like Wedekind had already surpassed the level of social revolt in his work (*Spring's Awakening/Frühlingserwachen*, 1891; *Erdgeist*, 1895, best known today in Berg's operatic version, *Lulu*). As a result his primary influence there was as a stylistic model.

Since the term 'expressionism' was first appropriated for the drama by Walter Hasenclever in a series of essays on 'The theatre of tomorrow . . . the call for a spiritual stage',[38] it seems appropriate to use one of his plays as an example of expressionist drama. *Humanity* (*Menschen*, 1918) is representative of the way the structural qualities of Strindberg's dream plays were developed. The title itself underlines the abstract nature of the characterisation. Only the protagonist, Alexander, who is simultaneously a murderer and the murderer's victim (carrying his own decapitated head around with him in a sack), and the two figures symbolising the dual nature of woman, Lissi and Agathe, demonic sexuality and purifying spiritual love, have proper names. The other characters are described simply in generic human terms as the sufferers from whom regeneration might come – The Youth, The Girl, The Mother – or defined by social function as representatives of the corrupt and repressive materialistic world of society – Doctor, Banker, Whores, Beggar. Like *To Damascus*, Hasenclever's play contains an obligatory asylum scene and begins and ends on the same spot, though here the 'framing scene' is loaded with symbolic connotations. Instead of an everyday street corner the opening is a cemetery at sunset, and the first image sets the action firmly in the spiritual sphere. A stone cross topples over as the protagonist rises from the grave, and what follows is clearly signposted as a dream, since everything takes place during the course of the night, with the ending at dawn.

This is, perhaps rather over-obviously, the dark night of the soul in which daily existence is seen as a nightmare. The stock market is presented as a demonic roulette game where only the number thirteen comes up, the bankrupted losers are pushed down through a trapdoor by masked men and the table collapses under the weight of the stakes. Social revolution is rejected as a solution, since the workers are defined as brutally materialistic and the slogans of socialism – 'No more private property!. . . No wars!' – go together with a total disregard of individual values where the question 'Human beings?' only brings the response 'Slaves.'[39] The conventional alternative of romantic love, fulfilment in the family group and hope for the future in a new generation is also dismissed, because sexual constancy is impossible. Even before the first words of the play The Girl has already deceived her lover, who is seduced by Lissi and dies of syphilis; birth is a trauma of blood and screams; and even a lullaby makes it clear that the baby's innocence will not outlast the cradle.

Against this nightmare world of whores and death (no less than ten of the main figures are stabbed, throttled, strangled, literally disintegrate with syphilis or commit suicide) is set the possiblity of transformation or spiritual renewal through a Christ-like love of mankind. Lissi's nihilistic 'Dead is dead!' is balanced by Alexander's cry of 'Resurrection'.[40] On one hand we are given a series of vignettes demonstrating the fatal corruption of materialistic society, symbolised by the money that passes from The Banker at the roulette table to a tippler, to The Youth, to The Doctor who demands sex from his female

4 Apotheosis in *Transfiguration*. Stylised revelation – the rhetoric of salvation.

patients in return for performing abortions and grows rich from diag-
nosing incurable syphilis, to Lissi, the symbol of egoistic sexual perversion. All of them die for or because of it. Money is stuffed into the
mouth of a dying woman, whose funeral procession is disrupted and
whose corpse is stripped by a mob brandishing unpaid bills; and
money motivates the betrayal of Alexander to the police as a murderer by his follower, who claims the reward then hangs himself. On
the other side we are shown images of an alternate, spiritual reality in
the progress of Alexander, who gives everything to the poor and
brings The Girl back to life, when she slashes open her wrists after
her abortion, by drinking her blood as it flows from her veins. He
embraces all sinners as his 'family' and buries the abandoned corpse
of the dead woman with his own hands. And in typical expressionist
fashion Alexander's pilgrimage in search of himself repeats Christ's
Passion, betrayed by an obvious Judas-figure, a mock crown set on
his head. As in Toller's play *Transfiguration* (*Die Wandlung*, 1919)
where all that is needed for the 'caricatures of humanity', who have
let mechanical institutions enslave them out of fear, to leap up from
their crawling prostration transformed into 'unconditioned new
men', is the revelation that 'you could . . . still be human, if only you
had faith in yourselves and in humanity, if only you would grant that
spirit its fulfilment',[41] – so here the ending is emblematic of renewal
and hope achieved. Agathe releases Alexander from the condemned
cell by taking his chains on herself, 'the sky appears, chorals are sung
from spires', and the murderer, who epitomises the 'hatred' that
explicitly dominates the nightmare world where 'HUMAN BEINGS in
the shape of beasts . . . crawl about', is transfigured into an *ecce homo*:

The sun rises.
THE MURDERER, *spreading out his arms*: I love![42]

The main problem here, one that Toller and other expressionists
share, is that this humanist ecstasy is so vague. The pictures of social
evil and deformed humanity are graphic, imaginatively convincing in
spite of their one-sided extremism. Yet the transformation is so sudden that it appears unmotivated, and the images of salvation, of the
apotheosis of reborn man are merely rhetorical.

The structure of *Humanity* is also typical of expressionist drama, and
its qualities can perhaps be most clearly seen by analogy to the painting of the fauves, where autonomous structure (or in Kandinsky's
terms 'internal necessity') was substituted for composition after nature (or 'external necessity'). The free associations of images replaced

5 The prison of psychological repression in *Masses & Man*. Free association
of images, dream states & emotional intensity.

logical organisations of mimetic shapes, and the 'arc' of discontinuous
scenes (*Bilderbogen*) in plays patterned on the Stations of the Cross
(*Stationendrama*) is in many ways equivalent to the visual artists' pref-
erence for curvelinear forms. Time and space do not exist as
categories for organising experience, or rather the attempt to give the
action immediacy and direct relevance to all spectators leads to

abstract universalisation, and Hasenclever therefore specifies the time as 'today' and the scene as 'the world'. Hence too the cemetery, a setting in a sense outside time which had already been used in another play, Fritz von Unruh's *A Family* (*Ein Geschlecht*, 1916), where 'the tragedy is not confined to any temporal straitjacket [*Zeitkostüm*]: its action plays inside and in front of a churchyard on a mountain peak'.[43] Unlike a play such as *Transfiguration* in which key episodes 'are to be imagined as a shadowy reality, played out in the distant interior of a dream', or Toller's *Masses and Man* (*Masse–Mensch*, 1919) where various scenes are listed as 'pictures in a visionary dream distance',[44] Hasenclever has extended Strindberg's principles for reproducing the internal logic, rather than the visual impression of a dream. Scenes are not only linked by associations, rather than cause and effect. They become almost independent moments – a montage of single images, each making a specific effect, out of which a composite picture emerges. Strindberg's 'contrapuntal structure' has been given a new meaning on Hasenclever's multi-level stage with separate acting areas to left and right. The short scenes can be played out almost simultaneously or formed into extended sequences of comparison and contrast, with the spectator's attention following the spotlights as they pick out one group of figures, then another; all of which corresponds to the concept of the dream as a state of awareness, not experience measured by temporal duration.

There is a corresponding development in the use of language. Where Strindberg's dialogue tended to the poetic or metaphoric, Hasenclever's characters are reduced to emotionally charged and evocative single words. Already in Wedekind or Sternheim speech had been condensed to a staccato telegraphese, intended to express emotional intensity. Here this has become the full-blown expressionist '*Schrei*'. The intellectual, denotative quality of language has been excluded by removing practically all grammatical structures and connectives. Assertion takes the place of discursive argument, and there is no room for a character's utterances to express personality or indicate motivation. This of course reinforces the status of the figures as archetypes, either representing caricatured aspects of external society versus intrinsic moral qualities, as in *Humanity*, or projections of the protagonist–poet's spiritual struggle, as in Sorge's *The Beggar* (*Der Bettler*, 1912). But, as a perceptive critic like Brecht immediately realised, this is a form of inflation that devalues its own symbolic currency, and a figure like Hasenclever's Alexander at times

appears almost a parody, Strindberg's Unknown reduced to an algebraic lowest common denominator:

THE FATHER: Who are you?
ALEXANDER: I seek myself.
THE FATHER: A Man!![45]

At the same time this type of dialogue must be seen as an attempt to
reflect the uncontrolled emotional depths of the subconscious in such
a way as to appeal directly to the same pre-rational levels in the
spectators' minds. Strindberg's images are intellectually formulated
and interpretable as allegory. This expressionist simplicity is designed
to reach a more basic stratum of awareness on which men are united
by instinctive and emotional qualities shared by all, so the appropriate verbal forms are assumed to be the spontaneous cry or unpre-
meditated image. There are obvious parallels to Nietzsche's concept
of tragedy, in which the 'spirit of music' liberates man from individuality and reunites the Dionysiac audience with the universal will in a
'collective ecstasy'.

Ultimately then, what is significant is a particular expressive quality, the means rather than the meaning, as the self-adopted label of
'expressionism' indicates. The structures of action and dialogue are
not only intended to embody the fundamental operations of the mind
through intensification and condensation, but to speak directly to the
audience's collective subconscious. Hasenclever's use of isolated key
words – Life, Death, Love, Brother, Money, Syphilis, Atonement,
Sunrise, Resurrection; always capitalised and followed by two, sometimes three exclamation marks – is the equivalent of a painter like
Franz Marc's belief that certain colours automatically trigger specific
emotional associations. Responses are to be subliminal, almost Pavlovian, and the essential criteria are therefore directness, immediacy,
intensity. In short, the expressionist play or painting should ideally
be a transparent conductor, transferring the artist's subjective vision
to the spectator's mind without being filtered through the intellect or
socially conditioned perspectives, so that it is experienced as 'lived
truth'. In no sense is the artistic process intended to create an objective reality that an audience, as observers, could consider critically or
react to individually.

The subjectivity of this dramatic form, in which internal acts become externalised, and the external stand only for internal states, is
close to the single voice of lyricism. The world only exists on stage as
a vehicle for the soul or a reflection of the will, so objects and figures

can be transformed to correspond to the emotional state of the dreaming or visionary mind. There can be oppositions, contrasts, but no real conflict; and if *Humanity* can be seen as an extended monologue, many other expressionist plays literally culminate in monologues. The thematic tendency carries over into the form. The climax is introspective, the crisis being formed by the point at which feeling ('*Seele*') becomes so forceful that it bursts through the dramatic structure into incoherence, not by the decisive nature of physical action (death, marriage, etc.). Drama becomes concentrated to a point of 'pure' emotion, and the ending of one monologue, the 1,000-line declamation in the final act of *The Beggar*, is worth quoting because it is particularly revealing about the expressionist author's intentions:

Oh tears! Tears!... Joy!... ETERNAL LIFE!!! And not to be able to live it! Indeed I know I can't live it – oh curses! Curses! To be condemned to words! Yes, I am damned by words! I must become a sculptor of symbols, must renounce the priesthood... Poet... Holy only on the surface... Hypocrite... Think... Think... Symbols... *Leaps impetuously upward with hands outstretched.* Oh consoling lightning... Illumination... Agonising consolation of the lightning... SYMBOLS OF ETERNITY... End! End! Goal and end! If the blood, the sum of unreality, of tumult, of the desire for tumult in me... in my blood, if this is condemned to speak in symbols, then so be it: SPEAK THROUGH SYMBOLS OF ETERNITY. *Exhaustion.* [46]

Speech is at several removes from spiritual reality. To find a frequency that avoids the noisy static of daily life, the artist must use symbols. But conventional symbolism is too limiting because of its intellectual connotations, and as a result the pauses on an expressionist's page are made to carry more meaning than what is said. Visual images, keyed in by emotionally charged words and accompanied by suggestive vocal sounds, become the primary means of communication, comparable to Artaud's 'hieroglyphs'.

The problem (for the expressionists) is that any form of symbolism is by nature indirect, still standing in an oblique relationship to reality, but the attempt to short-circuit the twin gaps between external representation and internal states, and between expression and reception, leads to a form of vacuum. Particularly when read as a text and divorced from performance, expressionist dialogue seems loaded with more weight of emotion than the words can bear. Pathos has been exaggerated to the point where it turns into bathos, and symbolic meaning is so inflated that it loses contact with the particular, becoming emptied of significance. Theatrical conventions are only effective when they appear the natural form for a particular concept of existence, when the medium is so well integrated with the message that it goes unnoticed. By contrast these techniques tend to attract attention to themselves and, partly because of the expressionist fixation on emotional absolutes, frequently seem to be used with all the subtlety of sledgehammers. Paradoxically then, the attempt to abolish form, to turn it into a transparent conductor, makes the formal elements obtrusive.

At the same time the most frequent criticism of the expressionist approach is its undramatic abstraction.[47] But this negative evaluation is mainly based on reading the plays in literary form; and with the relegation of dialogue to a minor role, these are not so much texts as deliberately incomplete scripts. They should be seen as a framework for mime accompanied by exclamations; and if the stage directions are too abbreviated to give more than bare indications of the desired effect, this is because the expressionists were writing for a recognised style of presentation that had developed in response to their requirements.

Expressionist staging

Obviously, since expressionist figures are not naturalistic individuals in the context of a specific social environment, the mimetic approach to acting, which combines different characteristics drawn from observation and portrays psychological nuances, was inappropriate. Instead the effects aimed at were artificial and exaggerated, comparable to the conventionalised rhetorical gestures of neo-classical and romantic acting though in an even more heightened form. But at the same time the actor was to be an example of 'the new man' for the audience, revealing his innermost being directly in movement, gesture and facial expression. Kornfeld's 'Epilogue to the actor' (1913) shows the dual requirement clearly. Not only is the actor to create 'his characters from his [own] experience of the emotion or fate he has to portray ... and not from his recollections of human beings he has seen filled with these emotions or victims of this fate', but he is not to conceal 'the fact that he is acting. Let him not deny the theatre or try to feign reality.'[48] This basic antithesis remained unresolved, perhaps because it corresponded to the contradiction inherent in expressionist characterisation: as the 'self' is made the subject of analysis it becomes increasingly elusive and ambiguous, escaping into role playing where the face dissolves into multiple masks.

On one level the actor searches for absolute emotional truth, which only subjective experience can guarantee, and which any element of pretence or illusion discredits. 'Not counterfeit thoughts, but his emotions alone lead and guide him. Only then can he advance and approach absolute ecstasy', an emotional transcendence which is to be achieved through trance states and self-hypnosis.[49] Again the principles are those of spontaneity and immediacy, ruling out the prior selection of feelings to be exhibited, since these would have been distorted by the process of intellectual reflection. Behind this is the expressionist concept of humanity. If the opinions and behaviour patterns that define individuality are associated with the conscious, rational side of the mind, then the essential qualities of a human being are universal, relating to the idea of a 'collective soul', and the aim of the actor is to divest himself of personality. He presents 'nothing but the most sublime and the most miserable: HE BECOMES MAN... not a puppet dangling on the strings of a psychological philosophy of life'.[50] Following this line, techniques were developed to project archetypal emotions directly in physical terms through rhythms of movement, posture and symbolic gesture. In an approach Grotowski was to develop to its limits in the sixties, the actor's body becomes an expressive instrument, literally incarnating his spiritual being, at least according to one of the leading expressionist exponents, Erwin Kalser. He had made his name as the Student in Falckenberg's 1915 production of *The Ghost Sonata* – a classic example of the 'ecstatic' acting style, where the actor playing the Old Man came to blows with Kalser during the dress rehearsal because of the hate built up by their roles, a telling symptom of the extreme emotional states and degree of involvement in expressionist acting – and while performing the part of the Cashier in Kaiser's *From Morn to Midnight* (1916) he commented:

Of what else does the actor's training consist, but removing the obstinacy of the body, which he himself resists, to make it completely and totally the organ of the soul? The soul must reach deep into the hidden core of the body, so that nothing is impossible for him; he can completely forget himself in his soul... The actor who is conscious of his inner strength goes onto the stage as someone sleepwalking.[51]

On this level the actor always plays himself, though trying to reach beneath the merely personal, and came to be compared with shamans and mystics, paralleling Strindberg's claim that the actor should function as a spiritualist medium in a trance – a transformation from within that actors themselves believed they achieved, referring to 'tremendous spiritual ecstasies' experienced when they were able to reach a semi-unconscious dream state in performance.[52]

On the other level expressionist actors clearly conformed to a highly rhetorical style. Their exaggerated gesticulations show the influence of the traditional series of six distorted hand gestures developed by Hans Sachs to depict character in the German Passion Play – a deliberate return to the archaic which indicates the expressionist concern with the primitive, and parallels the way Kokoschka organised movement on lines derived from early medieval art. Their faces were transformed into 'masks' (again with all the primitive connotations) by the rigid tension of facial muscles. Hands became stretched into talons, arms curved sinuously as swans' necks to form exterior 'signs' of psychological states. Movement swung between an almost epileptic dynamism and cataleptic stasis, creating driving rhythms in which rapid and highly patterned moves continually froze into a series of emblematic positions comparable to the schemata of classical Greek theatre. Voices were harsh, emphatic, staccato, matching the compression of dialogue into isolated nouns or telegraphic phrases. The whole surface effect was angular, corresponding to the crooked arches and oblique perspectives of the expressionist sets in which the actors were framed. It was grotesque, gothic and sharply conventionalised.

However the expressionists themselves saw no contradiction between rigid stylisation and subjectivity, contemporaneity and archaism. For them what provided a synthesis was the concept of the universality of emotion, the continued presence of atavistic instincts in modern man beneath the surface of superficial rationalism imposed by western civilisation, and the belief that personal emotion, if intense enough and expressed in archetypal forms, would release primitive responses and automatically evoke the same emotional state in the spectators. As Stefan Zweig commented, announcing 'the new Pathos' in 1909, 'technical proficiency' must 'no longer be an end in itself, but only a means of inspiring pathos'. And this would only be achieved by 'a return to the origins' of art, since primitive poetry was idealised as 'a scarcely verbalised cry' that expressed 'the excess of a sensation – full of pathos because it arose out of passion – solely with the aim of generating passion'.[53]

This ecstatic style was undoubtedly powerful. Even the artificiality contributed to the effectiveness, as in the way rhetorically exaggerated gestures, originally designed for Reinhardt's mass spectacles in gigantic staging areas like the Circus Schumann, Reinhardt's 'theatre

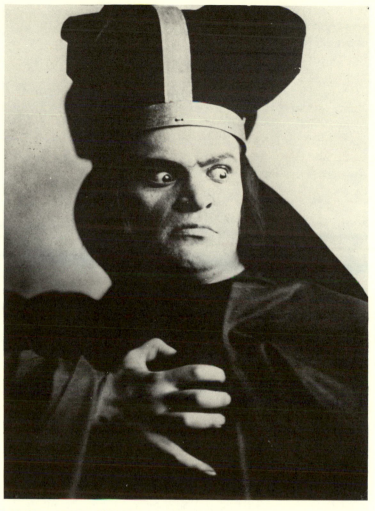

6 Kortner as Richard III. Ecstatic acting – facial 'masking' & exaggerated
gestures.

of the 5,000', were transformed unchanged to smaller stages like the
intimate Kammerspiele, where Falckenberg's production of *The Ghost
Sonata* was performed on an acting area barely 26 ft wide and without
depth. The emotional projection would have been overpowering,
particularly when united with the compulsive tempo intended to
sweep the audience along and with the communicative impulsiveness
of the acting. And it is hardly surprising that Fritz Kortner, whose

performances in Karl Heinz Martin's production of *Transfiguration* and Leopold Jessner's of *Wilhelm Tell* (both in 1919) set the standards for expressionist acting, had gone through an apprenticeship with Reinhardt and had been the leader of the chorus in his monumental version of *Oedipus Rex*.

In light of this impassioned presentation, the number of insane characters and mad-house scenes in expressionist drama is hardly coincidental. It corresponds to the image of the ecstatic actor as 'a man possessed', even if this tended only too literally to mean bared teeth and rolling eyes. In addition to this over-obviousness, as Zweig's stress on 'the excess of sensation' implies, plays like *Humanity* require a performance to start on such a high level of intensity that it leaves little room for building to any crescendo. As a result the aggressive emphasis and sustained emotional pitch could become a form of overkill, exhausting the spectator's ability to respond by its unremitting violence. At the same time the schemata that are intended to crystallise meaning become clichés through repetition, the clearest example being the Christ image which recurs at the climax of so many expressionist plays. Indeed this was effectively emptied of meaning through being used to signal a whole range of emotive states from ecstatic transfiguration, as in *Humanity*, to the agony of sacrifice, as in *From Morn to Midnight*, where Kaiser's dying Cashier stands 'with outstretched arms slumping against the cross sewn on the curtains. His gasp sobs like an *Ecce* – his expiring breath sighs like a *Homo*.'[54]

Despite such flaws, this ritualistic style of performance had a wider currency than is generally realised. In particular it provides a working model for visualising what Artaud intended when he described his ideal actor as 'signalling through the flames', creating 'violent physical images' of 'energy in the unconscious' which 'crush and hypnotise the sensibility of the spectator'; and Artaud's description of the qualities he admired in Lugné-Poe's acting could be applied word for word to the expressionists: 'his surprising changes of voice, his fingers which became rigid points, his inflamed glances evoked thoughts of a tradition now lost to the theatre. One would have said we were in the presence of an actor from the mystery plays of medieval France.'[55] Significantly too, bearing in mind the expressionist rejection of discursive language and their reduction of dialogue to rhythmic exclamation, this style of acting carried over into silent film and had strong affinities with contemporary dance. Indeed some of the aims of expressionism can be seen more clearly in dance than theatre, because here the essential qualities are presented indepen-

7 Laban, *Titan*. Musical rhythms and archetypal movements.

dent of the traditional dramaturgical elements of characterisation and
plot still retained in the plays.

The work of Dalcroze and Laban is mainly discussed today in terms
of time-and-motion study. But 'eurythmics', Dalcroze's system of
movement training, focussed on the emotions aroused by musical
rhythms and translated these into attitude and gesture, while Laban's
theory of 'eukinetics' reduced all movements to opposed pairs of
stylised 'shapes' – for instance centripedal or 'scooping' versus centrifugal or 'scattering'. Being distilled to their essential elements, such
movements held strong archetypal associations, and the dance group
that Laban established to demonstrate his ideas repeated variations of
these 'pure shapes' to express clearly defined emotions such as anger,
joy, love or fear, until all the dancers reached a 'universal celebratory
state'. Both the stress on performance as therapy for the performer
and the abstraction of physical expression to universal shapes were
carried over into ecstatic acting in modified forms. The use of repeated and rhythmic movement for hypnotic effect, heightening
emotional states to the point where the subjective turns into the ar-

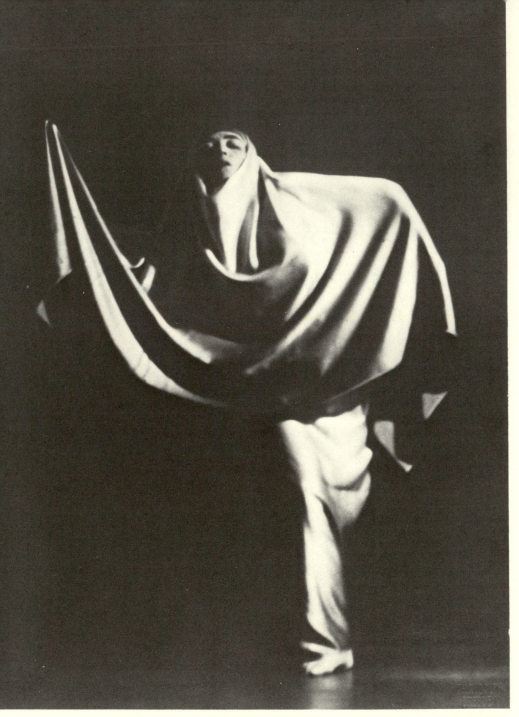

8 Wigman as 'Veiled Figure'. The visionary psyche & ritualised movements.

chetypal, which is so clear in this type of dance, illuminates the ritualistic aims of expressionist theatre. And the closeness of the connection between modern dance and expressionist drama can be seen in the way Laban's principles were developed by Mary Wigman, whose Dresden dance school was already attracting notice by 1920.

Choreography for classical ballet is allegorical, with highly conventionalised mime indicating the feelings and actions of figures who are represented rather than embodied by the dancers. There is no sense of improvisation and the ballerina's focus is on a level of aesthetic harmony, the illusion of an effortless rising above physical limitations, which precludes identification with the characters. By contrast, in Wigman's dance–drama sequences of movement based on the tension between extension and contraction were developed as group improvisations and in her view 'each impulse, to be valid, must come from the heart, the depths of a nature shaken by the sacred fury'.[56] To demonstrate the intensity of this personal emotion physical effort was emphasized, instead of concealed, and the dance steps were not orchestrated by external musical accompaniment. Instead the dancers created their own expressive patterns of sound from the rhythms beaten out by their feet or drum beats, which were regulated by the tempo of the dance and (as in O'Neill's *Emperor Jones*) not only echoed the heartbeat of the performers, but helped to excite a corresponding pulse rate in the audience. As might be expected from this stress on subjective authenticity, there was no characterisation. The dancers presented their own inner states, although these were frequently given idealised mimetic expression in the sense that repressions or personal fears might be embodied by the image of a pinioned slave, panting and writhing against imaginary chains, lust by animalistic contortions, ecstasy by the spinning whirl of a dervish.

Observers were struck by the trance-like or somnambulistic impression given by Wigman's troupe – an impression given as much by the frenzied 'nervous energy verging on hallucination' as by the fixed eyes and mask-like rigidity of their faces – and described what they were watching as the 'visions and spectral obsessions of a nightmare'. Descriptions of the 'spasmodic violence' of these performances also stress the total absorption of the dancer and the absence of pretence, qualities which apply equally to the expressionist actor, since the movements and gestures correspond so closely to those of the ecstatic acting style: 'Most of the dance-dramas . . . demand a painful tension of the whole being. The dancer's eyes exclaim; her fingers flare; her body writhes with terror; she squirms on the ground, stamps furiously, collapses exhausted.'[57] Favourable critics praised the Wigman school's approach as 'liturgical'; the disapproving condemned it as 'barbarism' – and both terms point accurately to an intrinsic quality. Even more obviously than expressionist theatre, this dance identifies emotional intensity with religious belief, the primitive with the spiritual, and searches for quasi-mythological forms. Mary Wigman's repertoire was composed of titles like *Totenmal* (*The Call of the Dead*), *Ekstatische Tänze* (consisting of four parts: Prayer, Sacrifice, Religious Rite, Temple Dance) or *Die Feier* (*Rites*, including The Call, Migration, Chaos, The Turning Point, Vision, Greeting), and the sub-title of *Rites*, 'ceremonies of a cult devoted to an unknown god' indicates the abstraction of this sort of mythmaking which simultaneously retreats into the exotic and attempts to gain relevance through universality. The epitome of this type of dance, of course, is Stravinsky's *Rite of Spring* (*Le Sacre du printemps*, 1913) which the Wigman group also performed. Set in prehistoric Russia and depicting a pagan ritual of mating and human sacrifice, in which a virgin possessed by ancestral spirits dances in an ecstasy to music of increasing violence and volume until she falls lifeless to the ground, this ballet brings together all the primitive and mythic tendencies we have noted in expressionism. It also preserves the intended effect of ecstatic acting in musical terms, with atavistic rhythms, rapidly changing metres and conflicting polytonal chords which produce a febrile and unsettling restlessness, and *ostinati* (the constant repetition of melodic figures) building in intensity to create overpowering dissonances.

If dance reveals the atavistic, one might almost say Jungian aspect of expressionism, with its search for ritualistic or mythical archetypes to incarnate emotions so deeply felt that they become universal and transfigure the individual by a return to the roots of human nature, the work of Jakob Moreno brings out the complementary or Freudian aspect of subjectivism: theatre as therapy.

Moreno, the Viennese founder of group psychotherapy, did little more than extend current expressionist practice when he drew up his plans for a 'theatre without spectators' in 1923. The architectural design for his ideal theatre gives a quasi-religious impression that accurately reflected the expressionist belief in the divinity of man and the realisation of God in every individual through the full release of human potential (however odd this may seem from the standpoint of psychiatry today). The shape was that of a circular basilica with a stage in the centre and broad steps rising like terraces in concentric circles up to the outside wall, where there were four equidistant semi-circular 'chapels', each with its own stage and surrounding steps. This was the prototype of the egg-shaped Bauhaus design for a 'total theatre' by Walter Gropius (1928), and both were architectural attempts to integrate the audience in stage action. But Gropius' spectators were to be passive, involved only imaginatively and emotionally, although totally encompassed with external activity, scenes being played out around them on the perimeter, between them in broad aisles, in the middle of them on a central stage and extending above them by unbroken cinema projection over the curving ceiling. Moreno's concept was far more radical. His public were not spectators but active participants. There were no seats. Standing encouraged more overt responses and allowed free movement from one centre of action to another or even onto one of the stages, making a constant interchange possible between reacting and enacting. And since the focus of this psychodrama was the relationship of the individual to the group, those participants less directly involved acted as both the antagonist and the setting. Instead of an audience there was a responsive environment literally standing for society as the wider, normative context within which the individual moves. There were no scripts, no professional performers, no aesthetic appreciation, no scenery. Ordinary members of the public led others in improvised 'scenarios' dealing with personal psychiatric problems of general relevance to the group, and modified their actions following suggestions or alternatives demonstrated by those surrounding them. In practice Moreno gathered a nucleus of particularly interesting 'case-histories', who reappeared to act out the on-going saga of their personal and sexual relationships night after night. In theory however this was 'Theatre for everybody . . . not an expert actor surrounded by an open-mouthed attentive mass; all must play with it . . . must make the stride from awareness to improvisation';[58] and the structure Moreno developed reflected these desired elements of spontaneity and equality. First a preparatory phase, releasing inhibitions, finding a common problem and discovering the most suitable exponent, who would function as a protagonist for the group. Then a series of situations acted out impromptu following (ideally) 'the free play of the subconscious', with the protagonists playing the role of the 'self', others coopted as 'auxiliary egos' or antagonists, and the mass giving 'resonance' through comparisons and corrections. This was followed by discussion.

Moreno's 'theatre of improvisation' developed from his work with children, which led him to conclude first that meglomania was normal, since the self is inevitably a central concern for the individual, and secondly that spontaneity is the ultimate basic human trait, even prior to sexuality or other drives. The form of his theatre reflected his belief that blocks and repressions were created by the distorting pressures of an unhealthy social environment, not as in Freudian theory by infantile traumas; and performances were based on the premise that 'acting is healthier than speaking', which gave a therapeutic rationale for replacing 'the logical/verbal emphasis of traditional theatre' by 'improvisational situations'. In short Moreno's theatre offered a psychological value for the egoistic focus of expressionism and its elevation of *'Seele'*, the uncontrolled emotional aspect of the subconscious that was expressed by the *'Schrei'*, to the essential constituent of art. It also held out a justifiable rationale for the expressionist repudiation of society, one which – being psychological – was more consistent than the sort of ideological rejection that led various artists to a communist position. (The incongruity of attempting in practice to transfigure the population into 'new men' by revolutionary politics was aptly demonstrated by Toller's self-defeating idealism as president of the short-lived Bavarian communist republic, where he was reduced to running helplessly between the battle lines trying to stop a civil war, or desperately hiding the bodies of hostages he had been unable to save in an unsuccessful effort to avert a massacre of revenge.) Equally significantly, Moreno's psychodrama also gives a rationale for elements in expressionist plays which otherwise might appear arbitrary stylistic devices, for example the structure of short, independent tableaux and the substitution of montage for temporal sequence:

Scenarios only radiate magical influence when they are performed with a special tempo and in a foreshortened perspective... The foreshortening of the play is essential because intensity can only be held for a brief time. Tension is followed by release. An improvisation must not be carried on past the player's moment of release... The performance progresses in upward spiralling leaps with interpolated pauses. In the improvised theatre the 'drama' is not decided by the totality of the whole but by the scenic atoms... 'Time' is not presented but moments. The acts of a play are loosed from one another; they form a chain of independent, illuminating impulses.[59]

The stylistic characteristics of expressionism are generally dismissed today as outdated, the thematic aspirations as inflated and pretentious. But much of the subsequent avant garde development either repeats or derives from their experiments. The varied attempts to create a 'total theatre' – whether through Wagner's symphonic *Gesamtkunstwerk* in which all the other elements of drama were subordinated to the romantic absolutes of idealism and emotion in the music – or, as in Dullin's work at L'Atelier, uniting a multiplicity of theatrical styles to create a specifically theatrical form of fantasy 'more expressive than reality'[60] – or in Barrault's stripped-down version where 'lived truth' is created by using the actor alone to project all aspects of the world through vocal and physical expression – or in Artaud's total immersion of the spectator in the stage action, establishing 'direct communication' by a level of physical involvement that acts 'directly and profoundly upon the sensibility through the organs' and creates a receptive state in which 'all the senses interpenetrate':[61] all have their roots in the symbolists' exploration of 'correspondences' between colours and sounds or the expressionists' appeal to the pre-rational, primitive levels of the mind. Above all the Polish Theatre Laboratory repeats and extends the ecstatic acting style, with Grotowski's criterion of emotional sincerity, his use of physical discipline to free 'elemental impulses' in his actors, allowing them to 'go beyond' themselves to spontaneous self-revelation under extreme physical stress, achieving a 'translumination' directly comparable to the expressionist 'transfiguration', and his ideal of performance as 'communion'. Even Moreno's work finds definite echoes. Again in Richard Schechner's Performance Group the audience becomes the 'environment' for the actors; and it is a short step from Moreno's use of theatre to deal with the psychoses of an 'abnormal' group or his rejection of scripts and verbal communication to Artaud's concept of using theatre as corrective therapy for a sick society or his search for 'scenic rhythm' and 'concrete gestures' with 'an efficacy strong enough to make us forget the very necessity of speech'.[62]

Theory and practice

When critics discuss the use of ritual in contemporary drama or avant garde directors describe their attempts to rediscover the primitive ritual function of theatre, Artaud's name is usually the first to be mentioned. Although he can hardly be said to have initiated the trend, he did introduce the term itself into theatrical vocabulary, which up to then had relied on concepts drawn from psychology. With Artaud the focus on dreams and the primitive levels of the psyche becomes extended to include savage roots and primitive culture. Although expressionist painters like Nolde had already turned to African sculpture for inspiration, Artaud was the first to search for theatrical forms that would not only be non-European but specifically 'uncivilised' (as distinct from Strindberg's thematic borrowing from Indian religion, or Yeats' imitation of the Japanese Nōh as a 'noble' and highly refined art). And what impressed him about the Balinese dance–drama was 'the instinctive survival of magic' in what he mistakenly believed were involuntary and visionary gestures that caused 'the movement of religious terror which seized the crowds at the Paris Colonial Exhibition'. This was the effect he aimed at, and he believed that both his Théâtre Alfred Jarry and the Balinese theatre 'fed off the true magical sources of the same primitive unconscious'.[1]

In an 'Open letter to the schools of Buddha' Artaud rejects logic and reason as 'the chains that bind us in a petrifying imbecility of the mind'. What he proposes as positive values in their place are irrational spontaneity and delirium, which would release repressed tendencies in an emotional purgation analogous to the classical/tragic effect of catharsis. Significantly, the model outlined in his theories follows the two syllogistic modes of reasoning that dominate mythological systems, which Frazer defined as the 'laws' of 'sympathetic' magic (like causes like) and 'holophrastic' magic (the part stands for the whole). 'Images of energy in the unconscious and gratuitous crime on the surface' of a stage presentation are assumed to evoke a mirror state in the spectator's mind, if these 'can be projected with the necessary violence';[2] and this delirium will be contagious, exorcising repressive behaviour patterns in society as a whole by its presence in the tiny percentage of the population who attend Artaud's theatre, an analogy to the plague that in Artaud's confused metaphor is 'spiritual freedom' causing 'all social forms to disintegrate' and spreads 'without rats, without microbes, without contact'.[3] The linkage of physical and spiritual in this metaphor is typical of Artaud's approach. Metaphysics are to be imprinted in the mind through the skin, the dynamics of consciousness are embodied in scenic rhythms, the linear harmonies of a picture affect the brain directly. Theatre therefore had to develop a ritual language by rediscovering universal physical signs, or 'hieroglyphs', while verbal expression became incantation. These, in brief, are the elements that can be pinned down as the basics of Artaud's 'Theatre of Cruelty', to which must be added the thematic inversion of good and evil. This has been characteristic of the anarchistic avant garde ever since Strindberg, and as Artaud defines it in the letter appended to his 'Journey to the land of the Tarahumaras' or his 'Letters on cruelty', nature is anti-social by definition, while civilisation – and particularly the moral demands of Christianity – are debilitating lies designed by effete elites to subjugate the strong. To exist at all our supposedly artifical culture has had to label everything physical or natural as 'evil', so that to be true to our proper nature and therefore free to reach our real potential as 'total' men, no longer split by the western body/soul dichotomy, we must do what we have been taught is 'evil', while to force ourselves into the mould that society considers 'good' is the ultimate perversion. Quite apart from the philosophical shakiness of this argument, Artaud is uncertain about the exact status of actual cruelty. At times violence is seen as a symptom of the spiritual distortions breaking out as the repressive behaviour patterns imposed by society become unbearable. Alternatively it is presented as proof of the intrinsic violence of European civilisation compared with Rousseauesque noble savagery. At other times cruelty appears as the law of nature itself, sadistically Darwinian, creative through destruction. But whatever the case, the solution is to be a return to primitive existence, to pre-logical consciousness.

So Artaud's name elicits a formula: Primitivism. Ritual. Cruelty. Spectacle. But what is generally understood as his theory is contradicted in certain important ways by the theatre he actually created, and the closer one looks at what he wrote, the more ambiguous his influence seems. This is partly because his style is positively Delphic in its poetic obscurity. As a result it is the critics and interpreters of his ideas who have given definition to what is seen as 'Artaudian' in modern theatre – and their average approach is curiously uncritical, perhaps because Artaud is in many ways our *alter ego*. He mirrors the contemporary disillusion with conventional forms of society and religion, and pioneered the experiments with hallucinatory drugs. He anticipated the search for new modes of spirituality which today range from the popular interest in eastern religious figures to the following gained by even an ex-conjurer such as Uri Geller, from a widespread belief in the ancient superstition of astrology to the research into parapsychology and ESP at various university centres.

Artaud in fact is closely associated with our existential uncertainties, which may be why he is almost everywhere accepted on his own valuation. 'Prophet', 'magician', 'visionary', 'shaman', 'tragic hero' – this is the common currency of description. Artaud has been attacked on various grounds: that his theatre was unrealisable, inaccessible or divorced from the social and political context of the audience; that it destroys the conventionally accepted principles of drama (which of course was precisely its intention); that it reveals basic misunderstandings of key fields (e.g., psychology and Balinese theatre).[4] Alternatively Artaud is credited with a total 'reinvention' of theatre; creating a compelling harmony from the dialectics of the theatre by transcending his own schizophrenic psychosis; aligning art to the 'solar' and 'lunar' dualities of existence and thus tapping the essence of being.[5] In either case the evidence is drawn solely from his theories. Arguments revolve around abstract concepts which are oracular, and conclusions are derived largely from different attitudes towards Artaud's extraordinary personality. On this level Artaud is all things to all men, an inspiration, for example, to the communard students of Paris in 1968 even though he dedicated one of his poems to Hitler, because his writings are sufficiently vague to allow for almost any radical or anti-traditional interpretation. His basic position may be clear – 'our present social state is iniquitous and should be destroyed. If this fact is a preoccupation for the theatre, it is even more a matter for machine guns'[6] – but his programme is elusive and contradictory. As Adamov has noted, there is 'something effervescent about his dramatic ideas and when one ... thought one had grasped them they vanished'.[7] By contrast the events of his life are known, his actions and ideas are fascinating in their irrationality and his character comes strongly through his writings. Artaud is frequently hailed as the father of modern avant garde theatre, but in fact the relationship is one of immaculate conception. His theories have acted as a catalyst, but his work on the stage has been dismissed without even being explored. The typical reaction has been that 'it is difficult to speak of a theatre that did not take place', and starting from this premise critics take one of two lines. One claims that in a more supportive environment (such as the present) he would have 'transcended the purely spectacular aspect of his Theatre of Cruelty. No doubt he would have led us further into the Promised Land.' The other argues that 'Artaud triumphed not just in spite of failure but in and even through failure'; that because his theories are 'the direct expression of his vital torment', it is his life itself which 'incarnates' his vision, so that 'reading Artaud we are not dealing with the reflection on theatre but a truly theatrical action: the tragedy plays itself out literally before our eyes'.[8] Esslin, for example, combines both lines in the most recent study of Artaud (1976). Apart from one short chapter on 'Artaudian theatre – theory and practice', in which the practice is presented as the work of Barrault, Brook, Grotowski or the Living Theatre, the whole book is a biographical portrait. Since it is published as one of the 'Modern Masters' series, one is left with the irony that Artaud's 'masterpiece' is his life.

This is a curious blurring of the essential distinction between art and life, without which theatre cannot exist – a distinction that Artaud's practice shows he was well aware of, at least until his voyage to Mexico when his most serious mental breakdown began. Artaud's theories in fact do presuppose a dialectical relationship between the stage and the world; despite his followers, who believe that what he claims is true art cannot exist as an independent artifact (a 'product') but only when indistinguishable from the continually changing experience of life (as 'process'), and who seem to have been misled by Artaud's well-known inability to express himself precisely in words. It is perhaps indicative that the most frequently quoted passages are those with least logical sense, and statements such as 'every real effigy has a shadow which is its double'[9] are made no less gnomic by familiarity. But Artaud was capable of being more lucid, and his gloss on the title for his book in a letter to his publisher preserves a clear distinction between drama and daily existence even if it reverses the normal relationship of the stage to society: 'if the theatre is the double of life, life is the double of the true theatre'. Instead of passively mirroring the world, art is seen as a higher form of reality, with material life as an imperfect copy of what art symbolically expresses.

Clearly, this 'true theatre' will consist of something which, though it may be potential, is not present in the experience of modern man: 'the reservoir of the energies made up of myths which man no longer incarnates is incarnated in the theatre'.[10] *The Theatre And Its Double* shows how Artaud, feeling incapable of expressing himself with words, tended to take refuge in arcane mythologies and confused metaphors even before his travels in Mexico; but it is only then that he transfers his focus from the theatre to the cosmos. He still claimed to be seeking the means to stage 'true drama', but now this is divorced from the performing arts and 'may not have anything to do with theatre on the stage'.[11] After this point Artaud, suffering from an increasing mental breakdown accelerated by his use of drugs, obsessed by a desperate search for himself in a series of asylums and institutions, has little relevance for the theatre whatever value his interior drama may have as poetry. Some critics have claimed his last major poem *To Have Done With the Judgement of God* (*Pour en finir avec le jugement de Dieu*, which was divided between various voices for radio production in 1948) as the only true example of his Theatre of Cruelty. But this ignores explicit comments in the poem itself:

> There is nothing I loathe
> And detest as much as this idea of a play,
> Of a performance,
> Because of the appearance, the unreality,
> Attached to all that is produced and that is
> Shown . . .
> This whole broadcast was only made in order to
> Protest against the so called principle of appearance
> Of unreality,
> Of a play anyhow . . .[12]

Few contemporary directors have totally escaped Artaud's influence, but there has only been one consistent attempt to test Artaud's theories in practice. Unlike such self-styled disciples as Schechner or Beck and Malina, who adapted what ideas they borrowed to hybrid forms of their own, Peter Brook and Charles Marowitz specifically took Artaud's writings as the basis for their work in 1964. Their 'Theatre of Cruelty' had the limited focus of a controlled experiment. It was designed as a training for actors and culminated in a series of demonstration performances which included the first staging of *The Spurt of Blood* (*Le Jet de sang*). The results of that experimental season, which were incorporated into the productions of *The Screens* and *Marat/Sade* – a new freedom and directness in action, the filling of a stage space with movement and swift changes of mood from horror to farce – seem less 'Artaudian' than might have been expected. But at that time neither Brook nor Marowitz knew anything of Artaud's work outside *The Theatre And Its Double*. Interestingly, the conclusion that Brook came to was indeterminate: 'you should take Artaud un-adulterated as a way of life, or say that there is something in Artaud that relates to a style of theatre'; and this 'something' was defined as being 'certain limited, specific – almost technical – things, the use of yoga and breathing exercises, the expression of emotion by imagi-natively locating specific feelings in different parts of the body'[13] (in other words those suggestions contained in Artaud's essays which have least to do with metaphysics or the state of western culture, 'An affective athleticism' and 'The seraphim theatre').

Artaud's far-fetched mythological metaphysics in fact have as little to do with his development and practice of theatre as Bernard Shaw's quasi-religious theories of vital economy. If Artaud's essays have eclipsed his practical achievements it is as much as anything else because they promise something much grander than could ever be achieved in practice. Artaud had the habit of exaggerating to an ex-treme degree. He was himself aware of this as a defect, and in an illuminating postcript to a letter asking Jean Paulhan not to publish one of his theatre reviews since what he had written bore little rela-tion to what he had seen, he commented 'I cannot write without enthusiasm and I always go too far.'[14] This, rather than any lack of financial backing, is the reason for the gulf between Artaud's theory and his practice; and a good example of this gulf is the emphasis on drama as 'process', not finished product, in what is commonly con-sidered 'Artaudian' theatre.

His essays (and his followers) claim 'direct staging' and improvisa-tion as the basis of 'true' theatre. In his outlines for productions and his own actual stagings, however, he stressed that a performance should only *seem* to be improvised and merely 'give us the impression of not only being unexpected but also unrepeatable'[15] – a normal, indeed conventional standpoint. Even his attack on language in the theatre is not what it appears. With the possible exception of Yeats, who once expressed the frustrated desire that his actors rehearse their lines in barrels to make it impossible for them to substitute gestures and movements for the rhythms and sense of his poetry, one can hardly imagine any director or playwright believing that the logical meaning of words is the sole means of theatrical communication – yet it is this (non-existent) attitude that Artaud seems to be attacking. In fact his aim was to bring every element of a performance, including the script, under his rigid control, and his rejection of dramatic texts is really an argument for a more exclusive method of recording the totality of a production. Hence his wish for a system of notating gestures, facial expressions, attitudes, movements, tonal variations and breathing, and his search for ways of making these subtleties of expression exact, controllable and reproducible. What he wanted was 'a work *written down*, fixed in its least details' so that the 'final result' would be 'as strict and calculated as that of any written work' since 'the theatre, less than any other means of expression, will not suffer improvisation'.[16] This did not mean that Artaud approached a script with a preconceived interpretation or with moves already blocked out. According to actors who worked with him, he required that initially every line become a basis for 'free fantasising', and whatever emotional states might be evoked were translated directly into physical terms. But although he refused to allow the use of any traditional acting techniques, free expression was not encouraged. Rather he acted out all the roles himself and imposed a uniform if highly idiosyncratic style by demonstration. The moves, gestures and intonations arrived at were then carefully noted and rehearsed so that there was nothing accidental about the final performance, however frenetic and arbitrary the effect might have seemed. As Raymond Rouleau, who acted the part of the Officer in Artaud's production of *A Dream Play*, noted:

He did not prepare his productions in any precise way . . . His direction was a kind of introspection; he seemed to listen attentively to the promptings of his subconscious. At the first rehearsal, Artaud rolled around on the stage, assumed a falsetto voice, contorted himself, howled, and fought against logic, order, and the 'well-made' approach . . . When he felt that he had found the truth, which his interior voyage had disclosed to him, he fixed it very meticulously.[17]

From Artaud's early programmes of the Théâtre Alfred Jarry to Roger Blin's production notes in the prompt book of *The Cenci*[18] what was stressed is disciplined precision and strictly organised performance; and even Balinese theatre was not just an ideal example of magical and mythological drama. It was as valuable to Artaud for the 'reflective mathematics' of its precise gestures, regulated and impersonal, 'all producing methodically calculated effects which forbid any recourse to spontaneous improvisation'.[19] But the extent that his essays are open to misinterpretation can be seen in the example of certain contemporary directors, such as the Becks in America or Juliani in Canada, who claim to be following Artaud in seeing a performance as a living process and rejecting the idea that it should be a polished or fixed product. In the light of his stage work, however, it becomes clear that even when he refers to theatre as 'not . . . an end but a means'[20] Artaud is simply transferring the emphasis from the play as such to its effect on the audience's imagination. A performance still has to be a finished product; the 'process' takes place in the spectator's perception of it.

Not surprisingly, Artaud's theoretical writings overshadow his practical work in the theatre. Details of performances, after all, tend to be forgotten while essays can be reprinted, and even if his productions are mentioned they are usually dismissed as compromises with the conventional taste of the public, abortive because without financial support or simply dated. But in spite of the material difficulties which prevented him from entirely realising his aims in production, Artaud's focus was the stage. His primary intention was to create a new theatre through 'concrete examples' – concrete (that is, what was physically representable) being one of his key adjectives – and his lack of faith in his ability to communicate through words made performance not only the test but also the expression of his ideas. Hence the detailed outline of how the different elements of his theatre should actually function, together with a specific programme of works in his first manifesto; hence the detailed scenario, for which the statement of ideas seems merely a preface, in his second. Other manifestoes of the time, dadaist or surrealist, are mainly proclamations of principle. Set beside them his commitment to practice is striking; and it is in line with this that he announced that the public should look for the ideas of the Théâtre Alfred Jarry in its performances; 'better than any theories, our programme is there to make our intentions manifest'.[21]

Basing conclusions about Artaud's work on just the three full-length productions and four one-act plays that he managed to stage between 1927 and 1935 would be foolhardy, particularly when the text of one, *Burnt Breast* (*Ventre brûlé ou la mère folle*), is missing and the descriptions of sometimes prejudiced reviewers have to be relied on for many details. But if his scenarios both for screen and stage, the suggested production outlines which he submitted to Jouvet and Dullin and his work in film are taken into account, it is possible to reconstruct a fairly complete outline of his theatre.

Artaud's basic insight was that theatrical reality is different in kind from ordinary reality; that it is self-defeating for the stage to attempt to copy everyday life. As with the expressionists or surrealists, this reaction against naturalism implies a rejection of the philosophical assumptions of western civilisation. Presenting conventional social themes or psychological characterisation exacerbated the fundamental inauthenticity of stage performance, because it simply reinforced the falsified world of appearances; consequently theatre could only escape from pretence by setting its own standard for what is real. Not that this meant creating something unique and independent. The stage was to present inner rather than outer truth, which would be validated by audience response: a 'world touching the real' through its 'direct relation to the agonies and preoccupations' of each spectator.[22] In simple terms Artaud's criterion was emotional relevance, and this remained constant although his techniques developed. Compare his earliest example of 'ideal theatre' in the original manifesto for the Théâtre Alfred Jarry – a police raid on a brothel – and his use of colonisation as the theme for *The Conquest of Mexico* (*La Conquête du Mexique*) scenario in his last manifesto for the Theatre of Cruelty. Both subjects have sexual overtones and deal with basic human drives that arouse highly ambivalent responses. Both represent forms of exploitation that society disguises, but do so objectively as a 'spectacle' without a moral standpoint. Each shows a large number of people in conflict, which is one way of focussing on the event rather than the individual, and uses patterns of movement to suck the audience emotionally into the action. In Artaud's actual stage work the 'cruelty' which appears as a definition of existence in his metaphysical writings is no more than an agent to heighten response by magnification similar to Jarry's use of *Grand guignol*. It is in fact the dynamics that are primary not any intrinsic violence: 'the spectator... will be shaken and set on edge by the *internal dynamism* of the spectacle'.[23]

It is this dynamism that was Artaud's major concern in staging his only full-length play, *The Cenci* (1935). Although based on historical events – via Stendhal and Shelley – this is not just 'a tragedy' in Artaud's view. In his rather idiosyncratic terms it was 'a Myth', because it embodies his Sadeean vision of 'cruelty' in which spirituality is a delusive ideal formulated by the weak to subjugate the strong, an inversion of true values condemning the universal 'laws' of instinct as evil, while elevating a perversion of nature that prevents man from realising his full potential as 'good'; and this debilitating idealism is epitomised in Christianity, which 'consists of ascending into the sky as spirit instead of descending deeper and deeper as a body into hell, that is into sexuality, soul of all that lives'.[24] Hence the choice of a story which deals with the destruction of the heroine's soul, the context of the medieval age of faith and the characterisation of the figures as 'incarnations of great forces' to be judged (*à la* Nietzsche) 'outside of good and evil'.[25] Artaud has reduced the traditional plot to an outline of brutal simplicity by cutting the self-justification and self-analysis, the tremors of motive or conscience out of which conventional dramatic psychology is built up. Count Cenci, who identifies himself with destiny, obeying his 'own law' as 'a force of nature', has the sole ambition of personifying absolute evil. He holds an orgiastic banquet for the rulers of Church and State where he symbolically drinks the blood of his sons, celebrating their destruction by God for which he has prayed, in a parody of the Mass. He rapes his daughter Beatrice, who is driven to murder him, is immediately arrested, tortured, then executed. The effect of Cenci's practice of evil is to liberate the demonic in all the people around him; and the nature of the crimes about which the play revolves, incest and parricide, break the deepest taboos and most fundamental social relationships – those of the family – being given their particularly horrifying character by Artaud's stress on Cenci's status as a father. But it is here that the logic of the play's statement falls apart, since the image of fatherhood also represents social repressions, being repeated in God the Father and his regent on earth, the Pope, who refuses to intervene against Cenci:

'Am I to set myself up against the natural authority of a father? Am I to enfeeble in this manner the principle of my own authority?' Then he answered himself: 'No, never.'

Thus God is both 'the cruel necessity of creation' that Cenci embodies and the Christian divinity he rebels against; the Pope is both as much a criminal as Cenci and the epitome of society; and even Cenci has a contradictory dual signification, not only 'a demon whose task is to avenge the whole world's sins' against nature but a figure symbolising those 'sins' as the representative of the social structure that denies man's true being. Coherence of vision is obviously not as important to Artaud as the intensity, passion and extremity of the action, just as the script itself is only a framework to be filled with 'a whole language of gestures and signs in which the anxieties of the age will blend together in a sort of violent manifestation of feeling'.[26]

However, the stage works most effectively through indirect suggestion. There is far more erotic stimulation in Genet's clothed and masked emblems of prostitution than in the nudity of Tynan's *Oh Calcutta!* – and similarly the violence and cruelty of Artaud's themes were represented by opposites in the 'scenic rhythms' that he had defined as the most important aspect of the theatre's language. Many of his more startling acting effects were shocking because of their unconventionality rather than any impression of sadism, as in Raymond Rouleau's example of the sort of performance Artaud called for where an actor might start a speech standing, continue on his knees and end it flat on his back, presenting his own inner states without reference to the sense of the speech. And the *Cenci* prompt book contains more notes on patterning and tempo (the controlling elements of a production) than on any other aspect.

The banquet scene demonstrates the effect of the dynamism in Artaud's work most clearly, since it employs the largest number of figures: not only all the characters but – echoing Jarry's *Ubu roi* – life-size dummies as well. The opening stage directions in the published text, with their reference to Veronese's painting of 'The Marriage at Cana' (also underlining the sacrilegious theme), suggest a static tableau which erupts into chaotic movement, but Blin's notes show that this movement was highly organised. Starting from a hierarchic pattern of order in three ranks of three, the guests dance in circles of carefully gradated size and speed; the smaller the circle the slower it moves, with the dancers in the wider circles curving around and through the others. Superimposed on this is a repeated vocal pattern: a cry, followed by a laugh, then a sob – and the formalised effect is heightened by being contrasted with the erratic caperings of a dwarf. There is also an overt element of depersonalisation, since certain of the guests are dancing with dummies. The impression aimed at is a dehumanised mechanisation which Artaud compared to the workings of a clock – the opposite to what one normally expects from 'a scene of orgy'. This openly inorganic structure is carried through into even small gestures. For example, when Count Cenci enters, the guests, now arranged in two parallel rows on each side of the set, throw glances at each other diagonally across the stage in an alternating and duplicating sequence. All the actors are required to move as a part of a whole – either in progressions, as when Andrea approaches with the goblet and Blin's note reads 'G, 3 paces; F, 2 paces; E, 1 big pace; J, 1 little pace . . .'; in opposition, or in unison, as when a guest calls for ' . . . torches to light my way; I am leaving':

Here Beatrice draws herself erect. Lucretia droops. Everyone rises. All throw themselves into the centre then draw apart when Cenci says to them: 'Wait.' They move in groups to the right, to the left . . . all rise, they take one pace . . . take 2 paces . . .

This calculated symmetry, which Artaud calls variously a 'dizzying' or 'inhuman rhythm', is undoubtedly how he would have staged even the most apparently chaotic scenes in *The Conquest of Mexico*. Take for instance Montezuma's rebellion where space is described as

. . . gorged with a brawling mosaic where sometimes men, sometimes compact troops tightly pressed together, limb to limb, clash frenetically. Space is stuffed with whirling gestures, clenched fists, manes, breastplates, and from all levels of the scene fall limbs, breastplates, heads, stomachs like a hailstorm bombarding the earth with supernatural explosions.[27]

What sounds orgiastically wild on the page would have been organised into a similar dynamic of clearly defined patterns – as the inconspicuous 'mosaic' and 'whirling' indicate.

Artaud took considerable pride in the 'precision' and 'rigour' of the movements worked out for *The Cenci*, and when he referred to the 'mathematical comings and goings of the actors around others which traces in the air of the stage a true geometry'[28] he was being quite literal. Actions are broken down into mathematical sequences throughout the production; mass movements are based on simple geometric forms which would be instantly recognisable to the audience, parallels, circles or triangles – as when the published stage directions state that the guests 'are huddled in one corner' and Artaud's notes translate this into: 'Colonna places himself on the right, the others fan out into a triangle behind him . . . each, all together and very marked, one pace . . .' These movements are even worked out to give the impression of familiar laws of gravity; for example when the guests 'surge back from all sides in disorder. Panic stricken . . .' Artaud choreographs the actors into a pattern based on centrifugal forces:

Colonna returns towards the guests who each describe a spiralling circle. Colonna moves in a large circle around them . . . as this whirlpool comes to an end the men find themselves flung outside the circle, the women in a heap in the centre.

The striking thing about these detailed directives is not only that the words in the text are, as one might expect, little more than catalysts for extended passages of physical activity. The dynamics of these movements have a very precise and surprising (in view of Artaud's attacks on rationality) intellectual content. In a very real sense they carry the meaning of the play through symbolism. The number three, used widely in the groupings and as a structure of sound, has for many people an almost mystical significance as a prime number with religious connotations, and the basic geometrical shapes are associated with the Greek ideals of harmony and order. Artaud in fact gave a very precise symbolic meaning to the dominant image of the circle which forms the pattern for the majority of individual and group movements and culminates in the torture wheel on which Beatrice swings. It directly represents both the 'circular and closed world' that Artaud associated with cruelty, and the force of necessity, the 'gravitational movement' of that world.[29]

If the rigid patterning, indeed rationality of this physical, visual expression (to say nothing of its cultural base) runs directly counter to Artaud's well-known rejection of intellect and western civilisation, it only suggests that Artaud was more practical as a director than the reader of his theory might suppose. What is perhaps surprising is that this manifestation of order has been used to illustrate a story of both 'corporal' and 'moral' excess which 'goes to the extremity of instinct'.[30] But the extreme dichotomy between style and subject actually follows the precedent established by Jarry, where the incongruity of meticulously applying mathematical formulas or scientific logic to a world of the imagination in his pataphysical writings, or the impossible juxtapositions and fantastic distortions in the *Ubu* plays are designed to have a hallucinatory effect. Jarry's aim was to liberate the subconscious, and Artaud after all had named his theatre after Alfred Jarry. Artaud in fact is after a similar effect in the way he organises his alternative stage world by substituting the laws of the mind for those of physics. Geometry is an abstract summing up of how we see our material environment and as such determines our estimate of our positions *vis à vis* objects, our orientation to reality. By applying geometric shapes to a vision of anarchy and primitive excess, which would make the perspectives on life that they represent seem artificial and arbitrary, Artaud could hope to make his audience uncertain of their familiar assumptions about the physical universe. Simultaneously the dynamism is intended to draw the audience in, to involve them in this stage world, while the rigidly patterned movements give this imaginary creation a visually logical structure analogous to the way we customarily view reality. This was Artaud's way of creating an 'actuality of feeling and thoughts more than of facts' – discrediting

our conventional concept while using its basic organisational principles as subliminal support for an alternative vision: 'reality seen
simultaneously from recto and verso. Hallucination chosen as the
principle dramatic means.'[31]

Form and theme

The opposition of two realities, emotion and instinctive thought versus facts and intellectual constructs, has to be accepted to understand
Artaud's work, even if in the light of common sense this dualism of
his is an oversimplification. The world of facts is all around us and
interpenetrates emotion; to find feeling and thought in a pure state
Artaud turned to dreams.

It is a commonplace that Artaud's scripts and scenarios are mental
dramas, the Mexican revolt against Cortez for instance taking place
simultaneously on the historical plane and on 'every level of
Montezuma's consciousness' with the struggle of white against red,
repressive civilisation against primitive instinct, explicitly located as a
'battleground in the mind of Montezuma'. But it is also far too often
assumed that his work is purely subjective, a realisation of his own
subconscious state. It has even been suggested that Artaud's self-
expression is mainly dramatic in nature (the basis of drama being
conflict) because he suffered from a split personality, so that Artaud
was 'using his "disease" as a dramatic subject *par excellence*'. This may
be an accurate description of his poetry, and Artaud was certainly
involved subjectively in his productions to such a degree that Barrault
accused him of lacking 'sufficient distance' to stage a play successfully.[32] He also projected himself totally into a role like that of Count
Cenci, and even claimed that there should be an identity between the
psychology of the actor and his part, putting himself forward as the
only person capable of doing justice to the figure of Usher in a film
version of Poe's story on the grounds that his personal experience of
mental illness fitted him for playing characters in torment. But Artaud's work is distinct from the characteristic expressionist approach
in which the central figure is the artist, the victim–saviour of mankind, dreaming the other characters who are no more than projections of different aspects of his psyche and together form a complete personality – his own. Apart from one early film scenario, *Eighteen Seconds* (*Les Dix-huit secondes*), where the central figure has strong
autobiographical features, being an actor suffering from a mental
breakdown, Artaud's stage world was not intended to be a

psychological reflection but to achieve an objective existence. From the opening of the Théâtre Alfred Jarry with Roger Vitrac's *The Mysteries of Love* (*Les Mystères de l'amour*), when Artaud claimed that 'for the first time a *real dream* has been produced in the theatre',[33] to his essays on cruelty, dreams are set beyond the personal by being consistently qualified with adjectives like 'true', 'concrete', 'the theatre's dreams'.

The expressionism of *The Road to Damascus*, then, was not Artaud's road. But there is a definite link between his aims and the way Strindberg was perceived in France, since his term 'cruelty' was first coined to describe *Miss Julie*: 'M. Strindberg is not a true realist; rather his harsh and acrid eloquence, his indictments against society, the taste which leads him to depict the ugliness of life and the soul without restraint . . . without shame, epitomise the literature of cruelty.'[34] In spite of Artaud's rejection of psychological subject matter and 'research into human personalities' as being 'what disgusts us most',[35] the surrealist ideal of staging dreams led him inevitably to Strindberg; and in his experimental production of *A Dream Play* (1928) he developed some of his most characteristic techniques. When his earlier productions qualified as dreams it seems to have been because of a certain thematic quality. *The Mysteries of Love* (1927) with its violent and unmotivated action, its illogicality and the suspension of cause and effect (as when a murdered man reappears laughing), as well as its direct assault on the audience (ending with a spectator 'killed' by a shot from the stage), is described as a 'real dream' because it reversed normal assumptions and presented a view of existence freed from conventions. Thus its value for Artaud was that it 'realised on the stage the anxiety, the mutual isolation, the criminal ulterior motives and the eroticism of lovers'[36] – a parodistic synthesis of spiritual ideals and animality which also found expression in Vitrac's *Victor*, where the stage effect that Artaud seemed to have prized most was a Jarryesque offence to sensibility – the contrast between the beauty of the leading actress and requiring her to break wind every time she spoke; childishly scatological but seemingly effective since some critics commented with disgust, and the first actress engaged for the part resigned loudly when she found out what was required.

Vitrac is one of the few successful playwrights produced by the surrealist movement. The dramatic output of Aragon, Breton or Ribemont-Dessaignes is hardly conceived in stage terms, and the surrealist principles of rejecting any compromise between art and the material world, or opposing the conventional reality principle, as in the proclamation at the end of Breton's *Manifeste du surrealisme* that 'Existence is elsewhere', are inconsistent with the physical nature of theatrical presentation. Artaud's expulsion from the surrealist movement, together with Vitrac, which forms the background to the surrealists' disruption of the *Dream Play* production, was inevitable. His concentration on staging was seen as a betrayal, emphasising the medium (theatre) over artistic content (the presentation of subconscious reality) and creating work within a conventional genre – an aesthetic quarrel further complicated by Breton's conversion to communism that led Artaud to declare, 'in the theatre only what is theatrical interests me, to use the theatre to launch any revolutionary idea (except in the realm of the spirit) appears to me the most base and repulsive opportunism'.[37] But Artaud's intentions continued to follow the basic surrealist line. Thus his aim of creating 'profound transformations on the level of appearances, in the values of signification' by using the material of dreams and the subconscious to spark off 'that intense liberation' or 'metamorphosis of the inner condition of the soul' which can 'push back reality' ('A la grande nuit ou le bluff surrealiste', June 1927, a pamphlet rebutting Breton's attack on his work in 'Au grand jour') is a restatement of an early proposal, welcomed by the surrealists, that in his ideal theatre 'all that is dark, buried deep, unrevealed in the mind, should be manifested in a sort of physical projection, as real'.[38]

With such aims it was natural that the Théâtre Alfred Jarry should become the interpreter of Vitrac, who had described his work as subconscious images for a 'Theatre of Conflagration'. Indeed an early play like *Poison* (1923), 'a drama without words' which adapts silent film techniques to the stage in a visual montage of dream-like images, logically unrelated and distorted in scale, anticipates many of Artaud's principles. Another early play, *Free Entry* (*Entrée libre*, 1922), clearly shows the influence of Strindberg. Three tableaux, each representing the projection of a dream by one character in a love triangle, lead to a central scene where the dream images are re-enacted in a realistic dinner-table setting, causing violence to break through conventional behaviour and the murder of one of the characters. This is followed by three further tableaux, each relating again to one dreamer but in reverse order, echoing the symmetrical structure of *To Damascus*. In this amalgam of arbitrary and subjective images, events are deliberately confused and unclear, even the identity of the victim is uncertain, giving the atmosphere of violent cruelty and emotional distress the imaginative force of fact. The same ambiguity recurs in

The Mysteries of Love, where political realities become images of obsessions, with characters transformed into Lloyd George or Mussolini, while again at the climax of the play the dream is shown to have sufficient emotional power decisively to affect reality when the melodramatic multiple murders spill out into the auditorium with the death of a spectator. However this merging of different levels of reality places too great a strain on the suspension of disbelief. It may correspond to the 'revolutionary' aim, outlined by Artaud in 'A la grand nuit', of throwing 'the existing basis of things off its axis, of changing the angle of reality', which can also be seen in the play's opening where the action begins, while the house lights are still up, with an argument between two ostensible spectators (the main characters) that becomes more disjointed and associative as it grows louder and attracts attention. But these dislocations of perspective and conventional assumptions are crudely artificial, and Artaud cut them in performance. For him it was 'a question of shifting the spiritual centre of the world, of changing the levels of appearances, of that transfiguration of the possible... beginning with spiritual derangement',[39] and *Victor, or the Children Take Power (Victor ou les enfants au pouvoir,* 1929) is a far more effective realisation of these aims. The title itself indicates the thematic inversion of conventional values, and the action is a Jarryesque mixture: simultaneously a parody of boulevard drama and a dream. The total experience of life is telescoped into a bare three hours for the outsize Victor – 6 ft tall and visibly growing during the performance – on the evening of his ninth birthday. Brought face to face with the hypocrisy of his parents' bourgeois society, he changes from a model child to an anarchistic iconoclast. He smashes Sèvres china, disrupts his father's adulterous romances, drives their cuckolded neighbour (patriotism in the shape of an ex-soldier from the 1870 Franco-Prussian war) to hang himself in uniform trousers and nightshirt from his flagstaff to the tinny sound of a military march on a gramophone, and dies because experiencing every aspect of existence has shown him there is nothing worth living for. The distortions of time and scale, together with syntactical dislocations and nonsense language, reach a peak in the father's erotic daydream, where the figures from a soft-porn serialised romance (*Les Hommes de l'air,* 'a novel of sport and love') take on more reality than the 'real life' characters. The focal point in Artaud's production was Ida Mortemart, the ethereal *femme fatale* with a gross physical disability. Her entry signals a psychic liberation, even for Victor's socially repressed father, whose speech breaks through into stream of

consciousness – 'Ida Mortemart, croupissant comme la mer Morte
... Ida, dada, Ida, dada, Morte? Mortemart? J'en ai marre, marre,
marre'[40] – and the power of dream to affect the real world was supposedly demonstrated by throwing stink bombs across the footlights
every time she farted. This was also intended to bring home 'the
poisonous effect of matter and moral grief' that 'spiritually crucified'
the potential 'intelligence and superiority of the other world' that the
dream-woman represents.[41]

There are structural parallels between *The Mysteries of Love* and *A
Dream Play*, and Vitrac still claimed to be following Strindberg in
Victor, calling him 'one of the most admirable liberators of the
mind'.[42] But here Strindberg's influence is only retained in a general
emphasis on the falsity of external appearances contrasted with the
reality of dream states, and (following Artaud's defense against the
surrealist disruption of his *Dream Play* production) in the negative aim
of 'vomiting on his fatherland, on all nations, on society'. As the
father's verbal associations on the name of Ida proclaim, it was dada
that determined the way Vitrac developed Strindberg's concepts, and
the dadaist influence was already clear in *Poison*, where the twelfth
tableau which 'depicts a mouth that pretends to speak'[43] echoes Tristan Tzara's *Gas Heart* (*Coeur à gaz*, 1920). The dada movement was not
simply the artistic iconoclasm that it is still frequently seen as today.
In Berlin its attack on bourgeois principles had a positive political
rationale; in Paris dada shared the surrealist belief that the free flow of
imagination and release of the subconscious could liberate the individual from repression. Despite André Breton's desperate attempts to
preserve the immaculate conception of his surrealist movement, as
Barrault has commented, Louis Aragon, Robert Desnos, Breton,
Tzara and Artaud continued to mix; and beneath even the most negative statement of the dada attitude lie values of spontaneity, intuitive
response, creative irrationalism and immediacy that the surrealist
manifestoes also proclaimed:

Every product of disgust capable of becoming a negation of the family is
Dada; a protest with the fists of its whole being engaged in destructive action:
Dada; knowledge of all the means rejected up until now by the shamefaced
sex of comfortable compromise and good manners: Dada; abolition of logic,
which is the dance of those impotent to create ... Dada; abolition of
memory ... Dada; abolition of the future: Dada; absolute and unquestionable
faith in every god that is the immediate product of spontaneity.[44]

The lines between the two movements in fact are almost indistinguishable when Tzara describes his artistic aim as embodying 'the

forms, common to all men, of that poetic activity whose deep roots draw on the primitive structure of affective life'; and looking back on his activities after a quarter of a century Tzara put the dadaist 'will to destroy' in its true perspective: 'much more of an aspiration toward purity and sincerity than the tendency toward a sort of vocal or plastic inanity, satisfied with stasis and absence'.[45]

Traces of dada can be seen too in an early work of Artaud's like *Burnt Breast* (*Ventre brûlé ou la mère folle*) when he was just beginning to formulate his theories of cruelty. Part of the same bill as *The Mysteries of Love*, this play can only be reconstructed from hints provided by reviews. It combined a dadaist parody of conventional authority-symbols, such as a king and queen, and of materialistic society and its surrogate experience in bizarre figures like 'the Horn of Plenty' or 'the Hollywood Mystery', with surrealist elements that already show Artaud's attraction to the primitive and ritualistic. While Vitrac's play is fairly literary, although the protagonist demands that the author write plays without words and is told to spit out the words put into his mouth, *Burnt Breast* was almost pure mime, with dialogue limited to single words or isolated sentences that were apparently delivered with such overcharged emphasis as to be (deliberately?) incomprehensible. However, both plays shared the same disregard for cause-and-effect logic. Modern life (presumably) was represented by a young man suffering – in a deep armchair – extremes of ennui despite the material plenty poured by a cornucopia in female shape. A violent storm announces the entry of another woman, embodying the celluloid fantasies of Hollywood, and gives the signal for wild dancing (variously described as a tango or a fox-trot) which culminates in the death of the king. His queen steps disdainfully over his body with a vulgar comment about cuckolds, and the performance ends with a long funeral procession (comparable to the frenetic cortège in René Clair's *Entr'acte*) that dances around the stage with flaring candles to what was obviously intended as primitive and atavistic music. However little justice such a bare-bones description does to the play, it would need to have been acted with extraordinary skill to be effective. The use of imagery is, to say the least, unsophisticated and over-exuberant; but Artaud's aim was clearly to induce a hallucinatory vision which would provoke Pavlovian responses from the spectators' subconscious. His choice of rather hackneyed atmospheric effects – the grotesque funeral march in ultra-violet light, the savage dance in almost complete darkness, strokes of lightning and portentous symbolism – has to be seen as an indication that his search for techniques was in a rudimentary stage. Probably the most effective aspect was the music, described by the composer as 'almost entirely for percussion; monotonous or frenetic pulsations, rudimentary rhythms...'[46]

With *A Dream Play* new perspectives opened, and it was the work on this production which brought Artaud to formulate his idea of a stage reality quite separate from naturalistic illusion:

> Nothing is less capable of deluding us than the illusion of fake properties, of cardboard and painted canvas which the modern scene gives us... There is in the simple exposition of real objects, in their combinations, in their order, in the relationships of the human voice with light, a reality which is self-sufficient and has no need of any other to live. It is this false reality which is theatre, and it's that which it is necessary to cultivate... The false in the context of the true, that is the ideal definition of this *mise en scène*.[47]

The effect in this particular production was crude, and the highly stylised acting was presented on a bare stage with a screen for projections as the only scenery and a ladder for ascents into heaven, an uncomfortable clash of fluid abstraction and over-literal concreteness. But this new awareness gained from working on Strindberg was seminal for Artaud's development. On one level it led to the parody of naturalistic conventions – as in the first act of Vitrac's *Victor* where Artaud suspended empty window-, door- and picture-frames from the proscenium to literally create a fourth wall and so make the spectators' role as 'voyeurs' explicit. More to the point, it resulted in his use of real objects for the décor instead of either the customary pretence of flats and backcloth or the conventional way of representing dreams by impressionistic, atmospheric vagueness. These objects were not symbolic in the way the 'Horn of Plenty', coffin or crowns of *Burnt Breast* had been, but gained significance from being out of scale or out of context; and where symbols were called for they were presented as deliberately artificial.

Artaud's production proposals for *The Ghost Sonata* provide a good example of this use of the stage. In Strindberg's play there is a surface level of 'crime and secrets and guilt' that corresponds to the adulterous or corrupting past revealed by the action of plays like Ibsen's *Ghosts* or *The Wild Duck* and Hauptmann's *Before Sunrise*. But here the patterns of guilt are so complex and convoluted that they act as a parody of typically naturalistic concerns, exaggerated to a point where they become unreal. The mummified wife of the Colonel is the mother of the Girl by the Old Man (Hummel), who had seduced her in revenge for the Colonel's seduction of his fiancée. She has also been the mistress of the Baron, who is divorcing the heiress of the dead Consul to marry his illegitimate daughter, his Janitor's wife's child, who is already the Baron's lover and pregnant with his illegitimate baby. But this network of relationships, any single part of which would have been the primary focus for a naturalistic drama, is treated like a mirage of false appearances, beneath which facts of existence on a far more basic level are revealed. The play moves inward from the street to the hyacinth room, growing progressively more grotesque as the action becomes internalised. Fake social roles are peeled away, with Hummel stripping the Colonel of his spurious family name, uniform, wig and false teeth, only to be unmasked himself as a murderer by the Mummy, until the physical world becomes transparent and we reach the dream level of subconscious reality. Here the embodiment of material existence in Hummel's double appears, the vampire cook who drains the spirit of its vitality, and the saviour Student liberates the Hyacinth Girl from life by making her realise that 'she was withering away in this air charged with crime and deceit and falseness of every kind'.[48] Corresponding to this, the settings Artaud envisaged were to be representational though not naturalistic, the background for Act I being composed of three-dimensional free-standing houses lining two streets receding up a hill, but with subtly conflicting perspectives and details picked out in unnatural clarity. Various objects – the fountain, a cornice, perhaps a window or a pot of flowers – were to function as focal points highlit with '... an intense halo of light. Most would be larger than life... the paving stones in the street climbing in the background in sharp relief as in a cinema set.' In some ways this corresponds to Otto Falckenberg's expressionist production of the play, in which physical details were exaggerated, with the cook carrying an oversized ladle and sauce bottle and with the clock dwarfing the characters. But Artaud's hallucinatory mix of actuality and distortion was a logical extension of the way he had staged *The Mysteries of Love,* where an early concern for the geometrical patterning that characterised *The Cenci* was also already evident:

For the first time on the stage real objects could be seen: a bed, a cupboard, a stove, a coffin, all subject to a surrealist order, which is disorder in terms of ordinary reality, responding to the profound logic of the dream at the point where it abruptly materialises in life. Multi-coloured lights responded to the same strange logic, to an identical preoccupation with equilibrium and musicality.

The same selective heightening of reality was carried over into the characterisation. Strindberg's desiccated mummy was presented as an elderly high-society widow, the desired effect of horror being created by a subtle contrast between the visual impression of normality and her unnatural, poetic lines which were delivered in a 'special' voice. This would probably have repeated the effect Artaud had achieved with Génica Athanasiou's acting of Léa in *The Mysteries of Love*; not the artificial and dissonant vocalisation of Jarry's original *Ubu roi*, but rather: 'a gilded, quivering, mysterious voice ... the true voice of archaic Greece, when in the depths of the labyrinth Minos sees the sudden crystalisation of the Minotaur in the virgin's flesh'.[49] The intention was to lift the action onto a visionary level, while the conventional appearance of the character, being seen as independent of the inner personality, as an autonomous and objectified surface, would make the audience question their assumptions about social reality. Similarly 'the acting should give at times the impression of slow motion in film' – the effect of this specific technique being to make us aware of the musculature of motion while paradoxically divorcing this from its function, so that the details we never normally see, broken down into separate elements, become real while the overall movement seems illusory. By contrast an overt symbol such as the monstrous, life-sucking cook was deliberately artificial, being (literally) an object and one which could only be given movement, personality, purpose through the individual imagination of each spectator: 'The character of the cook will be represented by a mannequin and its speeches projected in an enormous and monotone voice through several loud speakers in such a way that it isn't possible to perceive the source exactly.' The consistent principle is that the objects should be understood for what they actually are in an immediate sense. They are not transposed into intellectual signifiers. A movement is a series of motions, a street is built up of separate paving stones, a symbol is a symbol. Even where there is to be deliberate distortion, this is created by exaggerating a normal perception; say the effect of reflections on glass or unexpected soundproofing, setting totally silent movement in one area against the ordinary sounds of life on the rest of the stage, as in Act III where

to the right and rear the little round salon will be set up, separated from the front of the stage by a large glass comparable to those of windows in department stores, of such a kind that everything which happens behind it will be flat and as if deformed in water; and above all no noise will come from this part of the stage.[50]

The mixture of magic realism and Daliesque distortion in this *mise en scène* is clearly intended to be hallucinatory. But it is worth noting that it is through a conviction of reality (in theatrical terms) rather than pretence (in terms of life) that this dislocation of perception and freeing of responses is to be achieved.

These techniques were extended in Artaud's subsequent stage work, scenarios and production outlines. *The Cenci*, for example, has distortions in scale (miniature men in armour 'like the figures on the face of the great clock of Strasbourg cathedral'), cinematic slow motion (characters 'moving extraordinarily slowly... walking at the same statue-like pace'), contrasts between mannequins and living actors, and juxtapositions of the everyday with the abnormal (as in the torture prison which 'sounds just like a busy factory').[51] In Artaud's production the acting was highly stylised, with the figures in the Banquet Scene presented as animals to symbolise the bestial nature of society beneath the fine robes; while the setting isolated significant objects, distorted perspectives through staircases built on opposing diagonals and was constructed of three-dimensional shapes which were evocative rather than naturalistic. As one impressed reviewer described it:

a *décor* at once interior, symbolic and Italianate in which everything falls into place with extreme simplicity and force... The built-up scenery on which people walk is essentially architectonic and is reminiscent of a gigantic prison palace by Piranese... there is a scaffolding like a huge ladder and a round column against the sky which raises the Cenci palace to a frightening height.[52]

Sound effects in the *The Cenci* were designed to have the same qualities as the visual elements of the production: unmistakable reality, heightened and transposed. The dialogue was neither conversational nor conventionally dramatic, but orchestrated for musical effect with the delivery formalised to create clear rhythms. Noises-off were as far as possible real sounds, rather than rolling a barrel in the wings for thunder; but, like the speeches, lifted out of their expected context. For example, although borrowing huge bells from a church proved impractical (to Artaud's disappointment), he still insisted on actual bells, making a recording of peals from a specific cathedral – and then amplified the reality of this sound by projecting it through loudspeakers at all four corners of the theatre, so that the spectator was placed in 'a net of sonorous vibrations', set in an unusual and overwhelming relationship with the familiar. This effect was also used to transpose the characters directly into the audience's minds, with the performers' steps at times accompanied by recorded footsteps, amplified at full volume over the loud-speakers surrounding the auditorium and given symbolic resonance by the beat of a metronome oscillating at different speeds, so the rhythmic stamping must have echoed like footfalls in the audience's skulls. Similarly, the musical accompaniment by Roger Desormière came from an electronic keyboard capable of producing a far wider range of sounds than orchestral instruments. Being free of the 'art' connotations of conventional music it could only be called 'Musique Concrète', sounds organised into patterns instead of notes composed into tunes, though in fact its structural principles were based on the seven-beat rhythms of Inca music and intended to give a primitive, exotic tone. Artaud summed up Desormière's achievement as managing 'to catch the noise of machines in an urban factory which would not be out of place in a torture chamber of the middle ages', and indeed this impression came across – reviewers found themselves unable to describe the music except by comparison to 'Negro fan-fares at the Exposition Coloniale' or 'the cry and the railway catastrophe'.[53]

This stress on actuality portrayed with hallucinatory precision or

9 *The Cenci.* Evocative setting & the transposition of reality. Note also the stylised and choreographed movement.

perceived from unusual angles (and doubly unnatural in the theatrical context of pretence) is the keynote of Artaud's approach. Where
figures are overt symbols they are presented on a purely symbolic
plane as 'concrete images', like the sixteen-foot-high mannequins
proposed to Jouvet for the dream scene in a play by Alfred Savoir,
which were to have recognisable faces of French politicians but carried such props as the Arc de Triomphe on their shoulders, or the
giant mask of the head of Montezuma in *The Conquest of Mexico*. With
live actors, Artaud's aim was to create a new sense of man and his
relationship to the universe by distortions of scale, movement,
perspective – as with Cortez and his men larger than their ships, or
the crowd forming patterns out of 'diverse and contradictory
movements as an ant heap seen from very high up'.[54] Verbal expression and gesture were always heightened and unnatural, while real
noises were used for sound effects, as in the *mise en scène* submitted to
Jouvet for Vitrac's *Battle of Trafalgar* (*Le Coup de Trafalgar*). Here, instead of attempting to reproduce the sound of a crowd of one
hundred thousand with ten extras, an actual mob was to be recorded
on disc then amplified through loud-speakers 'in all parts of the stage
and auditorium'. The proposed set of this production was also typical, houses and streets were to be constructed 'in relief . . . like a film
set' or seen from a viewpoint foreign to the stage: 'the scene will
appear through a cutout in a wall, not painted but showing on one of
its sides its true thickness, as in certain film sets'.[55] It would have
been along the lines of these examples that Artaud's lost play, *The
Torture of Tantalus* (*Le Supplice de Tantale*), was intended to create 'a
new reality' out of '*extreme* realism'.[56]

The influence of film

The constant comparison to film is significant, and its relationship to
Artaud's work was obvious enough for reviewers to apply the expectations and standards of cinema (usually unfavourably) to his stage
productions – as for instance one comment on *A Dream Play*: 'This
performance has confirmed me in the opinion that dreams or nightmares should go back to being the property of the cinema.'[57] Yet surprisingly little critical attention has been paid to the influence of Artaud's
film experience on his theatre. His film career, where dealt with at all,
is treated as completely separate to his theatrical experiment, and the
only cross-references that have been made are tantalising in their
incompleteness.[58] But to see the one in terms of the other can be

illuminating. His early film scenarios and *The Shell and the Clergyman* (*La Coquille et le clergyman*, 1927) pre-date the Théâtre Alfred Jarry, while his film acting and script writing continued while he was formulating his 'Theatre of Cruelty'. In 1928 he was praising film as the new art form through which alone his ideas could be realised, and it was only in 1933 with his essay on 'The premature old age of the cinema' that he rejected the screen – not as a medium in itself but because it had become commercialised, turning art and artists into 'commodities', and because the 'talking cinema' was 'an absurdity. The negation of cinema itself.'[59] The silent film in effect was seminal for Artaud. Not only can its influence be traced in his stage work, but it explains the nature of some of his techniques and also accounts for why certain aspects of his productions were less than successful.

The relationship between reality that is accessible to the senses, the physical world of matter, and the 'mystical reality' of emotion and spirit, the instinctual world of the unconscious, is frequently referred to by Artaud in his discussions about cinema. His estimate of 'the present epoch' wavers from a belief that no time in history has been a better seeding ground for 'sorcerers and saints' because of the reaction against nineteenth-century materialism and the questioning of the validity of sense data, to a conviction that the feeling for anything but the immediate has been 'lost'. But film always lies in the interstices of this equation and its development as an art form is seen as a direct response to what Artaud thought was the twentieth century's growing inability to communicate with words or to represent the whole of life in conventional artistic forms. 'True cinema' for him was not representational, not story telling. Nor was it abstract or psychologically based. It was the camera's power to focus the attention on apparently insignificant objects that was important to Artaud. This could not only heighten details into images but make the inanimate seem alive; while cutting could create metamorphoses and rhythms through which the physical world became a subliminal image. As in *The Cabinet of Dr Caligari*, human figures could be stripped of their all too solid flesh and appear as phantoms in settings which were the shadows of the mind; and for many critics this instant classic epitomised the nature of cinema as an art form, so that 'film requires the ultimate in exaggerated and rhythmic gestures, the expressive possibilities for transformation and variation inherent in the screen'.[60]

At one stage Artaud considered that this new art form as a 'remarkable excitant' would relegate theatre to 'the wardrobe of memory', and it seems to have been only when commercial pressures turned it into a 'hybrid' art through substituting words for images that he began to work for 'total spectacle' on the stage – in conscious opposition to talking cinema.[61] But, not unnaturally perhaps, he attempted to transfer to the stage those unique cinematographic elements which gave film the 'magical' ability to transform the world into an alternate reality. Practically all his theatrical devices discussed so far correspond to film techniques, which Artaud believed acted directly on the brain. His description of *The Shell and the Clergyman* as 'the mechanism of a dream' is equally applicable to his structuring of theatrical performances. The spotlighting of objects in *The Ghost Sonata* or the perspective through a hole in the wall in *The Battle of Trafalgar* is the equivalent of focus. The rhythms of movement in *The Cenci* or the flying transformations of images in *The Conquest of Mexico* are intended to gain the same effect as cutting and montage. Even his plastic concept of sound (as in the stage directions to *There Are No Heavens Anymore* – *Il n'y a plus de firmament*, where sound is described as falling 'from very high' and splashing 'widely out, forming arches, parasols')[62] is related to his film experience. The parallels between film and stage are perhaps most obvious in his use (or disuse) of dialogue, single words as the catalyst for extended movement, cries as an accompaniment for action, which corresponds very closely to the use of sub-titles in early silent cinema. Being brief sentences or single words, these were limited to the key phrase of a whole conversation, the summing up of a complex emotional situation already acted out in physical movement or facial expression on the screen, sometimes an editorial statement independent of the characters – and always, like small placards, presented in visual terms. Although he was not so unrealistic as to think the theatre available to him was technically capable of achieving the fluid freedom of the cinema in moulding images, and much of the dialogue in his full-length play, *The Cenci*, functions conventionally in building character, expressing thought, explaining situation, yet his film scenario, *The Butcher's Revolt* (*La Révolte du boucher*), indicates what Artaud was working toward in the theatre. This can be seen as an attempt to come to terms with talking cinema by using dialogue to extend the effect of sub-titles. All the speeches are short and some are separated from the scenario by being printed centre page with a surrounding border. As Artaud announces in the introduction, 'the words pronounced have only been put there to make the images reverberate. The voices are there *in space* like objects . . . Voices and sounds [are organised] on the visual plane . . . in and for themselves and not as the *physical consequence* of a movement or an act.[63]

Some of the films Artaud acted in are as influential for his theatrical ideas as his own scenarios. He placed a great deal of importance on his major roles, Marat in Abel Gance's *Napoléon*, Massieu in Carl Dreyer's *Passion of Joan of Arc* and the Intellectual in Léon Poirier's *Verdun*; and some of the techniques, even the atmosphere of these films, can be paralleled in his stage projects. *Napoléon*, a landmark in the cinema's technical development, used simultaneous projection on three screens, the central action being flanked by rhythmically repeated images to give a subliminal impression of energy, transmitting emotion through movement. Gance also sought to involve the audience by giving the camera the viewpoint of the characters. He set the camera in motion on the saddle of a galloping horse, threw it from a cliff for Napoleon's dive into the sea and identified it with the emotional rhythms of the action – as when he attached the camera to the chest of a tenor while recording the Girondins singing the 'Marseillaise', so that the filmed scene pulsated with his breath. *The Passion of Joan of Arc* was originally intended to be a talking film, but since there were no studios equipped for sound in Paris in 1927 Dreyer used close-ups and all the expressive possibilities of camera angles to compensate. The faces of the actors were without make-up to accentuate the interior play of thought or emotion and to give the impression of reality, by contrast with the more usual film practice of the time where actors were made up as for the stage. Dreyer's comments on the film are remarkably like some of Artaud's statements about his stage intentions – 'I seek nothing but life itself . . . what is important is not the objective drama of images but the subjective drama of souls'[64] – and according to one observer the cast became so emotionally involved in the production that there was a remarkable merging of fictional action and reality. This account is worth quoting at length, because in many ways it represents in ideal terms Artaud's aim of creating a hallucinatory or alternate reality, which he was developing less than a year later in his work on *A Dream Play*. It also helps to explain his insistence on the director's control of every detail of a production, though here the effect was on the actors rather than on an audience. Apparently the atmosphere created on the set was so effective that the actors,

caught up by the will-power and faith of the director remained unconsciously in their roles after the shooting had finished . . . living the drama as if it were actuality . . . Particularly impressive was the day when, in a silence as of an operating theatre, in a pale light as of the morning of an execution, Falconetti's [Joan's] hair was cut close-cropped to the scalp. Our sensibilities . . . were moved as if the mark of infamy had been carried out in reality. The electricians, the mechanics held their breath and their eyes were full of tears.[65]

Despite Artaud's emphasis on them, his roles in these films were relatively minor. Marat was a bit-part in an epic treatment of the revolution, which included the deaths of Robespierre and Saint-Juste as well as Marat, and covered Napoleon's career from infancy. Massieu, Joan's confessor, only appeared in scenes with Falconetti where the dramatic focus was on her. The Intellectual in *Verdun* was the centre of only one scene, in which he goes mad and has to be restrained from rushing over the parapet in the middle of a bombardment. But these characters echoed Artaud's concept of dramatic figures, and his portrayal of them explains what seems a very odd style of acting in plays like *The Cenci*.

The characterisation in *The Cenci*, deliberately unnaturalistic and allowing barely enough personalising traits for psychological plausibility, was intended to work on a metaphysical rather than a social plane. The figures were conceived as superhuman 'beings' who incarnated the great forces of nature because they were in direct contact with the 'cruelty' at the root of existence. They were beyond moral judgement, because (like such natural disasters as lightning or tidal waves) their acts were not the result of individual will. This, of course, is exactly what one would expect from reading *The Theatre And Its Double*, where stage figures are seen as reflections of myth, so being objectified into 'nervous magnetisms', 'passionate manifestations', and the actor is expected to depict 'total man' instead of an individualised personality.[66] But Artaud had already formulated this concept of dehumanised, moral rather than psychological characterisation with reference to his film roles before he wrote the essays on 'Cruelty' or 'the Plague'. Talking about his acting of Marat and Massieu in 1929 he described these characters as complementary opposites, absolutes of moral existence. Marat he called 'the first role . . . where it was given to me not only to try to be true, but to express the concept that I have of a figure, a character which appeared as the incarnation of a natural force', and he contrasted this with the Monk, Massieu, whom he saw as acting on the same universal level: 'this time I incarnated a saint, no longer in turmoil, full of paroxysm and perpetually torn away from himself, but calm instead . . .'[67] Artaud saw these characters as 'decisive' for his development, and his portrayal of them was remarkable. There is a magnetism in the mobility of facial expression and a stylised force in movement and gesture which has considerable emotional impact.

These portrayals in fact approach that degree of 'incandescence' which action, situation and images had to reach at least once in a performance if a *mise en scène* was to qualify for Artaud as Theatre of Cruelty.

Looking at early silent film today one is struck by an exaggerated style of acting in otherwise conventionally dramatic roles, which seems to falsify the emotion of the characters by raising it to an unnatural height. A comparatively minor thwarting of a character's purposes is enough for bulging eyeballs, success of any sort brings out symptoms of ecstasy, every situation is an occasion for large gestures and statuesque poses. This is partly due to the use of stage actors in film. The visual rhetoric they had learnt for the theatre, which has to be defined and broad to carry to the gallery, appears oversized in the intimate lens of the camera, which acts as a magnifying glass. It is also partly deliberate; a way of making silence speak, since subtle nuances are easily misread. Artaud took this film acting as a model – intensity being his criterion for effectiveness, and exaggeration, heightening, loudness apparently being mistaken for intensity. Artaud's theatre was also subject to some of the same limitations as the early cinema,

10 Artaud as Count Cenci. Metaphysical characterisation – 'incandescence' & visual cliché.

since his downgrading of verbal communication to incantation in effect meant (as in silent film) replacing speech with a 'concrete language intended for the sense', in other words 'sign language'.[68]

His search for a physical, visual mode of communication follows logically from using the stage to appeal to the pre-rational and primitive level of the mind and the related attempt to create myths, which in surrealist terms were 'precipitates of the universal dream'.[69] This meant finding a symbolic vocabulary that had no allegorical connotations and could not be translated into discursive terms. To evoke a purely subconscious response it had to have the force of apparently involuntary expression; and Artaud's aims correspond to Jung's analysis in which 'the primitive mentality does not *invent* myths, it *experiences* them. Myths are original revelations of the pre-conscious psyche, involuntary statements about unconscious psychic happenings', while his ideal of physical signs foreshadows Cassirer's later definition of mythopoeic thought in which 'the "image" does not represent the "thing"; it *is* the thing'.[70] Unfortunately 'things' only acquire symbolic significance from gathering conscious associations through repeated usage. Conventional symbolic forms were therefore inextricably linked with the 'artificial' culture Artaud rejected and could only be presented as parody, as in *Burnt Breast*. This led him to explore Egyptian hieroglyphics, Chinese ideograms, Mexican pictograms – but these were alien to his audience, and although their strangeness itself had a positive imaginative value it prevented them from having the 'precise intellectual meaning' that he repeatedly stated his concept of 'physical thought' required.

Artaud realised the dangers of obscurity, and fearing (quite correctly) that his work would be misunderstood, he asked Gide 'to prepare public opinion in advance' for *The Cenci* just as he earlier suggested to Germain Dulac, the director of *The Shell and the Clergyman*, that because his film was composed of 'pure images . . . a few articles might be necessary to explain what you are trying to do'.[71] The uncertainty of physical communication made him search for 'concrete signs' which would be 'precise and immediately readable symbols', and this led him to adopt a theory something similar to the 'correspondences' of French symbolist poets. Hence statements such as 'even light can have a precise intellectual meaning', unrealistically hopeful at first sight, turn out to mean only that different intensities and colours of light could produce sensual impressions of heat and cold or emotional states of anger and fear.[72] A more exact vocabulary was needed. Visual symbols, like words, only communicate in so far as they have agreed and familiar definitions; and in practice this meant that Artaud was driven back to conventional forms and adapted his style from silent film and expressionism, as photos of the *Cenci* performance indicate. The actors' gestures are 'evocative' to the extent that they correspond to the typified expression of the screen, and the 'emotive' attitudes compare to the archetypal schemata used in German expressionist theatre. Here arms out-stretched in a cross stand for sacrifice or loving forgiveness, one hand raised to the heavens and the other in a fist beating the heart signifies furious determination while the head bowed in the hands is for defeat or grief.

The danger is that using formalised symbols to express emotion

11 Iya Abdy in the torture scene of *The Cenci*. Heightened emotion & archetypal poses.

formalises the emotions expressed, particularly when the aim is to portray feeling with an intensity which depersonalises it. This is one of the major flaws of early-nineteenth-century melodrama – and the comparison is not coincidental. Quasi-religious, employing devils, ghosts and the machinery of the supernatural, embodying a metaphysical vision of life in the conflict of absolute virtue and vice, stressing events at the expense of characterisation and justifying itself solely by arousing emotional involvement in its audience, gothic melodrama shares many of the qualities of Artaud's Theatre of Cruelty. It mixed visions with realism of a spectacular kind. It subordinated words to action and replaced them with music, and it used stock formulas which became ritualised by repetition. Not surprisingly, Artaud looked on 'the great romantic melodramas' as the last 'valid' form of theatrical spectacle and praised them as being 'dramas of almost ritual situations'.[73] His output included adaptations of *The Fall of the House of Usher* and Lewis's *The Monk. Thirty Years* (*Trente ans, ou la vie d'un joueur*, 'a melodrama in three acts and in prose by Ducange and Dinaux') was at one point on the programme of his Theatre of Cruelty, and when Jouvet criticised the melodramatic basis of *The Cenci* Artaud defended 'the simple elements which you despise: the good, the evil and the traitor' on the grounds that what 'moves' an audience is very different from the type of play which aimed at sophisticated understanding.[74] His dramaturgy echoes these thematic qualities, and there is a close correspondence between the finale of a nineteenth-century melodrama, *The Miller and His Men,* in which a fortress is blown up hurling miniature bodies and stones high into the air, and the visual effects called for in his *mise en scène* of Act III of *The Battle of Trafalgar*:

towards the middle and in the background facades of buildings are terraced on both sides of a street. At each bomb explosion one will see panic-stricken men running across the road and thrown up in fragments into the air from both sides!!![75]

The style of acting that would be appropriate in such a context is not hard to imagine, and quite apart from the few photographs of *The Cenci* practically every line in his film scenarios describes it. A brief glance through them give us 'a gesture of cursing'; a man with 'his head in his hands, as if he held the terrestrial mass' being 'sunk in thought'; a man who opens a door by striking it with his fist 'like one exalted', tearing off a woman's dress 'as if he wished to lacerate her breasts', shaken by 'a paroxysm', gesturing 'with intensity, frenzy, passion', his face in a 'hideous grimace'; a man who 'raises his eyes in the air' to indicate how engrossed he is in a book, while 'an unnameable fear' is 'marked by his fixed features, his trembling lips, his face pale as a corpse, the whites of his eyes'; and these extreme physical manifestations of emotion vary with extreme rapidity – 'he falls into a mad anger. He is sad. He sits down and wipes his brow'. Females are similarly afflicted: 'fixed', or in 'fresh convulsions', or 'trembling from top to toe'.[76]

By naturalistic standards, where psychological nuances are the key to plausibility, this passionate rhetoric would be (to say the least) unconvincing, and Esslin sums up critical opinion by dismissing Artaud as 'certainly an uneven, probably rather a bad actor'. Artaud however was trying to do something rather different, and ought to be judged by other standards. Undoubtedly, as Barrault commented, there were 'dissonances' – effects which failed. But he also acknowledged that Artaud reached 'sublime moments', and even eyewitnesses of *The Cenci* who slated the performance commented that his acting was 'so bad that it ended by interesting us'.[77] As might be expected, one of his greatest acting triumphs was in a melodrama, *Monsieur de Pygmalion*, where he played an incarnation of evil with the appropriate name of Urdemala, but descriptions of Artaud's acting indicate an exaggeration that clearly goes beyond melodrama: 'Whenever Artaud had to move he tensed his muscles, he arched his body and his pale face turned hard with fiery eyes; like this he would advance using arms and hands as well as legs; he would zig-zag, stretching out his arms and legs and tracing wild arabesques in the air.'[78] Perhaps the nearest equivalent would be the rhetorical effect of theatrical acting in film, and it could be suggested that Artaud's aim was to create a similar 'unnatural' level of representation on the stage. The reviewer who commented that Iya Abdy, who played Béatrice Cenci, 'could have had a brilliant career in earlier days – in silent movies'[79] may have unconsciously touched on a key aspect of Artaud's approach. Yet it would not have been sufficient for Artaud simply to transpose the quality of acting in silent film back to the stage – in a theatrical context it would have lost its heightened effect.

Unlike some of his contemporaries (particularly Germans like Piscator) Artaud never seems to have considered using a screen as part of a stage set and merging acted with filmed scenes, even though he had himself acted a variety of roles for a film sequence that was integrated with Ivan Goll's theatrical parody of materialistic life, *Methusalem*, in 1927. The conventional use of film in the theatre was for documentary effect, extending the personal scale of a play into the social. But for Artaud the danger of transporting film onto the stage lay precisely in creating 'too familiar images'. What he wanted was a 'quasi-magical fabrication of life' as in surrealist films,[80] not the realism of the camera but its ability to create images; and from *Burnt Breast* on he experimented with gaining cinematographic effects by theatrical means. This first play was more concerned with stating the theatrical value of film than exploring it, although the montage of images and 'sub-title' dialogue might be seen as derived from film. But even this statement was confused by the satiric attack on the commercialised 'Mystery of Hollywood' – which might help to explain why Artaud's intention of 'humorously denouncing the conflict between the cinema and the theatre' apparently escaped the reviewers, though one did call the performance a stylistic 'potpourri which contains something of the cinema, the musical and college farces'.[81] But *The Spurt of Blood* draws strongly on film techniques with its visible alterations in characters' physical shapes, the contrasts in scale from the macrocosmic of stars colliding to the minute of scorpions or a beetle and the cascade of objects, bodies and even abstractions, together with swift transitions and variations in speed, from frantic acceleration to 'vomit-inducing slowness' – all elements which were to recur in *The Conquest of Mexico*. Like the perspective of crowds seen from above in *There Are No Heavens Anymore*, these effects require shifts of vision rather than changes in the object viewed and in fact could only be convincingly accomplished by the camera, which was perhaps why Artaud never tried to stage these plays, even though *The Spurt of Blood* had been advertised in the programme of the Théâtre Alfred Jarry.

The Spurt of Blood, which anticipates *The Cenci* in its thematic use of incest and blasphemy, combines a childish level of Jarryesque insult ('merde', made more offensive in the mouth of that symbol of chivalrous nobility, a knight) with the hallucinatory shock effects of surrealistic film. All the main characters represent varieties of spiritualised ideal love as grotesque perversions of nature. The opening parodies a romantic duet on the trite themes of 'I love you and everything is beautiful... We are intense. Ah, how well ordered this world is!', rendering the clichés meaningless by artificial tonalities, and contrasting them with the spectacular collapse of cultural values symbolised by the fragments of classical architecture, religious temples and human limbs (a highly ironic echo of the Sophoclean man as the measure of all things). The last line is the young girl's: 'The Virgin! Ah that's what he was looking for' as her lover flees with the whore.[82] All the figures standing for society – Priest, Shoemaker, Judge, Street Pedlar – are destroyed by strobe-like flashes of lightning intermittently illuminating images of earthquake and plague; and the death of God fertilises the world of sexuality when the whore, literally 'signalling through the flames' as her hair bursts into fire in the grip of an enormous hand, bites God's wrist and 'an immense jet of blood spurts across the stage'. The intention here is the same as the 'magical *mise en scène*' of *The Conquest of Mexico*, where 'Montezuma cuts the living space, rips it open like the sex of a woman in order to cause the invisible to spring forth', and the images that follow simultaneously illustrate the 'cruelty' of natural life and celebrate sexuality. The whore and the Young Man eat each other's eyes at the point of orgasm; an army of scorpions swarms out from between the Nurse's thighs and over the Knight's penis 'which swells up and bursts, becoming glassy and shining like the sun' – images which are comparable to the close-up slitting of the girl's eyeball with a razor blade in the Dali/Buñuel film *Un Chien Andalou*, using visceral shock to short-circuit rational response and release the subconscious.

One element of Artaud's staging worth noting is his inventive use of lighting, the most direct point of contact between film and theatre. His use of black light in *Burnt Breast* and the pulsating illumination of *The Mysteries of Love*, the aquarium effect called for in *The Ghost Sonata* scenario, or the strobe lights required for *The Spurt of Blood* were all revolutionary for the time. In these experiments light was clearly intended to disorient the spectator or give emotional colouring to scenes. But in Artaud's view the true value of lighting was its ability to dematerialise stage action, transposing it into a primitive, subconscious key, and he referred to Lugné-Poe's production of *Pelléas and Mélisande* as his ideal: 'here was truly living light; it was aware, it emitted aroma, becoming a new sort of active force and giving to his settings and his actors a luminosity like that in the ultimate absence of consciousness of the "dervish" '.[83]

When *The Spurt of Blood* was finally produced (in 1964 by Brook and Marowitz) no attempt was made to reproduce Artaud's extended stage directions illusionistically. Film projection or elaborate lighting effects were ruled out as 1930's anachronisms, too dated to be of value for the modern theatre; instead the play was performed on a bare stage, and the hurricane and earthquake were suggested in purely imaginary terms by symbolic gesture and movement. However, there was one visual effect which followed the text: an enormous, three-dimensional 'Hand of God', suspended from the flies, which broke through a paper screen to appear above the actors and gushed out blood when bitten. According to Marowitz, this was the high point of the performance. The contrast to the abstract mimesis-through-movement of the rest of this production may help to account for its imaginative effectiveness; but what is surprising, remembering that at the time neither Brook nor Marowitz had any knowledge of Artaud's *mises en scène*, is its closeness to the gigantic realism of Artaud's proposed dream-scene for Savoir's play. The only recent production of *The Cenci*, at the Brno State Theatre in 1967, provides another example. Starting like Brook from Artaud's essays, this production arrived at remarkably similar groupings and poses to Artaud's own production. Perhaps the elements of Artaud's staging are more closely related to the theories of *The Theatre And Its Double* than what is normally thought of as 'Artaudian' – and perhaps, in light of its comparative effectiveness, more attention should be paid to Artaud's practice.

'An aborted theatre'

It must be said, however, that there are inherent weaknesses in Artaud's concepts too. Some of these became very obvious in the Brook–Marowitz *Spurt of Blood* production, where sound was substituted for much of the dialogue and the whole performance lasted only three minutes. A picture may be worth several pages of words, but only if it is in front of the eye for the same length of time – and contemplation is not one of the strengths of theatre. Conventional drama extends actions by words and so allows for ambiguities, transformations, development, while movement alone is a kind of shorthand which coalesces to a single image, however striking. In addition, the lack of a developed and precise visual language (something Artaud was working on but never achieved) leads to triteness or obscurity. Another tendency is to mistake unremitting vehemence for intensity, which deadens responses rather than heightening awareness, and exaggerating (as Artaud did) any aspect of melodrama – a genre which in any case hovers on the edge of self-parody – can result in bathos. Even in Brook's short performance, there were still points where the audience laughed. But these flaws should not cancel out the imaginative and vital elements of Artaud's work.

That these were not more widely appreciated at the time seems only partly due to Artaud's lack of financial support, even though this did indeed cause great production difficulties. *The Mysteries of Love*, Claudel's *Break of Noon* and even *A Dream Play* had only one rehearsal on stage with costumes before the opening, while *Victor* didn't even have a complete run through. These were impossible conditions for achieving Artaud's ideal in which images were to be given meaning through the dynamic relationship of parts to the whole in 'a grand harmony . . . in the gestures, in the interrelated movements . . . fixed and adjusted as in a well-wound mechanism'.[84] Retraining actors who had been schooled in the conventions of naturalistic theatre was also a problem, particularly since, according to Roger Blin, Artaud was so completely inside his own ideas that he seldom tried to explain them to his performers; and as a result Artaud was driven to use inexperienced people even for major roles – in *The Cenci* neither Iya Abdy nor Cécile Bressant, who took the part of Lucretia, had ever been on stage before. With this lack of rehearsal, amateurism and his admitted difficulty in working with actors as a group, all of which led to the improvisation that Artaud considered the opposite of proper theatrical expression, it's surprising that he saw his productions as successful on any level. But *Victor* was looked back on as a valuable attempt – 'there was only a little lacking to have made it a brilliant success' – while he described *The Cenci*, which is generally considered a catastrophe, as 'total success' in 'a year of deceptions and failure'.[85] It is possible of course to see these comments as self-deceptions marking Artaud's inability to face the end of his theatrical career. But in Blin's view the *Cenci* production only had the limited aim of making the public aware of the concept of the Theatre of Cruelty. And if different standards to those outlined in *The Theatre And Its Double* are applied, so that instead of expecting an overwhelming psychological impact and a therapeutic transformation of the audience, the play is approached as a technical exercise demonstrating a stylistic model, then Artaud's satisfaction appears in a more realistic light.

In fact Artaud himself must be held to blame for the lack of critical comprehension, much of which was due to the publication of the Theatre of Cruelty manifestoes shortly before the performance of *The Cenci*. The reviewers had been led to expect an irresistible paroxysm of physical action which would have a direct effect on the central nervous system, comparable to acupuncture performed by a street drill and inducing a collective delirium with a spiritual healing power that would make the theatre the equivalent of Lourdes. The effect, they believed, was to be 'a true therapy' which Artaud had imprecisely compared to snake charming, medicinal music of North American Indians and the incantations of black sorcerers. In theory this would cure 'the patient' – the spectator, and through him society – by (confusingly) exteriorising his latent cruelty while at the same time forcing him to assume an external attitude corresponding to the state of interior order which one wished to restore.[86] Not unnaturally, the reviewers were sceptical as well as curious. In fact no performance could realise these aims; and the abstraction of the manifestoes, the vagueness of Artaud's advertisement for *The Torture of Tantalus*, where the sentences are repeatedly qualified by '. . . sort de . . .', indicate that these generalisations are not conceived in practical theatre terms. So Artaud had a point when he claimed that the critics had overlooked some of the stylistic factors and criticised him by inappropriate standards.[87]

There were also of course effects that failed. The most disastrous seems to have been the heightening of gesture and vocal delivery, which resulted in a single-level tone, a lack of emotional variation; and this destroyed the very intensity it was intended to create to such an extent that the audience broke into laughter at two climactic points in the action – the culmination of the storm when Orsino announces that the assassination has failed, and the torture scene with Camillo's 'I feel quite sick with horror.' But Artaud seems to have been satisfied because, by and large, the critics did concede the effectiveness of the elements he considered significant, even if the way their approval was expressed showed they had been looking for something else and their overall judgement was therefore unfavourable. They were receptive to the stylised presentation and found 'the continual animation of the stage space' effective in creating a 'hallucinatory spectacle' which had 'the symbolism of nightmare'. In short Artaud did succeed in realising the qualities he had sought in *A Dream Play* or *The Battle of Trafalgar*, as even the mixed reactions show, however grudgingly: 'never the less, with his absurd violence, his staring eyes, his scarcely pretended fury, [Artaud] does carry us with him up above good and evil', or

complex lighting, individual and mass-movement, sound, music revealed to the spectator that space and time form an *affective* reality . . . All the more then one can reproach the dramaturge, for . . . if Artaud had 'activated' certain fundamental acts of Cenci and Beatrice manifesting a total cruelty he might perhaps had better avoided the excess of verbal material[88]

Stylistically at least, then, Artaud achieved much of his theatre, although this was far from the total and revolutionary upheaval of traditional drama that his contemporaries expected and more modern critics credit him with. But style is not autonomous. It is the choice of a mode of communication, a rhetoric determining what subject the material expresses by reference to its effect on an audience. Leaving aside Artaud's metaphysical abstractions (those notional theatres of ordeal or exorcism), what he actually tried to achieve was an intense emotional response which would lead to a heightened awareness of inner potential and the rejection of a rationalistic and materialistic society. In this context one of the most serious criticisms levelled at Artaud is that he ignored the question of the audience and worked for psycho-social effects without considering exactly who would be affected.[89] For his style to be appropriate to his aims Artaud would have had to take the established behaviour patterns of the spectators into account, since only so could he predict responses accurately and select sequences of images to gain precise reactions.

How far did he do this? An open question, since he never spoke of his audience in detail. But he certainly worked on the principle that people from different backgrounds would have different responses to at least the political level of his attack, had a clear idea what social class the majority of his spectators would come from and chose techniques which relied on certain cultural assumptions. His productions were not aimed at a 'committed public' who might be predisposed to applaud, but specifically at 'what one is accustomed to call the *public bien Français*' and their antagonistic response was calculated into the total effect of a performance: 'their clownish reactions are an extra in the programme'. *Gigogne* for example was 'written and performed with the systematic aim of provocation', and the juxtaposition of 'the most ridiculous infirmity' (flatulence) with beauty and love in the heroine of *Victor* is sufficient indication of his approach: an undermining of cherished – but from his viewpoint fake – ideals which the audience would find 'cruel' because gratuitous. Nowhere is this clearer than in Artaud's staging of *Break of Noon* (*Partage de midi*) in 1928). This farcical treatment of a poetic celebration of Christian conversion, that Claudel had declared to be 'the first work in which I truly acquired the consciousness of myself', not only parodied the all too easy target of religion and automatically insulted the social establishment of which Claudel was a prominent member; it also implicitly rejected romantic assumptions about art as the expression of the unique self, and simultaneously attacked the traditional qualities of 'masterpieces' by turning *Break of Noon*'s rhetorical tirades, baroque imagery and Racinian psychological struggles into pretentious nonsense.[90] Farce, of course, is a double-edged weapon that tends to undercut the seriousness of its own intentions. But inciting anger or hate or fearful revulsion by denigrating all an audience stands for can create a more intense involvement through the antagonism focussed against the stage than through any conventional empathy, as a play like Genet's *The Blacks* (*Les Nègres*, 1959) has shown.

Farce, always an element in Artaud's work (the scatological joke in *Victor* and the operatic rendering of 'I love you' in *The Spurt of Blood*, the inanely grinning assassins in *The Cenci*, or 'the learned heads of the official spokesmen' in *The Conquest of Mexico*), is used for its corrosive effect, not for humour; and even the thematic 'cruelty' in his choice of material – for all his metaphysical justifications – is there to shock by reversing social assumptions. Civilisation, organising human relationships by legal curbs or religiously inspired spurs, is traditionally justified because it controls destructive urges and limits violence. Artaud turns this upside down: civilisation intensifies undesirable emotions by repressing them, so that society itself becomes an instrument of violence. The scenario for *The Butcher's Revolt* for example justifies the 'eroticism, cruelty, taste for blood, refinement of violence, obsession with the horrible, the dissolving of moral values, social hypocrisy, lies, false-witness, sadism, perversion, etc., etc.' as a 'stock-taking'. These elements are not deployed 'with maximum plainness' for any ritual or psycho-spiritual reasons, but because they are seen as a true reflection of the reality commonly disguised by social appearances.[91] *The Conquest of Mexico* is another formulation of the same theme. Both scenarios have political intentions: to destroy the justification of society's existence. One shows the repressive nihilism of civilisation from the inside, in its metropolitan centre; the other from the outside, tearing away the 'civilising' aspirations of colonialism by presenting the realities of conquest and revealing its essential evil through the psychological effect of the *conquistadores* on a people whom Artaud believed to be 'natural'. In other productions Artaud attacked the principles on which society is structured. *Victor* was 'directed against the bourgeois family' as the basic social unit, while *The Cenci* was specifically an attack on 'the ideology of authority represented by the Father', seen as both the symbol and the root of 'the outdated ideas of Society, of Order, of Justice, of Religion, of Family, and of Fatherland'.[92]

There is a distinct absence of fine tuning here. Discredit the ideals held by the bourgeoisie who formed the body of any theatre audience, attack the basis of their society and use the resulting expression of disapproval, disgust and rejection as a demonstration of the thesis that civilisation is violent. Being crude this approach might have been expected to produce the broad effect Artaud anticipated, but he seems to have reckoned without the insensibility, self-assurance and cultural snobbism of his *'public bien Français'*. Certainly his estimate of the composition of his audience was correct. The opening of *A Dream Play* was attended by the diplomatic community, an aristocracy of counts, viscounts, a duchess and royalty, eminent literati including Valéry, Mauriac and Gide, and members of the French Academy. The première of *The Cenci*, under the patronage of Prince George of Greece and the Princesse de Polignac, attracted all the fashionable society of Paris. Artaud's expectations remained much the same from the very first performance of the Théâtre Alfred Jarry ('howling, bawling reactions') to this last production, the full-length prototype for his Theatre of Cruelty ('they will howl, weep, whistle perhaps'). According to programme notes, *The Cenci* was officially intended 'to grip the audience by the entrails and the heart' with 'true tragic emotion', but private letters showed that it was on account of the political provocation that Artaud expected 'the most violent reactions on the part of the spectators'.[93] Certain of Artaud's collaborators seem to have taken his wish for reality. According to Marc Darnault, who acted Victor, the production of Vitrac's play was 'terribly booed throughout the performance', while André Franck described a scene of chaos in *The Cenci*: 'the folding seats and chairs clattered; spectators rose crying in indignation or admiration . . . the public was still not ready'.[94] But in fact the audiences seem to have received Artaud with remarkable equanimity. Paul Block of the *Berliner Tageblatt* expressed his surprise that 'not a single protest' was raised against the social criticism in *Victor*, commenting that 'the audience by their amused reactions expressed a much more judicial judgement than the most experienced critics', while according to Paul Arnold, who was in the audience of *The Cenci*, Parisian society was predisposed to approve, being eager for 'strong sensations'. Other descriptions of the audience's response by the critics range from boredom to 'thirty people applauded wildly. The remainder of the room after a quarter of an hour took the tragedy with good humour.'[95] Only two productions caused violent reactions, *Break of Noon* and *A Dream Play*, and in neither case was the staging responsible. It was Artaud himself who caused trouble after the end of the performance of *Break of Noon* – the play was put on in defiance of Claudel, who had publicly refused his permission, and (perhaps because the audience had sat quietly through the performance in spite of the way long speeches had been reduced to nonsense by being lifted out of context) Artaud added insult to injury by striding onto the stage and accusing Claudel of selling out to an infamous establishment. In *A Dream Play* too it seems probable that Artaud incited the violent riot which occurred. Having just vilified the politics of his former companions the surrealists, he knew them to be hostile, yet no one else could have switched the place numbers of the central reserved block of seating to the balcony, which allowed the surrealists into the front rows; and the answers he shouted back at them from the stage could not have been better designed to anger the Swedes who had put up much of the money for the production.

None of this can be counted as successful theatrical agitation for the dismantling of society. But already, in plans for *The Torture of Tantalus*, he was transferring his attentions to a different audience, the uneducated working classes – and reading between the lines this move can be seen as a direct response to his inability to break through the intellectual defences of his Parisian public. *The Torture of Tantalus* was to be staged in Marseilles in a factory or public hall, and was aimed at 'the bulk of the masses' who, precisely because they had no time for 'subtle discourse' or 'intellectual gyrations', would 'not resist the effects of physical surprise, of the dynamism of cries and violent gestures, of visual explosions'.[96] One suspects that such spectators would have viewed Artaud's work with simple incomprehension, since his ability to communicate through symbols depended on prior cultural exposure; but at least when attacking society it is always more effective to appeal to the exploited than to assault the privileged. The failure of Artaud's techniques to produce any deep political effect however is due to more basic reasons than focussing on the wrong audience. As the dadaist experience demonstrated, it is contradictory to try to use artistic means to destroy culture, and Artaud's work in fact created new forms of expression in a very traditional way by building on established conventions. It is also counterproductive to measure theatrical effectiveness by immediate and obvious audience reactions, since evidence suggests that the influence of art is subliminal, that it can only modify, not reverse cultural images and may take a period of years to work through into social action.

Parallels: Oskar Kokoschka

In any other terms but his own Artaud would seem to have created a practical theatre, one capable of challenging the imagination by dynamic interrelationships of symbolic movements and forms, which could indeed create a heightened awareness of alternate realities. His idealistic theories, with their attractive combination of exoticism and obscurity, have been largely responsible for the way his stage work is ignored or disparaged; and ironically it is the view of Artaud as a unique innovator which has done most to undervalue his actual achievements. His work shows him to be firmly rooted in the culture of the twenties and thirties, even his flaws are symptomatic, and to reach a true evaluation he has to be seen in context.

Some of the theatrical forms mentioned by Artaud as if they were significant influences either seem to be imaginary ('Negro-American theatre', for example) or outside his experience (such as Soviet theatre, Artaud mistakenly looking on Russia as a country 'where theatre has become again a religion').[97] Others seem to have been misunderstood (for instance Balinese theatre, though this is hardly surprising since Artaud was exposed to only one performance).[98] But even these references indicate how close Artaud was to his contemporaries. The only thing that Artaud could conceivably be describing in the mysterious category of 'Negro-American' at that time are plays like O'Neill's *Great God Brown* (1925) or *All God's Chillun* (1923), and the similarities to O'Neill's experiments with masks and rhythmic drumbeats simply underline the links between Artaud's work and expressionism. The only Russian theatre Artaud had seen was Meyerhold's, and some of the recommendations in his essay on 'An affective athleticism' parallel the practices of bio-mechanics, while there are certain correspondences between Artaud's stage sets and constructivist décor. As for the interest in far-eastern theatre, that was a novelty that fascinated many of his contemporaries – including Brecht, who is commonly thought of as representing the opposite theatrical approach to Artaud.

Brecht of course developed along very different lines, but it is hardly a coincidence that his derogatory term for entertainment theatre, 'culinary', is so similar to Artaud's description of it as 'digestive'. Both started from the same point, the rejection of naturalism; and Artaud had a great admiration for the theatre that developed in the Weimar republic, an enthusiasm to be expected since German theatre in the twenties and thirties was exceptionally rich in technical experimentation and the formulation of new dramaturgical approaches. Artaud indeed had fairly close connections with this theatrical powerhouse. He collaborated with Ivan Goll on the French production of *Methusalem* in 1927, being responsible for the film sequence that counterpointed the stage action. He also acted in the film of the *Threepenny Opera*, which he disapproved of for much the same reasons that led Brecht to disown it, and visited Berlin several times between 1923 and 1935. He was greatly impressed by the work of Brecht's collaborator, Erwin Piscator, from whom he probably took the initial idea of merging film and stage media; and it is when referring to his experience in Germany that he first mentions his intention to replace psychological drama with 'a theatre of action and the masses'[99] – an aim which is very similar to Piscator's. His use of different stage levels, streets receding up hills or the balconies and staircases in *The Cenci*, is based on the same concept as Jessner's famous 'steps'; while the Bauhaus experiments with balletic sequences of forms and movement and their exploration of theatre as a spatial art also has similarities to some of Artaud's basic concerns. Even the stage space he envisaged for his Theatre of Cruelty – galleries around the perimeter of the auditorium, making it possible to transfer the action from the centre to the corners or play in the middle of the spectators, who were to be seated in revolving or mobile chairs – is an exact description of the theatre designed by Gropius, although Gropius allowed for film to be projected over ceiling and walls, as well as variable actor–audience relationships and the total immersion of the audience in a stage action.

Tracing influences is not particulary helpful for understanding Artaud's work – his selective use of film techniques, his updating of the melodramatic approach, even the replacement of verbal communication by the dynamic relationship of visual images seem to have been developed largely independently. But the correspondences show him to be an integral part of the wider European theatrical movements between the wars. It is generally acknowledged that Artaud's work is comparable on some levels to that of Craig and Appia, but parallels with his contemporaries of the twenties and thirties are more precise than many realise. It is even arguable that Oskar Kokoschka, whose work Artaud almost certainly knew nothing about, had already given an example of Artaud's ideal theatre some twenty years before the first manifesto of the Théâtre Alfred Jarry. Artaud's search for a visual language which is not a translation of words but a form of direct communication through using actions to form 'images that spring uniquely from themselves, which do not derive their meaning from the situation . . . but from a kind of internal necessity', is virtually a restatement of the position formulated by Kandinsky, Kokoschka and turn-of-the-century expressionist painters.[100] Reacting against the impressionists (the equivalent in visual art to reacting against naturalism in the theatre) their canvasses reflected autonomous interior images instead of the physical world, working with free associations which appealed directly to the senses. A key term for them too was 'internal necessity', and the characteristic elements in their pictures are the dynamic rhythms of curvilinear forms and the use of symbolic colours, both of which were designed to transfer emotional intensity directly to the spectator.

One of Kokoschka's plays, *Murderer The Women's Hope* (*Mörder Hoffnung der Frauen*, 1909), transposes these principles from canvas to the stage, and the results parallel Artaud's work so strikingly that it could almost be called a paradigm of the Theatre of Cruelty. *Murderer* is an intensely personal vision which embodies Kokoschka's fear of what he called 'the female principle', whose erotic advance causes the breakdown of intellectual and social balance, so revealing 'dangerous and intriguing' depths in the psyche. The play's aim is to open the spectator's subconscious to these depths by presenting archetypal sexual patterns of domination and destruction, and the theme is 'the fatal confrontation' between what Kokoschka saw as the fundamental poles of existence that form the basis of our dreams, Eros and Thanatos[101] – a comparable dualism to Artaud's which Kokoschka expressed (not surprisingly perhaps) in similar solar/lunar symbols. The action is composed of mythic elements drawing strongly upon erotic violence and designed to evoke strong emotional responses on a subliminal level – as in the consistent use of inverted Christian images (a cock crowing three times to announce murder and massacre, a woman's body spread-eagled into the shape of a white cross). The whole play in fact presents the seven Stations of the Cross as an extended orgasm with the sexual climax being the crucifixion. On one level the purpose is negative, to demoralise society by destroying unquestioned moral assumptions; but this also has its positive aspect, to open the spectators' minds by breaking down conventional responses through outrage – and these are precisely the tactics Artaud used in *The Cenci*. Even the weapon chosen, blasphemy, is the same. Kokoschka wanted 'the actors to offer the public a gesture of defiance', which would be an apt description of the Théâtre Alfred Jarry's intentions. But he was more consistent than Artaud. Instead of trying to attract society with gala openings, he took pains to insult public opinion in preparation for *Murderer*. He shaved his head like a condemned criminal to declare his rejection of social values in the most provocative way, and even the poster advertising the play was designed to shock. It was deliberately unaesthetic in execution and offensive in subject, a parody of the pietà in which a flayed male is being torn apart by a blue woman; and Kokoschka commented, with self-satisfied exaggeration, 'as I had intended, it sent the Viennese into paroxysms of rage'. Beneath this attack on society, again like Artaud, Kokoschka had a more idealistic aim: to reveal the religious nature of 'inner experience';[102] and a second poster was a variation on the expressionist *Ecce Homo*, a self-portrait with one hand pointing to a gaping wound in the breast.

The script of the play, which Kokoschka claimed was improvised in a single night of rehearsal – a claim clearly deriving from the value put on emotional immediacy and the direct externalisation of subconscious states by the expressionists, since in fact the play had been written over a year earlier between 1907 and 1908 – is little more than a framework for gesture and visual effects. Choreography and patterns of visual images and colours are used to communicate instead of a fully articulated text; and for the first performance each actor was given no more than a bare outline of the action and the key phrases he was to speak, but drilled extensively in movement and vocal rhythms. The speeches still contained the sort of evocative and poetic verbal images that Artaud avoided, but they were chanted or intoned, broken down into sounds – a scream, cries in various pitches, arbitrarily stressed syllables – and obviously intended to have an effect comparable to Artaud's incantation. Colours recur as motifs in the words and were repeated in the costumes, scenery and lighting. Primary colours were chosen for their emotional associations: blood for life, white for death, with red dominant – as it frequently was in Artaud's staging. Kokoschka's paintings of this period give a fair indication of how the stage-picture must have appeared under his direction. His illustrations for the play have strong but broken rhythms, the composition is geometric but the shadings escape through the boundaries of the forms, and the delicacy of line in conjunction with crude shapes echoes the tension between flowing patterns and the brutal gestures they represent. As an artist Kokoschka initiated the practice of using moving people instead of still-life sitters for figure studies, and the action of the play is not so much a series of events as a sequence of rhythms. Wheeling and circling movements are used as a structural geometry in a similar way to the 'gravitation' of *The Cenci*. However the style of movement was almost certainly different. Where Artaud was influenced by what he thought of as the heraldic gestures of Balinese theatre, Kokoschka rejected the influence of African, Mayan and Inca art, or that of 'the Pacific islanders', as a retreat from 'original creativity' into exoticism. He stayed instead in the European tradition and based his use of space on the tensions of gothic art. Rather than tending to tableaux, like Artaud's slow motion or the *trompe-l'œil* 'Marriage of Cana', Kokoschka used violent physical action, tribal dance steps and whirling fire brands carried by the actors to create 'a wild atmosphere'. Both however shared the aim of creating a new model of theatre in which the stimulation of the audience by dynamic movement in space would replace the traditional draining of feeling through emotional transference. The similarity of approach and the differences in execution can be indicated by Kokoschka's comment: 'my performers... were not acrobats, but even so they could run, jump, stand and fall better than any of the Burgtheater actors, who often took a quarter of an hour to lie down and die'.[103]

The comparison between Artaud and Kokoschka can even be extended into details. Kokoschka's actors were directed to use stylised gestures becoming progressively more animalistic (for the women) or godlike (for the men) during the performance, which contrasted strongly with the highly structured impression of choral orchestration and geometrically patterned movement – effects directly paralleled in the *Cenci* production. The music for *Murderer*, like that composed for *Burnt Breast* by Maxim Jacob, was limited to percussion and woodwind: drums to intensify the rhythms of the performance, cymbals and pipes for an atmospheric tone of primitive wildness. But the most striking duplication was in the visual appearance given to the actors. The costumes for *The Cenci* had the musculature of the body traced over the cloth, outlining the stomach, rib cage and limbs to give a skeletal effect. In exactly the same way Kokoschka painted 'face masks' for his actors, covering all their exposed skin (as primal beings they were scantily clad) with lines representing tendons and nerve structures. To some extent this was an extension of a familiar expressionist technique that can be seen in various pen and ink portraits, where abstract patterns of lines merge the face into the total design so that individual features dissolve; and it corresponds to the expressionist premise that external forms disintegrate under the intensity of extreme emotion, which paradoxically leads to the disappearance of the self in the movement down into subjectivity, and the transfer from ego to archetype. For Kokoschka it was particularly intended to represent the inner being of his figures, as if surface appearances had been flayed away, removing individuality and (in a typically Artaudian image) rooting deep emotional or spiritual states in the physical body:

The Greeks put masks on their actors to fix characters – sad, passionate, angry, etc. I did the same thing in my own way by painting on faces, not as decoration, but to underline [essential] character. It was all meant to be

12 Kokoschka's sketches for *Murderer The Women's Hope.* Archetypes & the externalising of spiritual being – nerves painted on the skin. (Compare the skeletal musculature of the *Cenci* costumes, plate 10). Note too the shaved head indicating the author's identification with his protagonist.

effective at a distance, like fresco painting. All I was after was this enhancement of expression. I treated the members of the cast quite differently. Some of them I gave cross stripes, like a tiger or cat, but I painted the nerves on all of them. Where they were located I knew from my study of anatomy.[104]

How effective was *Murderer The Women's Hope*? Kokoschka, like Artaud, had a certain artistic reputation or rather notoriety. Already by 1908 he was labelled the '*Ueberwilding*' (super-savage) and had been dismissed from his teaching post at the art school because the Minister for Culture thought an exhibition of his work was a 'chamber of horrors'. As a gesture of defiance the performance was undoubtedly successful. It caused a riot, order had to be restored by force and the reviews were savage, calling Kokoschka a 'criminal', a 'degenerate', a 'corrupter of youth'.[105] The violence of the reactions seems to have been partly fortuitous, being due to an unusual and unexpected mixture of spectators. The play was put on outdoors, and the atmosphere of extemporisation and the summer night might have had something to do with it. But, far more significant, the venue allowed a kind of spectator, who would never normally enter a theatre, to participate in the performance. Folding seats surrounded by a flimsy fence had been set up for the audience, and this enclosure was filled by reputable members of society (who had come to disapprove) and the intellectual elite (who were neutrally curious). On the other side of the fence common soldiers gathered. These were from a Bosnian regiment (renowned as the most primitive and backward part of a ramshackle empire) quartered nearby. The paying audience 'maintained a chorus of catcalls throughout the play', and this alone would probably have been enough to arouse the soldiers. Yet perhaps the fact that they intervened at the point of climax in the symbolic orgasm might indicate that the pre-intellectual involvement intended by Kokoschka worked – at least on naive spectators. 'As the foot stamping, scuffling, and chair brandishing increased in pitch, the soldiers stormed in and a free-for-all followed between them and the audience. In the tumult the police had to be sent for.'[106] The play however was more than just a *succès de scandale*. The text, originally published in 1909, was reprinted five times between 1910 and 1920, and an operatic version was published in 1921. The dadaists – for whom another of Kokoschka's plays (*Sphinx & Straw Man*) had 'decided the role of our theatre, which will entrust the stage direction to the subtle invention of the explosive mind, scenario to the audience, visible direction, grotesque props: the DADAIST theatre'[107] – performed it in Zürich.

Kokoschka produced it again in Dresden in 1917, and after the war it achieved a considerable reputation, being staged twice by Reinhardt in 1918 and 1919 as well as being performed in 1920 and 1921. Hindemith set it to music, and it was performed as an opera in 1921 and 1922.

The soldiers in Vienna, being infantry, had reacted with their feet rather than their souls, and industrial workers in France a generation and a war later were unlikely to be as unsophisticated or direct in their response as Balkan peasants. But the soldiers' enthusiastic involvment in Kokoschka's drama, however accidental on this occasion, indicates that Artaud's instinct to play to the masses rather than the cultural elite had possibilities despite the problems inherent in communicating with an uneducated audience. At the same time the spectacular stage history of *Murderer The Women's Hope*, taken up as it was by the whole theatrical spectrum from the iconoclastic dadaists to Reinhardt, the expressionist who became the representative *par excellence* of the grand tradition, suggests that Artaud's approach, which was so similar, would be as applicable to the conventional stage as to experimental anti-theatre. The failure of Artaud's productions, then, the lack of influence of his theatre (as against his essays) cannot be put down to intrinsic flaws. The reasons lay rather in his strategy, and his failure seems due as much as anything else to his habit of reaching beyond his grasp. First, the gap between his unrealistically idealistic theory and what he actually practiced raised expectations in his audience that his work was not even designed to meet. Secondly, his stage effects relied on complex technology and a high degree of control in the acting. His productions are conceived in terms of lighting which did not exist, scenery which was too costly for an *ad hoc* group to build effectively, and a precision of choreography that required long-term commitments by an expert troupe. By contrast Kokoschka issued no manifestoes and *Murderer*, although it does allow for spectacular effects, was originally performed on the bare earth and needs only one simple piece of scenery – steps with an open-work grille in the shape of a tower – while the savage atmosphere could be created by energy alone when there was no opportunity for discipline. Only in his later plays, when professional theatres were open to him, did Kokoschka introduce complicated or illusionistic effects.

Artaud, then, was very much a man of his time, a seminal figure for modern drama, but not in fact an innovator. Rather he should be seen as a theatrical litmus, sensitive to the cultural physiology of the twentieth century which has been given comparable but independent expression by others as far apart as Kokoschka at the beginning of the era and Grotowski, who only came across Artaud's ideas after his style had already been fully developed with such productions as *Akropolis* and *Kordian*, in the late sixties. Judged by what he did rather than what he said, and evaluated in the context of his contemporaries, Artaud turns out to be a less extraordinary but perhaps more interesting theatrical innovator. Less radical but more useful, giving us another model for anti-Aristotelian drama.

His theories (misunderstood or taken all too literally as in, say, the Living Theatre's *Paradise Now*) have produced only unrealisable strategies or self-indulgent, undramatic psychotherapy. However, the concepts that he picked up from the cultural currents of his time are among the most creative impetuses of modern theatre. His perception that the stage has a reality quite distinct from life, which can only achieve validity when presented with deliberate artifice, is mirrored in the overt theatricality of modern drama. His concept of extending the audience's imagination by destroying conventional assumptions and simultaneously presenting alternate visions of the world can be found in the work of dramatists as different as Genet or Robert Wilson, as can his methods of achieving this effect – hallucinatory distortions of scale and perspective, and overloading the brain with emotive images. On the level of technique his extension of stage language by emphasising symbolic gesture, patterned movement, speech as sound, has been developed by Peter Brook and others. Above all his ritualisation of theatre, with its accompanying aim to involve the spectator totally in the stage action, has become an ideal for much of the serious western drama. Artaud's name has been often invoked – indeed too often, since whatever the value of his ideas as a catalyst his practical work has had little influence, outside perhaps of Barrault, being almost unknown until recently. There is no 'school of Artaud'. But he has made a decisive contribution to the major current in modern theatre that can be defined as the contemporary form of tragedy, where archetypes from myth or dream shapes from racial memory replace the classical hero-figure, where the recognition affirms a comparable spiritual potential rooted in the blood in the context of a pitiless world and against an evil civilisation, and where what corresponds to catharsis is the total involvement of spectators in dramatic action with its therapeutic aim of liberating the natural man – instinctive, subconscious, cruel – from perverting social repressions.

Jean-Louis Barrault

The direct link between Artaud and the modern avant garde is Jean-Louis Barrault, whose work extends the more technical aspects of the Theatre of Cruelty to form a 'total theatre' based on Artaud's concept of the actor as 'an athlete of the emotions'. Barrault's first production, a mime version of *As I Lay Dying* (*Autour d'une mère*), was performed barely a month after *The Cenci*, and Artaud's enthusiastic response led to plans to work together on staging Defoe's *Journal of the Plague Year* in a specific attempt to give tangible shape to the ideal image of drama that Artaud had outlined in 'The theatre and the plague' (the key essay in *The Theatre And Its Double*). Artaud withdrew from the project because, as he wrote to Barrault, he was incapable of the compromise that collaboration entailed and believed there were fundamental differences in approach, Barrault's mime being primarily descriptive not symbolic and relating to factual reality instead of presenting hieroglyphic expressions of the soul. But if any modern director can be counted a disciple of Artaud, it is Barrault. Artaud introduced him to the eastern mysticism, Indian mythology and yoga that had such a decisive influence on his work – and, above all, to the Cabbala with its division of breathing rhythms into six main 'arcana', or combinations of masculine, feminine and androgynous principles, as exercises for inducing a trance state in which the body becomes the organ of the spirit. It is this ideal of psycho-physiological unity that forms the basis for Barrault's ideas and finds expression in his 'Little treatise on the alchemy of the theatre' or 'Alchemy of the human body'.[1] It has also been reflected structurally in his productions like *The Oresteia*, where each play in the trilogy was broken down into an 'organic' pattern of neuter, male and female phases. In 1936 Artaud acknowledged Barrault as the only practitioner exploring his concept of a physical 'universal language that unites the total [theatrical] space ... to the hidden interior life',[2] while Barrault has repeatedly underlined Artaud's influence on his subsequent work. Artaudian phrasing recurs in his writing – particularly in statements of intention like 'the plague is rigged up on the stage, and we lance the tumour with all our dark forces. This purifies us and we go away clean and fortified' – and he claims to have identified with Artaud 'to the point of mimicry', both in style of acting and directorial approach: Artaud's 'view of the theatre was totally *inner*. He was a mystic and visionary who . . . reached right into the core of things, of people and of situations. He taught me to do likewise . . . He despised the cerebral actor, the didactic director. He felt his way into plays. My attitude is similar in that I don't "intellectualise"; I act.'[3]

Yet despite the way he assimilated Artaud's ideas, Barrault can hardly be said to have simply trodden in his footsteps in his association with philosophical playwrights like Sartre or Giraudoux (whose 'gratuitous gymnastics and intellectual capering' Artaud singled out as the antithesis of his ritual theatre). As director of the Théâtre de France, he associated himself with the social establishment in a way that ran counter to Artaud's deepest principles; and considering Artaud's ridicule of all that Claudel stood for, it is significant that Barrault's career has been so closely bound up with productions of *The Satin Slipper* (*Le Soulier de satin*, 1943), *Christopher Columbus* (*Christophe Colomb*, 1953), and even *Break of Noon* (1948). Indeed Barrault effectively rescued Claudel's work from oblivion in using it as the basis for articulating his own spiritual theatre of 'total space'. Yet his focus always remained what Breton had called 'the latent content' of drama, seeing what made a play significant to be its status as 'a precipitate of the universal dream', rather than 'the manifest content' of surface intrigue or social theme, since for him 'the art of theatre is specifically the art of dreams'.[4] But in spite of his insistence on the revolutionary and subliminal nature of art, Barrault's aims are not comparable to the surrealists'. When he eventually attempted to carry out the project of staging 'the theatre and the plague' that he and Artaud had discussed, commissioning Camus' *State of Siege* (*L'Etat de siège*, 1948, a dramatisation of his novel *La Peste*), it was a failure because, 'insensibly, the subject slipped from the metaphysical plane (Daniel Defoe, Artaud) to the political (Camus, Hitler, Nazism); and the fallacy became apparent . . . The horror of the Nazi concentration camps no longer had anything to do with the saving epidemic, the power of a plague to bring good through the forces of evil.'[5] And his rejection of political strategies for opposing the *status quo*, his alternative that art 'should never stop putting ourselves in question', is a far cry from the fundamental surrealist challenge to accepted ideas of reality. Compared to Artaud, his concept of theatre as religion is conventional – hence the absence of contradiction in working with Claudel, the explicit advocate of Roman Catholicism – and he tends to associate 'sacred theatre' with 'ceremony' rather than primitive savagery. In a sense this is simply an extension of Artaud's actual practice, the formalisation and symbolic patterning that contrasts so vividly with the orgiastic wildness called for in his essays, yet it leads to a different relationship with the audience. Where Artaud's image is of transfiguration through torture and the violence is that of rape, Barrault's is that of communion, or in his favourite metaphor 'the act of love' in which a stage presentation is a 'coupling' between actors and audience (no irony intended, since Barrault conveniently forgets that one party has paid the other): 'To perform is to make love – one gives, one gives oneself in an interchange, an act of holy communion.' The sense of duality remains, but in the quasi-sexual emotional identification supposedly 'each individual recognises and shares with the rest a rediscovered Collective Soul'.[6]

Barrault's range has been eclectic, from the classics and Chekhov to Ionesco and Beckett, from Feydeau to Genet and Sam Shepard. But in those productions that he has picked out as defining his artistic credo – Claudel, and his own adaptations of *As I Lay Dying*, Kafka's *The Trial* (*Le Procès*, 1946) and Rabelais' *Gargantua and Pantagruel* (1968) – there is a continuing attempt to generate myths in T. S. Eliot's sense of large controlling images that give a meaningful structure to otherwise chaotic and fragmentary experience. The merely phenomenal is given spiritual significance by incorporating the whole natural world in the gestures and movements of the human body, an extension of mime into 'total' physical language where every aspect of stage presentation relates to a symbolic reality distinct from ordinary life. Being primarily a practitioner rather than a theorist, Barrault's statements of philosophy tend to be simplistic or solipsistic, and where he takes over Artaud's ideas he applies them all too literally to his work. For instance his rationale for presenting a symbolic level of reality repeats Artaud's concept of theatre as 'the double of life', the effigy of spiritual reality which stands in the same relationship to material existence as the world of pure forms to the shadows in Plato's cave: 'it is by exploiting [the duality of] Being and its double or reflection that the actor can exist'.[7]

The prominence of Barrault's public career, and his tendency to lump uncritical Marxism (the liberation of man) and vulgar Freudianism (the liberation of the instincts) together with oriental mysticism as the creative forces behind his theatre, have distracted from the main thrust of his work. This picks up where Artaud left off, and his 'total theatre' is a logical extension of Artaud's ideas. Many of the people he worked with initially had been trained by Artaud. Génica Athanasiou, Lea in *The Mysteries of Love*, took a major part in *As I Lay Dying* (1935); Roger Blin, whose first appearance on stage was as one of the assassins in *The Cenci*, acted the role of a 'double' to Barrault's interpretation of the protagonist in *Hunger* (*La Faim*, Knut Hamsun, 1939); Balthus, who had been doing only studio painting before *The Cenci*, designed the sets for several of Barrault's productions including *State of Siege*. And Artaud recognised *As I Lay Dying* as an authentic example of many of the essential elements in his Theatre of Cruelty, including his review of the performance in his 1938 edition of *The Theatre And Its Double*.

The elements that Artaud singled out were the creation of mythic symbols, like the 'centaur–horse' that Barrault created by simultaneously miming a stallion and its rider; the transfer of emotional states to the spectators by tempos of breathing; the use of incantation and stylised gestures to create a 'sacred atmosphere'; and the replacement of psychology and plot by what he elsewhere calls 'the theatre's physics' or scenic rhythms:

This spectacle is magical like those incantations of witch doctors when the clackings of their tongues against their palates bring rain to a countryside; when, before the exhausted sick man, the witch doctor gives his breath the form of a strange disease, and chases away the sickness with his breath... There is not one point in the stage perspective that does not take on emotional meaning.

In the animated gesticulations and discontinuous unfolding of images there is a kind of direct physical appeal...[8]

Significantly, these are also the qualities that Barrault has underlined as particularly fruitful for his future development. His *mise en scène* emphasised the image of man and horse by extended descriptions of running after the animal, leaping to seize its reins, leading it in a circle, jumping onto its back and breaking its bucking, rearing wildness into rhythmic dressage; while a letter of June 1935 singles out the essential qualities of his mime as 'striving towards a purely animal state, for example the face becomes a natural mask, the concentration is on the breathing'. [9]

Barrault described *As I Lay Dying* as 'pure theatre' – coining a phrase which has since been over-used – because it only existed as performance, and its basis was actors, not a text. In the two hours of stage time there were only thirty minutes of dialogue and much of this was in the form of choral songs or religious chants. There were no sets, and both costumes and props were minimal. The actors were practically naked, and the only 'costumes' were belts, to which were attached symbolic objects, each representing the character's dominant passion. They created the environment for the different scenes by vocal sound effects and rhythmic gestures, producing unaided the rasp of a saw for building the coffin or bird calls for the forest. It was solely their movements as an ensemble that evoked the dominating context of the natural world, flowing and tumbling for the river in flood, a light and leaping dance for flames in the fire or heavy mechanical bending movements for cotton-pickers in the fields. There were no atmospheric lighting effects and no external emotional tone from music, the only accompaniment being a tomtom. The only conventionally illusionistic element was the costume devised for 'the mother' when the actress playing the role fled (on discovering the degree of nudity required – shockingly revolutionary at that time) and Barrault took over the part in addition to acting the illegitimate son, Jewel. Even then, though the impression of femininity was essential for the maternal image, his dress was hardly representational. Barrault's chest was bare; and his skirt of ribbons, the long black wig falling below his waist and a stylised mask of black cheesecloth with reflective steel buttons for eyes transformed the figure into a monstrous totem.

As I Lay Dying was chosen because Faulkner presents a way of life that has returned to the primordial, in which man is integrated with nature and civilisation is seen as an artifical accretion. The central image of dying gives a spiritual perspective to the picture of crude physical life, which the extensive use of interior monologue has already transformed into subjective values. The simplicity of the story, the tragic extremity of passion where innocence and guilt become obsessions, and Faulkner's use of external description to reveal his characters' souls are easily translatable into mime.

The *mise en scène* focuses on the inner states of the characters and the emotional quality of landscape rather than events. The action opened with a mime of birth – anticipating a format that has become an archetype of ritual drama, one used both by Grotowski and the Living Theatre and brought to its fullest expression in Schechner's *Dionysus in 69* – 'A birth. The revelation of labour, the suggestion of suffering. Nothing individualised; a kind of annunciation . . . Relaxation. Each one turns back once more into a human animal; they dream of finding their true selves again.'[10] The family gathers around the dying mother, who signifies her desire to have her coffin made in her presence. Her body is taken by the father and her five children, including her illegitimate son (fathered by the village priest), to be buried with her parents in the town where she was born. Within this spare framework there were four intermingling levels of action: the physical journey and the family conflict caused by Jewel's presence; the world of nature that echoes the passions of the characters; a subliminal world of delirium, dreams, hallucinations; and a mythic reality of spiritual vision. In one sequence where the family cortège comes to the river, for example, Barrault himself presented at one and the same time the figure of Jewel, the curvetting horse he rides, and birds of prey circling overhead. Other actors mimed the water, as well as a floating tree trunk that is swept into the cortège in mid-stream, overturning the imaginary wagon to throw everyone into the river, and the dead mother rises out of her imaginary coffin. Contrasting with the struggles of the living, her movements are 'aquatic and feline, forming rhythms of suffering', and having passed 'to the other side of life' she is freed from the limitations of mute existence and can speak. But – in a way that strikingly anticipates Ionesco – language is only a block to communication: 'the words signify nothing, the words never correspond to what they strive desperately to express ... Sin, love, fear: the sounds for these are never sinning, nor loving, nor fearing, and those that are used for them have never been and could never be, at least until the words have been forgotten.'

Similarly in the mother's death scene realistic external actions, the sawing and hammering or kneeling by the bedside to pray, are set in a context of symbolic mime representing blinding rain and the primal violence of a storm surrounding the imaginary hut, while the most deeply affected members of the family act out their grief and jealousy in terms of delirious visions. 'Madness of little Vardaman. Hallucinatory journey of Darl [the eldest legitimate son] and Jewel.' In this, the focal scene of the performance, two further levels of ritualised and heightened reality were included. Onto a screen behind the death-bed was projected a strongly rhythmic shadow-play of the priest administering the last rites and holding a mass for the dead woman's soul, accompanied by a repeated funeral chant. These ceremonial rhythms were linked with organic rhythms established in the actual death sequence, particularly a stylised representation of the mother's breathing which was magnified into a pulse beat for the whole theatre.

Her eldest son is making the coffin. The wheezings from her chest fit in with the raspings of the saw. All the rest of the family, like an enormous jellyfish, contracts and relaxes in unison with the mother and the carpenter. The whole theatre is in death throes – a pump rhythm, an octopus rhythm, and all of a sudden at the climax of a breath: total stoppage. The mother's hand, which had been raised as when someone wants to look out into the distance, falls slowly in the silence, like a water level going down. Life is emptying out. The movement is prolonged throughout the body until the rigidity of a corpse is reached.[11]

The aim is to regulate the heart beat of the spectator by this driving pulsation which dominated every aspect of the stage image. This was a graphic example of Artaud's ideal that metaphysics should be made to re-enter the mind through the skin, and according to Barrault the effect

took us into the real regions of the sacred, of prayer: a rite as strong and primitive as if we had been in the middle of a tropical forest among witch-doctors. Rhythm is the only thing that can take us out of ourselves – I am thinking of trances of the soul:

> *corps de Jésus*
> *corps de Jésus*
> *corps de Jésus* . . .[12]

Each character was portrayed as existing on two opposing planes, social behaviour (man the individual) versus 'fundamental' behaviour (the double: primitive natural Man), and organic animal or religious rhythms were contrasted at the end with the artificial tempos of civilisation. When they reach the town the characters are plunged from 'the slow pace of the journey. The road without end . . . fatigue, insomnia, buzzards, anguish' into a vortex of frenetic, machine-like and purely external activity. In time to the beat of urban sound effects, a cacophony of motors, hooting, sirens, and phonograph music, pedestrians ran with jerky and extremely rapid movements, but covered practically no ground, while actors miming vehicles described painfully slow trajectories over the whole stage area, all movement freezing whenever a policeman on point-duty in the centre raised his arm. If the spectators have been brought to identify with the savage and spiritual by the earlier hypnotic rhythms, then this return to a surreal, Marx-brothers image of 'the town . . . in its everyday madness' should convince them of the essential unreality and shoddy unnaturalness of contemporary social existence. Something of this effect was undoubtedly achieved, at least for the artistic elite like Jouvet who invited Barrault to give a matinée performance of *As I Lay*

Dying at his theatre. But to the average reviewer this 'avant garde spectacle' was merely 'curious', 'an audacious experiment' but for 'a specialised taste', and by 1945 when its initial shock effect had been lost, this type of mimetic representation could be recognised as an artificial and partly conventional type of gestural language. As Gordon Craig perceived, what Barrault had created was 'an alphabet – the A.B.C. of Mime'; and when his 'rhythmic ballet' *Numance* (1937) was repeated in 1965 it seemed dated: 'Times had changed and Barrault had stood still.'[13]

It is partly the expressionist elements in his early work that were responsible for this. His concentration on emotional extremes in *As I Lay Dying*, his use of rhythms and symbolic characters, as well as the presentation of the external natural world as an extension of man, are all adaptations of typically expressionist traits, and his comments even contain clear echoes of Laban and Mary Wigman: 'We drugged ourselves chiefly with our own bodies: searching for ways of keeping balance, of slow motion, contraction, decontraction, relaxation, push–pull: the whole gamut. We would have liked to invent the impersonal masque . . .'[14] At the same time *As I Lay Dying* was close enough to Artaud's concepts for him to claim it as an example of his Theatre of Cruelty, and it was also only a short step from this to the 'total theatre' that has become Barrault's theatrical trademark.

Total theatre

The search for 'totality' in one form or another was one of the major motifs in French theatre between the wars, and from Barrault the line runs back not only to Artaud with his concept of a theatre that could totally involve the audience, both physically and emotionally: it can also be traced through Charles Dullin, Barrault's first mentor whom he claimed to have 'absorbed to the point of looking like him', to the symbolists and Copeau's Vieux Colombier, where Dullin received his training. Copeau united a visual stylisation derived from Gordon Craig with Adolphe Appia's concepts of rhythmic movement, sculptural lighting, 'musical space', in which actor and setting are united in a single plastic and expressive image (a section from Appia's *Music and the Arts of the Theatre* was printed as a note in Vieux Colombier programmes). Dullin's aim was a 'total spectacle', creating a strictly theatrical stage world 'more expressive than reality' through a synthesis of stylised conventions from circus and *commedia dell' arte* to the Nōh.[15] All these elements recur in Barrault's characteristic productions, where they gain a quasi-religious significance – which perhaps helps to explain his extended involvement with Claudel, who for the others in Barrault's anti-establishment and surrealist circle represented a 'monstrous mushroom living in a feudal world . . . a defender of the most reactionary forces, of bondage and stupidity'.[16]

Already in his early work Barrault was experimenting with combining different media (as in a film like *Les Enfants du Paradis*, where the highly stylised art of mime was dovetailed with the illusionism of talking cinema) and with creating new interrelationships between the different elements of theatre in the play between light, setting and the geometry of movement in an actor climbing a staircase, or between sound and sense in sequences where meaningless words 'plastically reproduced' conversation phonetically or spoken dialogue was answered by musical notes (Hamsun's *Hunger*). But it was primarily through his productions of Claudel in the forties and fifties that he developed his model of 'total theatre', and their importance to him is indicated by the way he revived *The Satin Slipper* (1943, 1953 and 1964), and the fourth section of the play, *Sous le vent des Iles Baléares* (in 1972), *Christopher Columbus* (1953, 1960, and several productions in Germany, 1961–3), *Break of Noon* (1948, 1961) and even an early play that Claudel had repeatedly refused permission to stage, *Head of Gold* (*Tête d' or*, 1959, 1967).

On a technical level Claudel's plays, with their multiplicity of short scenes and characters, their marvellously baroque, incantatory language, and their shifting transformations of visual imagery, provided a challenge that could only be met by radically new stage conventions. Even with cutting and doubling parts Barrault found that *Christopher Columbus* required a cast of thirty-three; while the setting in *The Satin Slipper* called for a globe, melting into the distant shape of the island of Japan, which looms up into the threatening figure of a warrior in dark armour and is transformed into a Guardian Angel, whose wings fold round, flowing back into the shape of the world, which slowly recedes into the depths of space, becoming one of the myriad points of light in a starry image of the Immaculate Conception spread out across the sky. Claudel labelled his theatrical work 'musical drama', but although it has general points of resemblance to Wagner's *Gesamtkunstwerk* and includes complex orchestral scores by composers like Honneger (*The Satin Slipper*) or Darius Milhaud (*Christopher Columbus*, which was originally conceived as an opera), 'music' is more a structural analogy than a formal description. Claudel rejected Wagner's concept because it subordinated setting, dialogue and actor – and with the actor, drama itself and human emotion – to a monochrome symphonic form that was self-enclosed and tended to stasis. By contrast his idea was to use music to amplify character and dramatic situation. And in ideal terms this meant that instead of being pre-composed and pre-set, the musical score would be orchestrated in direct response to the performance, 'giving impulse and pace to our emotions through a medium purely rhythmical and tonal, more direct and more brutal than the spoken word . . . music not only in the state of full realisation, as a cryptic language portioned out among the pages of a score, but in the nascent state, rising and overflowing from some violent feeling'.[17] In this concept music is not simply a resonator. It also has an active function, to unify the 'diverse voices' of a play into a harmonic 'enthusiasm', transforming the conflict of dramatic action into a 'final hymn'; and this is paralleled by a type of structural composition which weaves disconnected events into a single 'melodic' line.

Claudel's drama, which focusses on different varieties of religious conversion and sees human life in terms of the struggle of the flesh ('the Ordeal of Sin') against the spirit ('the Ordeal by Fire'), is yet another form of interior, mental drama. His plays are autobiographical and, as he openly acknowledged, in *Exchange* (*L'Echange*, 1914), as in *Break of Noon*, all the characters were projections of himself and reflected the 'painful bondage' of his life, while *Break of Noon*, *The Satin Slipper* and *Christopher Columbus* all repeat the same personal experience – sinful love for a married woman, who becomes the instrument of the protagonist's salvation, since his desire, which can never be consummated, leads to a victory over the self and his emotion is transferred by a natural progression from the woman, already idolised as an angel, to God. But instead of the expressionist or surrealist stress on dreams, the stage here represents the soul and the objects of the material world are veils for spiritual realities. Nowhere is this clearer than in *Christopher Columbus*. The play opens with Columbus on the point of death, impoverished and rejected by the king, to whom he has come to beg for the means to finance another voyage; and the scenes are the past as he relives it in the continuous present of his mind. The hero splits into two figures, the actor in an epic of discovery and the spectator who holds judgement on the temporal action from his standpoint on the threshold of eternity. A voyage into a spiritual geography, in which the materialistic preoccupations of social life in the form of greed, envy and disbelief, creditors, sceptical courtiers and mutinous sailors, is set against faith in the form of the luminous western horizon or the revelations 'from beyond the tomb' that Columbus receives when he reaches the Azores, and the world's ingratitude is balanced by one woman's saving love. The play is bounded by the image of the dove, simultaneously the Holy Ghost and standing for Columbus himself (through the double meaning of his French name, *Colombe*), which brings a message of hope from across the ocean to the child in Genoa at the beginning and carries the soul of man from a 'newly risen world' to the bosom of Christ Pantocrator at the end. In this world of symbols Columbus' life repeats the archetypal pattern of the Passion, with him lashed by rebellious menials to the mast of his ship. The stage is a metaphoric altar and the performance is a religious celebration, with a choir – adapted from the classical Greek chorus – representing the collective awareness of subsequent generations and mediating between the 'sacred mystery' being re-enacted and the audience, who are conceived as a church congregation.

In envisioning this religious drama Claudel was influenced by two traditional forms. He had been inspired by Ida Rubinstein's work and performances of the Medieval Studies Group to write a mystery play, *St Joan at the Stake* (*Jeanne au bûcher*, 1938), as an oratorio with a structure based on Aeschylus' *The Suppliants* and a chorus representing the French nation. But an earlier and even more significant model was the ritualistic traditional Japanese theatre. Unlike Yeats or Ezra Pound, he knew this at first hand from his diplomatic appointment in Tokyo, and even had an exercise in the formal Nōh style, *The Woman and Her Shade* (*La Femme et son ombre*) performed at the Imperial Theatre with music by a Japanese composer in 1923. *The Satin Slipper* was structured according to the Kabuki model of a tetralogy spanning four 'days', each of the first three treating the same material in different tragic moods, while the last 'day' transposes it into an absurd light; and his dramatic conception echoes the Nōh, with its symbolic acting of legendary histories focussing on spiritual recognition, its emblematic world and its on-stage musicians integrated in the action, whose drums and flutes both evoke the characters, creating appropriate emotional states in the audience before the entry of divine being or demon, and respond to the characters' passions. And it was explicitly this strong Japanese influence in Claudel that determined the style of Barrault's acting company. It is also significant that in Barrault's eyes there are definite correspondences between Japanese and Greek theatre in the masked *Shite*, the *mie* (a complex series of gestures, accompanied by percussive rhythms and climaxing in a motionless, stylised expressive pose, in some ways comparable to the Greek schemata) and the use of chorus and dance[18] – an attempt to trace parallels which indicates that for all its apparent modernity Barrault's 'total theatre' is another variant of the search for a contemporary equivalent of the imagined archaic, primal theatrical form.

Claudel's drama also dovetailed with Barrault's aims on another level. He was 'totally opposed to the rigid framework in which people want to imprison the theatre. Today there is the Comédie-Française where mass is said, and the Opéra where mass is sung. But I fail to see why another spectacle could not be devised which would utilise radio, dance, music and the cinema.' It was particularly to film that Claudel looked for the means to realise his drama of the soul. He believed that while painted scenery was by nature limiting and materialistic, substituting a cinema screen could produce 'a surface sensitive to thought'. By exploiting film as an 'infinitely subtle harmony of shadows' to express nuances of feeling through suggestion, 'that indistinct world where ideas are born from sensations' would become open to the stage;[19] and in Barrault's production of *Christopher Columbus* this was magnificently achieved by making the sail of his caravel, billowing in the wind, simultaneously setting, symbol and screen.

However, it was in this production too that Barrault developed his idea of creating a purely theatrical and non-representational world from the gestures, voice and movement of the naked actor. *As I Lay Dying* had been a crude but powerful prototype. Now this was revealed as a polished and flexible style. He added a prologue in which 'a troupe of men and women – although called "actors" all are primarily human beings – march onto the stage in procession, singing in unison . . . For their spiritual nourishment . . . they decide to re-enact the life of Christopher Columbus . . .',[20] a framing device which was to become characteristic of his work in emphasising the acted-out unreality of the spectacle, its supposedly spontaneous immediacy and imaginative nature, and in implying that theatre was an activity for all, not just for performing specialists. He also used the actors to represent nature and the elements, as well as the human condition. Thus in a scene where Columbus rescues an old sailor from drowning, the two actors expressed the impersonal surging force of the sea in which they struggled without going out of character, while other members of the cast hurled themselves across the stage like great waves or howled like the wind: a human universe. The same basic costume was used to suggest a court gown or peasant dress by simple alterations in shape, and, although Barrault tends to play down the

13 *Rabelais*, with Barrault in foreground. A bare stage & rhythmic gestures –
the actor as simultaneously character & natural environment (here a ship
at sea).

role of music, film and lighting in order to underline that '*the theatre is man*', in his most characteristic work all scenic devices do indeed appear subordinate to the human figures. Artaud had proposed that in his Theatre of Cruelty 'the set will consist of the characters themselves . . . and of landscapes of moving lights playing on objects and masks in perpetual interchange', and in Barrault's theatre this has been refined to the point that, in his most frequently repeated statement, 'as soon as there is, on four raised planks, no matter where, a man, and nothing around him, expressing himself in the whole range of his means of expression, there will be . . . *total theatre*'.[21]

In Barrault's terms the path from *As I Lay Dying* to *Christopher Columbus* found its logical extension in *The Oresteia* (1955). The drama of ancient Greece was the model for his ideal of the actor as an Artaudian 'emotional athlete,' where 'dance was the common factor' uniting the associated arts of sport and drama. 'Dances, chanting, choruses, trances. Drama reconstitutes these primitive ceremonies, which are theatrical play in its pure state',[22] and it was his observation of magic ceremonies in Brazil and occult séances, in which initiates were 'possessed' by spirits, that inspired his production of Aeschylus' trilogy. These formed the basis for his interpretation of Clytemnestra, whose invocation of the Furies became a black mass, and of Cassandra's prophetic frenzy. Again his premise was the universality of primitive cultural forms. The classical dance poses recorded in Greek sculpture and vase painting, normally taken to express rational harmony, were seen as identical to the trance dancing of a whirling dervish; and the style of the performance in gestures, costumes, music, masks, was 'inspired by African dancers'. On the surface this seems a rather facile and eclectic exoticism. But for Barrault the fundamental link between Greek, Japanese and other forms of 'archaic' acting was a tempo that 'makes one think of universal gravitation' (echoing Artaud's description of movement in *The Cenci*), and 'this organic rhythm', which in turn related to the cabbalistic 'ternary of creation', was read into the structure of *The Oresteia* – defined by Barrault as a neutral phase of mysterious preparation, the masculine phase of decisive action or fecundation, and the feminine phase of gestation, the gradual fruition of the act, 'fertilising history' to form another neutral phase and repeat the pattern in the next play of the trilogy. And it is on this level that Barrault's theatricalised drama of the soul, magically conjured up out of nothing by the actor's expressive power, ties into Artaud's 'metaphysics of the theatre', in terms of which Barrault defines the inner focus of his work: 'the world of the fantastic, death, blood, famine, fury, frenzy... *The river, fire, magic, my total theatre.'*[23]

These contrasting sides of Barrault's 'total theatre' were brought together in the two productions that epitomise the final stage of his career, *Rabelais* (1968) and *Jarry* (1970). The two works are closely connected. Both share the same subject in dealing with the human experience of living rather than life itself, following the trajectory of a human being through the imaginative universe of a writer's complete *œuvres* which Barrault had already experimented with in his *Connaissance de Claudel* (1955): a natural extension of his stylistic presentation of the universe in purely human terms. Both also treat the same theme, with the two protagonists representing 'free men' as satiric poets who confronted 'a world of total disorder' and reflected complementary aspects of 'truly contemporary experience' in their different epochs: Rabelais as 'Childhood grasping hold of life in both hands... An eternal student... fighting for new ideas', Jarry as 'identical to the conduct of certain contemporary youths who cannot adapt to the modern world, who turn their back on a bad world without working to mould an alternative world'.[24] They are also related by the incidental fact that Jarry himself had written a 'heroi-comic' stage version of *Pantagruel* (produced posthumously in 1911, with music by Claude Terrasse, who had composed the original music for *Ubu roi*) in which 'King Pantagruel' was another embodiment of Ubu and Rabelais' fantasy world became that of Dr Faustroll.

Inevitably, given the timing of the production, *Rabelais* appeared an act of self-defence in direct response to the youth revolution of May 1968, when the Théâtre de France was taken over and defaced by the students as the 'temple of bourgeois culture' and Barrault, fired by the government for compromising with the revolutionaries, found himself rejected by both the regime and its left-wing opponents. Initially however the show had been conceived as a counterblast to the public outrage against Blin's production of Genet's *The Screens* (*Les Paravents*, written in 1961 but unstaged, for fear of violence, until 1966). Barrault had not only sponsored this production but acted the key role of Si Slimane; and he took the riots which followed the first performance as evidence for the spurious morality and bad faith of 'right thinking people'. This radical perspective remained, despite the contemptuous and spiteful destruction of everything associated with Barrault's achievements by the student revolutionaries (led by the Becks and members of the Living Theatre, who had earlier been only too grateful for Barrault's support). Barrault obviously saw Rabelais as an *alter ego*: 'Caught between Roman repressive orthodoxy and the progressive fanaticism of the Protestant "gladiators", he chose the most uncomfortable side: that of tolerance.'[25] Yet his actual play lacked any sense of this objectivity, and the tone of its attack on hypocrisy and authoritarianism was taken from the youth sub-culture in an implicit plea for acceptance that made the treatment simplistic. The forces of repression were presented as cartoon caricatures – Picrochole's militaristic gestures were those of a Chaplinesque Great Dictator, while his henchmen were Marx-brothers' versions of Himmler, Goebbels, and Goering; the Church was a grotesque aviary of preening, rapacious and bird-brained poultry. Against this was set beat music and jive dancing to express the joy of life. Formal education was dismissed as 'Medieval' and deadeningly pedantic in being solely verbal and intellectual, while 'Humanist Education' was presented in mime illustrating the full development of the body as well as the mind and developing into an outburst of jive marking a student holiday. In the Abbey of Thélema figures representing moral deformities, physical ugliness and closed minds flung aside their cloaks to become the flower children of a 'hippy' commune, bare-breasted and mini-skirted in 'a blaze of light' where the cry

> Do as you will
> Because people are free!

is echoed by an orgiastic celebration as 'the music and dancing rise to a frenzied pitch followed by a strange torpor';[26] while the magic herb that Pantagruel takes with him on his voyage is translated into cannabis.

Quite apart from such political and social themes, the essential action of both *Rabelais* and *Jarry* takes place on an interior plane. The result was a variant of Claudel's spiritual stage, now interpreted psychologically, where expressionist and surrealist approaches were united with aims comparable to Alfred Jarry's own to produce psychomachia characterisation, dream realities and a structure designed to induce hallucinatory dislocation. In *Rabelais* Barrault divided man into Gargantua, the sensual appetites, Pantagruel, the thirst for knowledge and Panurge, the physical instincts – a simplistic separation of body, mind and emotion that he also applied to *Jarry*, where Père Ubu explicitly stood for the belly, Doctor Faustroll the head, and Sangle (from *Jours et nuits*) the heart, all of whom had 'a double' in the figure of Jarry himself. Both plays also present the same pattern of experience to the audience. The first half of *Jarry* attacked formal education, militarism and social institutions, setting 'the trauma engendered by society' against 'the desire for a new man', while the second half, like the psychedelic cannabis-voyage in *Rabelais*, moved into the subconscious as 'a surrealist dream, in the universe of drugs, which allows all hallucinations, all apparitions' and is designed 'to sweep us away' into an alternate reality.[27] The intention was liberty with a capital L, but unfortunately – symptomatic of Barrault's weakness as a thinker – the productions reduced this to simple eroticism. At the same time, on a technical level these 'spectacles' were fascinating and imaginatively powerful.

Barrault brought together all the techniques developed in his earlier productions, mixing conventions from the circus, music hall and puppetry with rhythmic chants, elaborate masks, the formalised movements of Kabuki theatre and choreographed mime to evoke the characters' environment and their unity with the natural world around them. Like *Christopher Columbus*, *Rabelais* was presented as 'a dramatic game' by strolling players, with the actors in modern dress mingling with the audience as they entered, carrying their props or costumes. And this close relationship with the spectators was reinforced by direct address to the audience during the performance, for

14 *Jarry*. The circus-ring stage: dream-like hallucinations & erotic ballets.

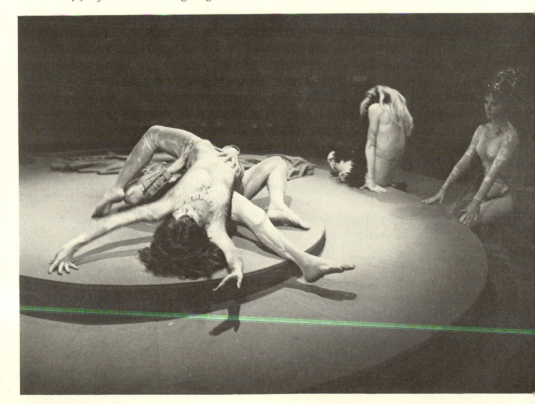

example discussing the way masks were being used by the actors to entertain not to deceive, as well as by the shape of the stage itself. In *Jarry* the action surrounded the audience on platforms constructed among the seats, as well as being played out in a circular central 'circus ring'. In *Rabelais* the acting area was cruciform, set in the centre of the auditorium so that actors entered through the spectators up steps at each of the four ends, and with ropes as the only scenery, functional and evocative. Spreading from a circular canopy high above the edges of the stage, these formed a circus-tent image for the first half, and simply by changing the place where they were tied down became the ship's rigging for the voyage. As in *As I Lay Dying*, Barrault mimed both Gargantua and his horse in the attack on Picrochole, and language was set against physical expression, as in a 'frozen words' fantasy where recorded voices were thrown by loudspeakers from different points in the auditorium and seemed to come out of the air. Rabelais' archaisms and obscure syntax were deliberately retained, sacrificing intellectual meaning to rich sound patterns, while in both plays the culmination was marked by strongly rhythmic music amplified to an enormous volume of sound enveloping the audience, and a pulsing kinetic energy in dance and acrobatics, accelerated by strobe lights to a 'mesmeric climax'.

However, as in Artaud's theatre, although the actors are required to be 'completely possessed' and the stage directions may specify that whoever plays Panurge 'goes into a positive ecstasy', the effect of spontaneity and anarchistic frenzy was always created from conscious and disciplined rehearsal. This became particularly clear in the 1971 British production of *Rabelais*, where Barrault's aim was 'to recreate as accurately as he could the sight and sound of his original production . . . the complex and precise ballet'.[28] A very high degree of precision indeed was required to integrate live dialogue with a multi-track, pre-recorded sound score of voices as well as musical effects, and a complete uniformity of mood and movement had to be achieved during the sea sequences to allow individual expression without destroying the image of a ship. Barrault's 'total theatre', then, is in various senses a theatre of total illusion.

It was also a style which could be applied independent of any thematic relationship to the material, as in Barrault's 'Connaissance d'homme', *Thus Spake Zarathustra* (1975). Nietzsche's agonised mind was turned into a colourful carnival, an emblematic masquerade which practically obliterated the dialogue, accompanied by elaborate slide and film projections on the walls of the theatre surrounding the audience that were striking but without discernible significance. This production in fact was an awful example of how the experimental could all too easily become an exterior effect, or eclecticism be substituted for synthesis, and critics noted that 'Barrault has, in fact, a prodigious, almost naive capacity for recouping what is fashionable'[29] – much the same criticism that has been levelled against a director like Peter Brook.

Peter Brook

It was a logical extension of his 'total theatre' for Barrault to found both the Théâtre des Nations – as a meeting-place where the traditions of the Far East, Bunraku, Kabuki, Nōh, could cross-fertilise with modern experiments by the Living Theatre, Grotowski (first exposed to the West through this festival) or Eugenio Barba – and its corollary, the Centre for International Theatre Research (CIRT) which he invited Peter Brook to direct. Like Barrault, Brook is a pragmatic director, who has a catholic appreciation of different dramatic forms while rejecting the theatrical *status quo* as a cultural garbage heap. Brook's concept of theatre as 'an empty space', the imaginative neutrality of which allows the actor to move freely through the entire physical world and into subjective experience, both presenting 'man simultaneously in all his aspects' and involving the audience collectively in 'a total experience',[30] is remarkably similar to Barrault's 'total theatre'. He also rejects naturalism as a style identified with the Establishment, 'the official art of every regime', and for him too the influence of Artaud was decisive, marking a radical change in his directorial approach.

For Brook, the 1964 'Theatre of Cruelty' season has a significance out of all proportion to its actual substance or achievement, as his frequent references to it in his book *The Empty Space* indicate. Initially, Brook and Marowitz described their aims in a typically inflated way – to create 'the poetic state, a transcendent experience of life' through shock effects, cries, incantation, masks, effigies and ritual costumes, changes of light to 'arouse sensations of heat and cold', different actions in separated areas 'all flooding one's consciousness simultaneously' and discontinuous physical rhythms 'whose crescendo will accord exactly with the pulsation of movements familiar to everyone' corresponding to 'the broken and fragmentary way in which most people experience contemporary reality' – and this eclectic mix of symbolist 'correspondences', dada and Artaud was labelled 'a rediscovery of the terror and awesomeness of the original semi-religious theatre'.[31] On this level the performance was a self-

15 Brook's experimental *Spurt of Blood*. Stylised simplicity & the exploration of basic theatre language.

conscious and pretentious failure, but beneath it there was a pragmatic and limited purpose. As an exercise preparing the traditionally trained actors of the Royal Shakespeare Company for a performance of *The Screens*, it was an exploration of theatre language designed to demolish conventional dramatic values, particularly 'the Stanislavski ethic', and return to the roots of physical expression. The experiment began by each actor attempting to communicate an internal state by pure thought transfer, adding vocal sound and physical rhythms 'to discover what was the very least he needed before understanding could be reached', and developing a body language 'beyond psychological implication and beyond monkey-see–monkey-do facsimiles of social behaviourism'.[32] This return to basics in order to develop in a new direction echoed Grotowski's aims in a remarkable way, even though it took place almost a year before the first reports of Grotowski's acting methods were published in English and two years before the first opportunity to see his work in Paris. And the parallel is not fortuitous. It indicates the fundamentalism of the avant garde approach.

The material presented – Artaud's *Spurt of Blood*; short abstract word collages by Paul Ableman; two surrealist sketches by Brook himself; a single scene from *The Screens* (replaced by Arden's *Ars Longa Vita Brevis* when the Lord Chamberlain demanded cuts in Genet's text); a montage of *Hamlet* by Marowitz, together with sequences of mime and improvisation – was little more than a series of acting exercises. When *The Screens* came to be presented three months later only the first twelve scenes were performed, the remaining two and a half hours being dismissed as repetitious elaboration, and it too was merely 'work in progress'; while the second half of the experimental season, which was to have followed Artaud's first Theatre of Cruelty manifesto with *The Jew of Malta* and Büchner's *Wozzeck* as well as *Ubu roi* and *A Dream Play*, never appeared (though recently Brook has reaffirmed his avant garde position in a practical form by staging, like Barrault, a compilation of Jarry's work, *Ubu sur la butte* – 1977). But the LAMDA experiment provided the principle of 'scientific research' into theatrical communication, on which all Brook's subsequent work has been based, and elements from it recurred in the key productions by which his search for a 'holy theatre' can be charted.

One of the improvisational exercises, expressing emotional states in fictional situations through Rorschach-like abstract action-paintings, which had been used in *The Spurt of Blood* and provided some of the most powerful moments in *The Screens*, was repeated in a more sophisticated form in *The Marat/Sade* (1964). Similarly the powerful erotic image of Charlotte Corday whipping Sade with her hair had its prototype in Brook's playlet *The Public Bath* where Glenda Jackson (who also acted Corday) as the scapegoat–saint, a double image of the notorious Christine Keeler and the bereaved Jacqueline Kennedy, whips the judge as he condemns her. The experiments with audience relationships, in which the spectators were surrounded by action or changed places with the actors, were extended in *US* (1966) where the actors with their heads covered by paper bags (as in *The Spurt of Blood*) stumbled groaning in among the spectators, representing the maimed of Vietnam and requiring physical assistance from the audience. This was an unfortunate confusion of symbolism with actuality, which was rapidly abandoned, even though it accurately expressed the focus of the production as an attack on the self-satisfied comfort of the 'uninvolved' British public ('us' rather than 'U.S.' – hence the absence of a coherent statement about the war). Like *The Marat/Sade* production, which had distorted Weiss' intentions by stressing the Artaudian images of sadism, violence and insanity, *US* was preoccupied by cruelty and in particular the self-immolation of Buddhist monks and Quaker pacifists. And this rather over-literal transliteration of Artaud's actors 'signalling through the flames', together with the ending, in which a butterfly was ceremonially burnt, followed by the full cast 'refusing' to leave the stage and thus forcing the audience into a 'decision' – to walk out, symbolising their avoidance of moral responsibility or involvement – illustrates two intrinsic flaws in Brook's approach, its tendency to simplification and aestheticism.

However, the attempt to go beyond language and to find more direct ways of relating the audience to the action has yielded some of the most exciting interpretations of conventional drama, like Brook's 1970 production of *A Midsummer Night's Dream*, quite apart from providing the springboard for his search for a ritual theatre, which had indeed been the rationale for his *Screens* project: 'the direction I want to explore is . . . a field in which ritual and what one calls outside reality completely overlap: and this is the world of Genet'.[33] For the *Dream* Brook rehearsed his actors intensively in improvisational exercises 'attempting to alter or strengthen the initial impulse that lay in the centre of the physical movement' and to form a 'vocabulary' out of acrobatics. This was extrapolated into the circus metaphor of the production, circus conventions being physical and presentational as opposed to the imaginative evocation of verbal poetry. And in poetic passages that Brook felt had become clichéed by familiarity, the words were reduced to sounds and merged into patterns of physical movement. The premise that the opposite worlds of the play were identical, with Theseus doubling as Oberon and Hippolyta as Titania, was extended to encompass the separate worlds of stage and audience, with Puck 'girdling' the auditorium, with Hermia almost forced off the stage into the spectators' laps, with the cast exiting through the audience at the end and literally enacting 'give me your hands, if we be friends' by shaking hands with the spectators. The formal parallels between Athens and the magic wood, together with the omnipresent fairies, who acted as stagehands bringing in props or created the lovers' environment by forming themselves into trees and even literally transported characters from place to place on the stage, all corresponded to the submerging of rational verbal communication beneath acrobatic activity. Beneath Shakespeare's poetry Brook revealed a 'secret play' of total 'anarchy' and 'wild joy', where the world of the spirit in 'the wood and its inhabitants pour forth a primitive wildness which infected all who came into contact with it'.[34]

This interpretation, like the rehearsal methods and the 'empty space' of the square white gymnasium set or the physical contact with the audience, clearly related the *Dream* to his experiments with Seneca's *Oedipus* and *The Tempest* (both in 1968). As in Brook's *Lear* immediately preceding the LAMDA season, where the perspective was explicitly Beckettian and the world was reduced to corroding 'facades and emblems' so that 'ironically, as characters acquire sight, it enables them only to see into a void',[35] the focus of both these productions was drawn from Jan Kott's existential interpretation of Shakespeare and Greek tragedy. In the *Tempest* exercise Prospero and Caliban were presented as complementary aspects of a single personality, with 'This thing of darkness I acknowledge mine' as the central motif and the intellectual, spiritual aspect of the mind losing control of the atavistic, instinctual Caliban, so that the performance became an exploration of the anarchic and primitive side of human nature. The choice of Seneca's *Oedipus* (rather than Sophocles' humanistic version where rational man is 'the measure of all things') also emphasised the violent and irrational side of life. Like Brook's *Lear*, where conventionally humanising elements such as the servant's protest against Gloucester's blinding were cut, the thematic point of both productions was to explore how much suffering a human being could sustain without splitting under the pressure. Brook's aim was to oppose a rigorous objectivity, of the kind he associated with Beckett, to the 'romantic' view, 'where we leave an experience of horror finally strangely comforted' because of the author's 'complicity'.[36] But neither production was intended to be nihilistic. Not only is Beckettian honesty itself seen as 'the most positive' attitude available in the twentieth-century context of genocide, political torture and total warfare, but the destructive anarchy of sexual urges expressed in these productions was itself considered liberating. The phallic golden spike on which Jocasta impales herself at the end of Ted Hughes' adaptation of *Oedipus* was paralleled by the farcically over-literal seven-ft golden phallus that the chorus danced around in a bacchanalian epilogue – to the tune of 'Yes, we have no bananas', an incongruity that highlights Brook's problems in updating archaic ritual to the modern day. The same theme was even more explicit in Brook's version of *The Tempest*, where Caliban led a mass revolution, raping Miranda then sexually assaulting Prospero, but this 'dark' side of sexuality was balanced against an innocent paradise of pre-civilised responses to nature, in which the final marriage ceremony was performed as a mating ritual.

By any definition Brook's *Oedipus* clearly counts as Theatre of Cruelty. The David Turner/Ted Hughes text drew parallels between the bloodshed in Thebes and Vietnam, modern agnosticism and Seneca's Rome where 'official religion... had lost any hold on private thought', being replaced by 'a mixture of mysticism and quasi-scientific humanism'. The speeches were patterned on Maori chants delivered in a 'depersonalised' monotone, with stylised emotional effects achieved by strong and irregular rhythms of breathing derived from recordings of a witchdoctor in a trance. The moves were abstract, devoid of feeling or contact, as in the slave's long description of Oedipus' blinding which was accompanied by cold and formalised gestures:

16 Emblematic stasis & abstraction v. verbal violence in *Oedipus* (chorus standing with hands over eyes on boxes at each side).

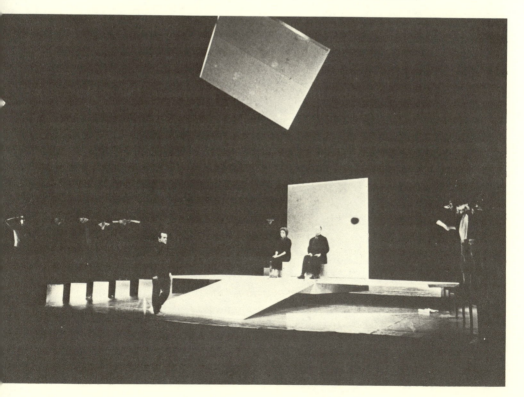

1. Slowly lifts arms.   2. Hooks fingers in front of eyes.   3. Raises arms, palms out, hands hooked.   4. Drops arms, X over Box to U/R – stands. TIRESIAS rises, X to OEDIPUS.   5. Slave sits as TIRESIAS puts hands on OEDIPUS's eyes.[37]

The same dichotomy between images of extreme violence and stoi-cally dispassionate expression – an avoidance of conventional rhetoric which paradoxically gives the sort of event conventionally associated with excessive emotion an impact of almost unbearable intensity by restraint, a technique that Peter Weiss also used to great effect in *The Investigation* (*Die Ermittlung*, first produced the same year) – charac-terised the whole presentation. The visual picture was one of extreme plainness, with the actors in dark suits and black roll-neck sweaters standing in an empty golden box of a stage, off which blinding light was reflected at high points in the action. And this impression of bareness was reinforced by the static immobility of the protagonists, with Gielgud in the whole of Oedipus' opening four-page im-passioned speech being restricted to one emblematic movement, rais-ing his arms to heaven. This was offset by emotive vocal effects from the chorus placed around the spectators, repeating the words to create echoing chants, accompanying the description of the plague with rapid rhythmic panting, punctuating the speeches with ulula-tions, ritually beating their chests at Oedipus' self-accusation. In the LAMDA experiment Brook and Marowitz had found that 'facial ex-pressions, under the pressure of extended sounds, began to resemble Japanese masks',[38] and the same effect was used here. A depersonali-sation equivalent to classical tragic masks, that could transform an individual actor into a representative of humanity in a communal sense, was gained by rigid and, at emotional peaks, distorted faces in which immobility combined with inner tension.

In the preface to the published version of *US*, written during the rehearsals for *Oedipus*, Brook commented that audiences instinc-tively close their minds to contemporary events which touch them on the raw, while conversely the potential power of myth is insulated in direct proportion to its distance from contemporary issues. This points to the basic problem facing all the inheritors of Artaud who seek to affect spectators directly by using rituals in the modern secular context where these have no religious significance, and therefore no subjective value for the public. The *Oedipus* production was an effec-tive attempt to overcome the audience's instinctive self-defence by presenting an archetypal situation, which had only an abstract rela-tionship to highly charged political realities, while gaining immediacy by throwing the subject of human 'cruelty' into stark relief through impersonal presentation and ritualised response. On one level this was a sacrificial rite, and reviewers found the primitive rhythmic orchestration hypnotic or compared it to *The Rite of Spring*. On another level it was a visceral assault on the audience, and so effective that some of the actors had moral doubts about presenting it at all:

The play is such a violent vehicle [but] to play it down would be dishonest... Blood, torn eyeballs, torn insides and torn gizzards are mentioned about every five seconds for two hours. Death, disaster, plague, sickness, horror are the main ingredients of the play... In fact I wondered whether it was right to perform this in front of people. In one of the speeches – the one in which the slave describes Oedipus tearing his eyes out – people in the audience became physically ill, and the St John's Ambulance Brigade was always on hand ready to carry people out. It happened quite often.[39]

In rehearsals for *Oedipus* exercises were developed from Tai Chi, using gravity as the only source of energy to achieve economy of movement, while the actors prepared by learning to express horrific personal experiences or Hieronymous Bosch visions of hell by sounds alone, or even just by rhythms of breathing: a reduction of expression to essentials that characterises all Brook's experiments at the CIRT.

The initial impetus for this research into theatre language came from the response of Eastern European audiences, who understood practically no English, to the RSC tour of *Lear*. Noting that the cultural or linguistic contexts within which any conventional theatre works in fact act as 'barriers' to communication on a deeper, universal level, Brook 'set out to explore what the conditions were through which the theatre could speak directly. In what conditions is it possible for what happens in a theatrical experience to originate from a group of actors and be received and shared by spectators without the help and hindrance of the shared cultural signs and tokens...?'[40] This determined the international composition of his company, which has included actors from Japan, Africa, Persia and Spain as well as France, Britain and the USA, and led to their African tour in search of audiences who lacked even the concepts of story line and pretence, the assumptions about linear narrative or acting out make-believe, on which theatre is based. In practice it has meant reversing the traditional priorities of communication, elevating the secondary elements of gesture, pitch, tone and the dynamics of sound or movement that give expressive values, over the primary element of intellectual meaning. The difficulty is that all forms of language, verbal, vocal, emblematic or physical, communicate with any precision only to the extent that their symbols are known and shared; and to counter the danger that in rejecting all shared signs expression would be reduced to the purely private, Brook's emphasis has been on integrating the individual actor in the group on the dubious premise that expressive forms created by a collective – however small – will have the force and universality of archetypes. This exploration of non-semantic body language implies that, extending Barrault's concept, theatre should not imitate life but directly create experience. And behind it lies a quasi-mystical belief in the metaphysical significance of the body as an 'organic root' uniting all men:

Our work is based on the fact that some of the deepest aspects of human experience can reveal themselves through the sounds and movements of the human body in a way that strikes an identical chord in any observer, whatever his cultural and racial conditioning. And therefore one can work without roots, because the body, as such, becomes a working source.[41]

In terms of *The Tempest*, which was presented as 'work in progress', this meant cutting all the surface play of plot, characterisation and 'pretty writing' that Brook found 'uninteresting' and 'hardly worth reviving', and concentrating on the 'buried themes' of social exploitation, violence, incest, sexuality and revolution that would turn it into a universal statement on 'the whole condition of man'.[42] The bare stage was set in the middle of the audience, some of whom were seated on multi-level mobile scaffolds that were pushed on and around the acting area, and over which the actors climbed, swung and performed complex gymnastics. As well as this integration of a token number of spectators, the audience was encouraged to mingle with the actors for close-ups on the action, both of which anticipate a characteristic technique of Schechner's 'environmental theatre'. In addition the opening 'mirror' exercise, with pairs of actors each facing the other and imitating each other's movements, provided an image of the ideal feedback between performer and observer, where every action arouses a corresponding reaction that in turn modifies the next action. In the performance itself the primary concern was the creation of physical images by articulating space through the movement of the group as a whole, as in the storm sequence where the ensemble huddled, trembled and swam trance-like through waves of sound from the Japanese Ariel giving vocal expression to a dream of tempest and terror, or in a mass copulation mime where an inverted pyramid was formed on the scaffolds with the violated body of Prospero as the apex at the bottom and Caliban triumphant on the top. And this stress on the collective was carried over into a thematic focus on power and isolation: how one actor could impose his will on the group as a whole, or in the way detached figures became reduced to machines or animals when contact with the ensemble was lost.

The text was treated in a similar way to the 'collage *Hamlet*' of the LAMDA experiment, where Marowitz had attempted 'to open up the play from the inside' as a montage of dialogue fragments and discontinuous scenes comparable to the film structures of Truffaut or Resnais with their cross-cuts, close-ups and slow dissolves, or to the dissonances in the music of Schönberg. It was also intended to correspond in a dadaist way 'to the tempo of our time'. But Marowitz's aim in the earlier production had been to create an expressionistic image of the subconscious mind, presenting the play in the form of 'subliminal flashes out of Hamlet's life' which mirrored the distorted perception of reality by a 'boy in... a stress situation', and presupposing 'that there was a smear of *Hamlet* in everyone's collective unconscious'.[43] By contrast, Brook's superficially similar juxtaposing of speeches reduced to single lines, merging of characters and rearranging of sequences in *The Tempest* was designed to transform Shakespeare's play into a mythic image of the primitive nature of man beneath the veneer of civilisation, and the dialogue was either transformed into hieratic chanting – like the final marriage sequence which was accompanied by repetitious elaborations on 'And my ending is despair' / 'Unless it be relieved by prayer' – or to show language as an instrument of oppression and exploitation – as in Prospero's attempt to control Caliban by teaching him single words related to identity, beginning with 'you/me' and ending with 'slave/master' in a remarkable anticipation of Peter Handke's theme in *Kaspar* (also first staged in 1968, and produced by Brook in 1972).

For *Oedipus*, Brook had introduced the cast to recordings of primitive native rites and required them to model their delivery on 'certain peculiar breathing methods' used 'for ceremonial purposes', and on

the pattern of [native] sounds and the pattern created by the use of hands and feet, and the extraordinary things the witchdoctor did with his voice. Brook talked a lot about what was the common root of *Oedipus* and the primitives. It was rhythms and the use of the voice to engender excitement... All this fitted in perfectly with Brook's idea of Theatre as Ritual [but] we didn't want to copy a native ritual; so we made up our own rituals. Breathing was our beginning.[44]

The CIRT work was based on the same principle, but extended from borrowing primitive speech patterns to using archaic ceremonial languages and integrating ritual, instead of merely applying it to their dramatic material. In order to compensate for the 'vocal poverty' of contemporary speech and what Brook saw as the limitation on auton-omous physical expression imposed by intellectual meaning, he trained his actors in the use of African chants, Latin and Avesti, the ancient Persian language of Zoroastrian incantation. The common factor was that these were 'dead' or incomprehensible languages as-sociated with religious ceremonies, where the expressive qualities of tone, pitch and rhythm could be explored to the full, without the interference of conceptual meaning, in his attempt to find a pre-logical, universal form of communication. The effect obviously relied heavily on exoticism and mystery, in that texts like Aeschylus or Seneca in the original contained specific content for the actor-initiates which the audience could sense but not understand, as well as gain-ing an abstract impression of spirituality from the pre-existing reli-gious connotations.

These linguistic experiments culminated in the remarkable produc-tion of *Orghast* at the 1971 festival in Persepolis, in which Brook's 'theatre of ritual' attained its fullest expression. Working with the group, Ted Hughes created a special speech, also labelled 'Orghast' to underline the organic unity of content and form in his play. This language was not only designed to reflect 'the sensation of a half-barbaric world' but to affect 'magically' the mental state of a listener on an instinctive level in the same way that sound can affect the growth of plants or the patterning of iron filings. Sounds were given specific emotive values, and words were invented intuitively to avoid what Hughes called the 'gabbled gibberish of static interference' in conventional speech and to return to an ideal of direct expression rooted in 'the experience of the moment'. The analogy to music struck many of the critics who attended the Persepolis performance, and in Hughes' terms

if you imagine music buried in the earth for a few thousand years, decayed back to its sources, not the perfectly structured thing we know as music, then that is what we tried to unearth. A language belonging below the levels where differences appear, close to the inner life of what we've chosen as our material, but expressive to all people, powerfully, truly, precisely.[45]

The intention was not to create a conceptual language which de-scribed a situation, but to compose blocks of sound that would have the status of physical action and be indecipherable by intellectual analysis. However, in practice the 2,000-odd words created all had semantic meanings and could be translated into other languages. Many of the roots were an onomatopoeic rendering of physiological states – GR... for 'eat', KR... for 'devour', ULL... for 'swallow' – and more abstract objects were either expressed by compounds such as BULLORGA (from ULL, 'absorb', and ORG, 'life') meaning 'darkness', or *KROGON* meaning the destructive principle, or alternatively became fixed when it was discovered that arbitrary formulations corresponded to words in languages outside the occidental framework, these coincidences being naively taken as evidence that in returning to the roots of language they were rediscovering the universal and organic sources of meaning. Thus Hughes' term for 'light', HOAN, was confirmed when it turned out to mean 'a ray of light' in Farsi, while USSA 'was just a provisional name [for his 'Woman of Light'] until we discovered it meant "dawn" in Sanskrit'.[46]

Perhaps not surprisingly, apart from its word-for-word translatability, 'Orghast' has strong similarities to the early dada experiments with 'plastic' sound that arose out of the surrealist interest in automatic writing as direct subconscious expression. The structuring principle parallels Zdanévitch's 'zaoum' language, which used onomatopoeic roots as 'the sense support' for other similar-sounding words. The intention is much the same as Kurt Schwitters' 'Sonata in Primeval Sounds'. And the general effect (with allowances made for the author's base in French rather than English) corresponds closely to Tzara's use of free association and African rhythms, as a brief comparison will show.

M. CRICRI: DSCHILOLI MGABATI BAÏLUNDA
LA FEMME ENCEINTE: TOUNDI-A-VOUA
                         SOCO BGAI AFFAHOU
M. BLEUBLEU: FARAFANGAMA SOCO BGAÏ AFFAHOU
       (*La Première Aventure céleste de Monsieur Antipyrine*, 1920)

GOD-KROGON: BULLORGA OMBOLOM FROR   SHARSAYA NULBULDA BRAR
             darkness opens its womb   I hear chaos roar

             IN OMBOLOM BULLORGA
             in the womb of darkness

             FREEASTAV OMBOLOM   NILD US GLITTALUGH
             freeze her womb   rivets like stars

             ASTA BEORBITTA   CLID OSTA BULLORGA
             icy chains   lock up the mouth of darkness

             IN OMBOLOM KHERN FIGYA GRUORD
             in her womb I make my words iron

                                                (*Orghast*)

'Orghast' itself was the name Hughes invented for the fire of being, in metaphoric terms the sun (from ORG for 'life, being' and GHAST for 'spirit, flame'), and the material for the play was a myth of creation compiled from the legends of Prometheus, Chronos devouring his children and the sun-worshipping cults of Helios and Zoroaster. It included passages from Aeschylus' *Prometheus Bound* and *The Persians* and Seneca's *Thyestes* and *Hercules Furens* in the original Greek and Latin as well as sections in Avesti; and in the same way that Hughes sought to return to the source of meaning in his language, this collage of mythical material was an attempt to rediscover the universal root myth buried under a wide range of archetypes. As a note in the programme stated:

Orghast stems from certain basic myths – the gift of fire, the massacre of the innocents, the imprisonment of the son by the father, the search for liberation through revenge, the tyrant's destruction of his children, and the search for liberation through knowledge–as reflected in the hymns of Zoroaster, the stories of Prometheus and Hercules, Calderón's *Life's A Dream*, Persian legends, and other parallel sources.[47]

Brook's interest in the Prometheus myth extended back to 1965 when he had commissioned a new translation of Aeschylus' play from Robert Lowell, and the action of *Orghast* not only revolves around the figure of Prometheus: it also takes place on a symbolic level within his being, as Hughes showed in an explanatory drawing of the 'physiology' of his play. This concept of mythology literally embodied in man – which has more than a coincidental family likeness to the human 'chart' of the Living Theatre's *Paradise Now* (1968) – carried over into the historical level of the play, where decisive battles like Salamis were presented as extensions of the primal conflict that take seed in the mind of future generations, on analogy to Lévi-Strauss' view of the way in which 'myths operate in men's minds without their being aware of the fact'. [48] This organic unity also brings the linguistic exploration into the frame of all-encompassing myth, with the connection (again following Lévi-Strauss) between the gifts of fire and language, the use of both being what distinguishes man from nature, the cooked from the raw.

Performed in a ceremonial balletic style avoiding all naturalistic expression of emotion, with vocal delivery stressing the 'animal music' of Hughes' text and choruses structured 'like a requiem, a solo voice rising in lament or rage above chanting', accompanied only by percussive rhythms on drums and metal pipes, the effect was paradoxically bloodless and abstract for all the 'organic' emphasis. This was partly due to Hughes' deliberate universalisation: 'at the level of generalisation, on which this myth works, the writings of most poets are one system and the same'. But it was also an inevitable side-effect of a production in which the anecdotal details and narrative side of the myths were stripped away so that 'the abstract, the hieratic spectacle, barbaric sound structures, would grip like music'.[49] The result was that few of the characters were well enough defined by the action for the audience to comprehend the mythology, and not unnaturally some reviewers reacted with considerable intellectual frustration – all of which indicates that despite T. S. Eliot's principle that poetry communicates before it is understood, its true message being subliminal, too direct an appeal to immediate experience can be counter-productive in attempting to bypass intellectual understanding altogether. In fact, despite the Artaudian emphasis on 'total man', like most of the ritualistic and anti-rational trend in avant garde theatre, *Orghast* was one-sided in its appeal. And ironically this appeal to the primitive night side of nature seems only to have worked with the over-educated, intellectually sophisticated spectators at the Persepolis festival – perhaps because of the highly literary sources for that collage of creative myths. When *Orghast* was performed to a supposedly primitive (and therefore in theory more receptive, even more susceptible) audience on Brook's African tour, apparently they found those dark primordial cries hilariously funny.

Even when restaged in Paris it fell far short of the desired liberation of the unconscious, and one can only conclude that it was the unique integration between theme, style and place which made the first performance so effective. Part I, which takes place in the spirit world, was performed in Ataxerxes' tomb and on the bare terrace in front of it looking out over the ruins of Persepolis; and the use of Avesti, the ceremonial language of the long-dead king and of the religion that constructed his tomb, the entry of Irene Worth as Moa, the female principle of creation, from the mouth of the burial chamber, and the ball of fire suspended above a carving of a fire-worship ceremony, all gave the ritual enaction of the myth intense imaginative force. The links between part II, in the world of the dead, and its setting on the cliff-face of Naqsh-e-Rustam (the City of the Dead) in which four emperors' tombs are carved, was equally striking, with Aeschylus' lament for the deaths of the defeated Persians and the fall of Xerxes in which Persepolis was destroyed resounding before the graves of Darius and Xerxes themselves. The use of fire as a natural form of lighting in the ball of flame suspended in front of Prometheus, chained high on the rock face, and the flambeaux carried by the actors

17 Ted Hughes' physiology of *Orghast*. Key: Orghast – creative force (the sun
+ conception). Krogon – the destructive principle (usurping God-King +
vulture). Moa – creation, chaos (womb + earth). Moasha/Ussa –
descendents of Moa (imprisoned light). Sogis – Krogon's liberating son.
Sheergra – strength. Furorg – enslaved life. Bullorg – darkness.

also had immediate symbolic power, as did the correspondence between the timing of the performances and Hughes' Manichaean vision of existence with its external conflict of light against dark. Part I, with Krogon's perversion of the original creative fire that represented divine harmony, took place at sunset, with the violation and enslavement of nature paralleled by the growing darkness. Part II ends the cycle at dawn, with the rising sun striking a Zoroastrian temple at the base of the cliff where Hercules' descent into the underworld had been enacted. This unity with nature, the reverberations of almost legendary history and the association of the artificially constructed myth with archaic religion gave *Orghast* a level of reality and intensity that could hardly otherwise have been achieved. As such it must be counted a vindication of Brook's Theatre of Ritual. But these qualities that gave it such effectiveness, being independent of the drama itself, made it unrepeatable in the normal theatre.

Jean Genet

It is no accident that Barrault supported Genet. Nor that it was Peter Brook whom Genet asked to direct the Paris première of *The Balcony* (originally intended for 1957, but banned until 1960), while it was Genet's play *The Screens* which had acted as the catalyst for Brook's exploration of Artaud and his subsequent attempt to create a ritual theatre. As Genet's translator Bernard Frechtman was the first to point out, he 'is endeavouring to create a theatre which is ceremony. In *The Blacks* and *The Balcony*, ceremony is achieved through the behaviour of characters who enact a ritual.'[50] On the surface Genet's plays appear to be making politically charged statements about contemporary society – class hatred and exploitation, revolution and repression, racial conflict, colonialism and third world liberation – and there have been various attempts to analyse his work in sociological terms. But such an approach inevitably leads to the conclusion that the plays are empty, or, as Norman Mailer put it, 'White and Black in mortal confrontation are far more interesting than the play of shadows Genet brings to it', and the most that can be made of them is Lucien Goldmann's contention that as 'mental structures' Genet's plays reflect the radical pessimism of the disillusioned European Left.[51]

In fact for Genet, whose work has links with the expressionists and surrealists, social realities are illusory and the human need for illusion is so strong that no social order can be based on reality. Revolutions are no more than 'someone dreaming' and, as the final words of *The Balcony* make explicit, the audience's daily life is falser than the 'house of illusions' represented by Genet's brothel, or in wider terms by the theatre itself. If what we take to be reality is illusion, then only undisguised illusion is real. If 'being' (in Sartre's terms) is defined as 'doing', but all action on the social level is self-deception, then only the achievement of a state of 'non-being', the negation of the self, can be authentic. Hence Genet's plots always centre on death, while his characters are roles, not personalities defined by a coherent set of internal qualities, but masks giving shape to a void or reflected images in a receding perspective of mirrors. The concept of the individual is the irreducible minimum on which all social relationships or political structures are based, whether individuals are reduced to statistics or seen as the products of environmental conditioning or elevated to an archetypal subjectivity where the world itself becomes a projection of the mind. And even when dramatists like Brecht, Weiss or Handke dismiss nineteenth-century ideas of individuality, their characters retain an inner core of motivations and experiences that distinguish single figures or groups. Pirandello was the first to show the social personality as an unstable agglomeration of imposed and self-adopted roles, but the comparison that has frequently been drawn with Genet is misleading. Behind Pirandello's naked masks is the face, while for Genet the masks are empty and the usual equation between appearance and essence has been reversed. The artificial appearance is the essence.

Nowhere is this clearer than in his first play to reach the stage, *The Maids* (*Les Bonnes*, 1946). The apparent reality of mistress and maid in the opening tableau, buttressed by a detailed naturalistic boudoir setting, is revealed as false. Both are maids, one impersonating Madame, the other impersonating her sister, and in Genet's original intention these parts were to be played by adolescent boys. In addition, these young boys were required to act incompetently to remove any impression of reality from this level too. Within the play there are references to an actual case of two maids, the Papin sisters, who murdered and dismembered their mistress, but this emotionally charged historical crime is at the furthest remove from reality. As women the maids are capable only of enacting their revenge for their degradation by society in fantasy, but as homosexuals this fantasy of class hatred becomes transformed into a transvestite fantasy of sexual domination, which in turn is undermined by emphasising that this too is imaginary, a performance. The essential level is that of the actor, which removes reality from even the final murder–suicide; and in theatrical terms the actor is a non-person, a blank whose personality is that of the character he is impersonating.

There are obvious problems in the way this reversal of reality and illusion is carried out, the main flaw being the breaking of the stage convention that the play itself sets up. If the maids are boys, what are we to make of the mental state of the mistress; and if she too is played by a boy, what place has this intruder in the private world of a homosexual couple? Yet when the parts are played by women, as Jouvet got Genet's permission to do for the first production, then the essential complexity of self-cancelling reflections is lost.

But this negation of reality through role playing is the premise of all Genet's subsequent plays. In *The Balcony* (*Le Balcon*, 1957), the social roles of the 'clients' – bank clerk, plumber or fireman – have exactly the same status as the brothel fantasies of Bishop, General, Judge, which can be transformed into functional figures when the rebels blow up the heads of the church, military and judiciary in the palace, since the 'reality' lies in the symbols imprinted on the public consciousness by centuries of tradition. The ceremonial accoutrements of mitres and copes, robes and uniforms, crowns and decorations are what have substance, not the men beneath; when these figures appear on the Grand Balcony as stiff gigantic effigies, the populace to whom they wave is represented by the Beggar, seen earlier as yet another role in the repertoire of the brothel; and as the rebel leader recognises, success is self-defeating since to succeed at all any revolution must find the emotional focus of an image, Liberty on the Barricades, thus denying not only its intrinsic puritanical reality principle but even its functional effectiveness by becoming a 'combat of allegories'. As the Envoy remarks, after we have been given a demonstration of how the symbols of social order are perpetuated by press photographers who ignore facts in favour of the 'definitive image', 'a true image' can only be 'born of a false spectacle'. And again the symbols, into which reality has been abstracted, are reduced to theatre. As in *The Maids* the characters are ultimately actors, wearing 'garish make-up' and 'tragedians' cothurni about twenty inches high'. Similarly in *The Blacks* the costumes 'suggest fake elegance', while the characters replaying the ritual murder of a white woman are not played simply by Negroes but are transformed into artificial images of absolute blackness by 'beautiful shiny black make-up', and each of the court who judges them wears a stylised mask representing 'the face of a white person . . . in such a way that the audience sees a wide black band all around it'.[52] Here the complexity of different levels of illusion is even greater than in *The Maids*. The formal court on stage is paralleled by a revolutionary court off stage, and the massacre of white images is set against the execution of a Negro leader who has betrayed the Black Power movement. Just as the re-enaction of a murder is a cover for revolt within the play against the judges who condemn the Negroes, a deliberate adoption of the image of ritualistic savagery and evil imposed on them by their oppressors, so this performance and symbolic uprising is intended to distract the actual audience from the political struggle against the social order they represent. But since it is explicitly presented as such, logically it can hardly be effective, and indeed the off-stage events are overtly fake. The execution is no more than 'the ultimate gesture' it is described as, and instead of revolver shots 'a firecracker explodes off stage, followed by several more. The sparks of fireworks are seen against the black velvet of the set.' It has no more substance than the body of the murdered woman in the centre of the stage, whose catafalque covered with funeral flowers is revealed to be a sheet stretched over two empty chairs. Even the political struggle is only a play, with each of the other levels of the action receding further into deception and illusion so that the love story between Virtue and Village, who walk away from the audience hand in hand at the end in the clichéed stage image of romance, becomes a play within a play (Diouff's ascension into heaven) within a play (the massacre of images) within a play (the murder trial) within a play (the revolution) – and on each level, as Archibald the Master of Ceremonies tells the court, the Negroes 'are actors and organised an evening's entertainment for you'. The reality is 'the theatre! We'll play at being reflected in it, and we'll see ourselves – big black narcissists – slowly disappearing into its waters.'[53] In Roger Blin's production, arbitrary change of vocal pitch and pace and stylised acting techniques were used in such a way that the presentation 'added to this willed multiplicity'; and according to him even 'the author himself gets lost in this labyrinth' of 'reflections of reflections'.[54]

The immediate effect is one of radical nihilism, an absolute negation of reality, which denies any possibility of change since revolutions are subsumed in the images they challenge, perpetuating the structure of reality they overthrow, and these images of domination and submission are complementary not conflicting. Genet's slaves can only revolt by intensifying the image of evil and worthlessness imposed on them in self-justification by their masters. Thus in order

18 *The Blacks*. Masks, funeral rites & fake images in a multi-level action.

to generate the hatred necessary for revenge the maids define themselves as 'the monstrous soul of servantdom' by their physical ugliness, filth and moral vileness – 'They're not of the human race. Servants ooze. They're a foul effluvium' – while the blacks define themselves as 'Darkness in person. Not the darkness which is absence of light, but the kindly and terrible Mother who contains light and deeds' by their blackness, cruelty, crime and 'odour of carrion... animal odours... the pestilence of our swamps'.[55] But this only serves to heighten the ascendency and attraction of the images of authority, and indeed legitimises them. Madame is transformed into a radiant symbol of beauty and spirituality precisely because the maids take on all the disgusting aspects of physicality, acting as 'our distorting mirrors, our loathsome vent, our shame, our dregs'. Similarly in *The Balcony* it is the sins of the penitent that make the Bishop holy, and this mutual dependence of moral opposites is emphasised by the Judge:

you've got to be a model thief if I'm to be a model judge. If you're a fake thief, I become a fake judge. Is that clear? . . . You won't refuse to be a thief? That would be wicked. It would be criminal. You'd deprive me of being![56]

Hence the only achievement of the revolution is to add two symbols to the nomenclature of the power structure, the Joan of Arc 'image of Chantal Victorious, our saint' and the black uniformed Chief of Police as an image of the brutal strong man in the modern dictatorial state – a pairing that embodies Genet's basic archetype, 'the eternal couple of the criminal and the Saint' aspired to by the maids. *The Blacks* affirms the identity of opposites even more explicitly.

THE MISSIONARY: For two thousand years God has been white. He eats on a white tablecloth. He wipes his white mouth with a white napkin. He picks at white meat with a white fork. (*A pause.*) He watches the snow fall . . .
FELICITY: To you, black was the colour of priests and undertakers and orphans. But everything is changing. Whatever is gentle and kind and good and tender will be black. Milk will be black, sugar, rice, the sky, doves, hope, will be black. So will the opera to which we shall go, blacks that we are, in black Rolls Royces to hail black kings, to hear brass bands beneath chandeliers of black crystal. . . .
THE QUEEN: And what about your darkies? Your slaves? . . . You'll need them, you know. . . . But you'll be strong. And we, we'll be charmers. We'll be lascivious. We'll dance in order to be seductive. Just imagine what you're in for. Long labour on continents, for centuries, to carve yourself a sepulchre that may be less beautiful than mine.[57]

The usual response to this nihilism is to make it acceptable in conventional terms by explaining it in the light of Genet's deprivation as an orphan, his criminal record or the sterility of homosexuality. And this view, a simplification of Sartre's point in his influential *Saint Genet: Actor and Martyr* (1952), has been put succinctly by Blin, the director most closely associated with his work: 'Genet was a victim of this society, which he now seeks to destroy . . . But he does not try to correct the society he denounces. He does not try to substitute one order for another since he is against all order.' As a premise, there is a certain obvious truth in this, and one of Genet's letters to Blin draws attention to the personal motivation in his work, emphasising that 'my books, like my plays, were written against myself . . . to expose myself'.[58] But Genet's biography is primarily an autobiography. He has given two very different versions of his initial crime, by virtue of which he claims his status as an outcast – alternatively stealing from his foster-mother's purse because he was hungry, or a murderous knife attack on another boy; one blaming the inherent evil in 'right thinking' society for his descent into criminality and perversion, the other claiming his nature itself to be intrinsically evil – and he has admitted consciously turning his life into legend, a pretext for poetry. Like his characters, he 'embellishes' his guilt into an image of absolute evil, not only asserting himself to be condemned by all normal standards, violating religion as an apostate, patriotism as an army deserter, property as a thief, sexuality as a male prostitute, but also declaring himself to be an exploiter of other outcasts as a pimp, even a traitor to his own underworld as a police informer; and there is at least one well-documented instance of his accepting the punishment (and status – life imprisonment) for a crime he did not commit. As for the conclusion that Genet is against all order, this is contradicted by the obsession with hierarchy in his plays from *Deathwatch* (*Haute surveillance*, 1949) with its alternative title of *Rules of Precedence* (*Les Préséances*), to the inverted hierarchy of criminality in *The Screens*, where, because their discipline and patriotism makes them equivalent to the colonial troops, the Algerian soldiers are inferior to the arsonists and child murderers, while they in turn are inferior to Leila, who steals from them, and Saïd, whose rejection of all values is so extreme that he even betrays the revolution which his negative example has inspired.

With their thematic consistency and the explicitness of explanatory statements embedded in their dialogue, Genet's plays are on one level didactic homilies expressing a coherent philosophy, or rather system of belief. In outline this echoes the theory of 'cruelty' Artaud derived from Sade, with its inversion of values based on the perception that 'in the manifested world, metaphysically speaking, evil is the permanent law, and what is good is an effort and already one more cruelty added to the other',[59] though this is modified by Genet's preoccupation with illusion and perhaps also by the influence of Sartre's study, Genet being apparently so overwhelmed by Sartre's image of him that he wrote nothing for over five years after its publication. If nature is 'evil', according to a society which represses natural impulses in favour of an artificial intellectual or spiritual transcendence, then to do 'good' is a perversion of man's true nature. So God and the Devil change places, and in Genet's 'rules of precedence' the more well recognised the merit the lower it is on the negative side of the scale, while the more infamous a deed is considered to be the higher the status it confers. From *The Balcony* on, this takes the form of images that correspond closely to Sartre's concepts of 'Being' and 'Nonbeing' (*L'Etre et le néant*). The dominant classes in society identify 'good' with existing conditions, which are defined as 'being', while labelling 'nonbeing', which Sartre sees as active since it is the power of negation, as 'evil'. From this comes Genet's association of the active principle with absence or death. Like 'the scenarios' in his house of illusions, his plays 'are all reducible to a major theme ... which is ... ? Death', and this is expressed in religious terms: 'The life which I lead demands the same unconditional renunciation of earthly things that is required by the Church of its Saints ... Saintliness leads to Heaven by the road of sin.'[60]

As its correspondence with the ideas of such different thinkers as Artaud and Sartre indicate, such a view of existence is not a personal aberration, nor can it be dismissed as simply a response to the unfortunate circumstances of Genet's life. In fact it is characteristic of the avant garde, and can already be found in a short mystery play from Strindberg's inferno period, *Coram Populo! De Creatione et Sententia Vera Mundi*. God is a usurper, who has deliberately created a 'world of madness' for his sadistic pleasure, and ordains sexual procreation so that life will continue to exist 'for the mockery of the gods' even after Lucifer has persuaded man to taste the tree of knowledge, which for Strindberg represents salvation through extinction because awareness of the true nature of existence makes suicide preferable: 'eat of it and you will possess the gift of deliverance from sorrow, the joy of death'. Since this false God 'calls evil good, and good evil', the polarities of light and darkness are reversed, Satan being presented as Prometheus and Apollo, the true benefactor of mankind. Christ in this inverted Pantheon is Lucifer's son, and his crucifixion is designed to 'abolish the fear of death', the final masterstroke in Lucifer's campaign to liberate mankind from a humiliating existence. And in the last scene God is dethroned, giving rise to a positive vision of destruction in which 'being' is transformed into 'nonbeing', since 'famine and plague ravage the nations: love is changed to hatred, filial love to parricide'.[61] The parallels to Genet here are striking.

The Screens is the most complete expression of Genet's beliefs. As in *The Blacks*, the basic elements of human life are polarised and their values inverted. White, standing for civilisation, is the colour of death-in-life. Black represents hatred and the void, the dark skin of slavery, savagery or the criminal in the night; and negation is the only creative force. To the colonists the Arabs are non-beings who embody crime, poverty and ugliness – 'how could *we* make the subtle distinction between an Arab who's a thief and an Arab who's not?... If a Frenchman robs me, that Frenchman's a thief, but if an Arab robs me, he hasn't changed' – and revolution is only possible in so far as they accept the image imposed on them. Like the Negro Earth Mother's call to the Soul of Africa, the impetus for revolt therefore comes from an invocation to evil – 'miraculous evil... impregnate my people' – but where Africa symbolises fertility, the evil evoked here is sterile. Its representatives are the unholy trinity of a mother, 'kicked out by the living and the dead', her son Saïd, whose descent from total poverty into absolute criminality counterpoints the rise of the liberation fighters from crime to recognised political status as an army, and his wife Leila, the ugliest of all Arab women, who makes herself even more hideous by adopting the gait of a cripple as well as becoming syphilitic and disfigured. Hatred is not just the only emotion available to outcasts, as in *The Blacks*, but is rigorously pursued in the relationships of this family as an apotheosis of evil. The mother deliberately makes her son's existence 'a dog's life, kicks in the ribs and maybe rabies', while Leila prizes her husband's cruelty to her:

Saïd, my nice Saïd, you put my eye out and you did right... As for the rest, yes I know, I've got the itch and my thighs are full of scabs... you delivered the goods. You were far ahead of me in rattiness, but all the same I'm the wife of a traitor. And that deserves consideration...[62]

For Genet, 'the crimes of which a people is ashamed constitute its real history', and it is Saïd's continued assertion of 'nonbeing' that sustains the Arab 'frenzy to the bitter end, or almost, heedless of the gazes that were judging us'.[63] Just as the colonists (like Madame) can see themselves as an image of glory because the Arabs take on all the negative human qualities, decorating a gigantic dummy with medals on the upper level of the stage while below them the Arabs are painting vicious images of cruelty and suffering on the screens – so when the revolutionaries take power (and with it the values of the now dead civilisation, singing 'Madelon' and the 'Marseillaise' as they parade) they have equal need of a symbol of shame to define their image. But on the surface the vicious circle of the identity of opposites seems to be broken in this play. The symbiotic relationship of Genet's eternal couple is dissolved, because Saïd and Leila achieve so pure a state of nonbeing that only her veil, the surface sign of her ugliness, enters the negative world of the dead, while he vanishes altogether. Consequently the illusions that define existence disappear, life ceases and 'the stage is empty. It is all over.'

This is the ultimate transcendence of reality, which lies behind the metamorphoses of his earlier plays, but to make it fully effective Genet must have reality to work with. Like *The Maids* the initial impulse for *The Screens* came from an actual situation, being based on a story Genet heard about an Arab labourer who was so poor that he could only afford to marry a wife no other man would look at; and even more than the reflection of Franco's Spain in *The Balcony*, the background of the Algerian war was a historical event of immediate significance to the audience. But despite the parallels to a study like Frantz Fanon's *The Wretched of the Earth: Black Skins, White Masks* (published in France the same year as *The Screens*), the oppression of colonised peoples is not depicted to promote political liberation. Their misery is exalted as a necessary step in a spiritual apotheosis, which (as the Missionary recognises) is dependent on the 'cruelty and injustice' of the colonisers. As Genet explained to Blin, the play is 'the celebration of nothing' and the intention was to 'act upon thousands of Parisians without disturbing the world order, and yet bring about a poetic, fiery release so strong, so dense that it would illuminate the world of the dead . . . The feast of the dead must be beautiful . . . so that whatever separates us from the dead will be transcended.'[64] As a homage to death, the play is intended to evoke a deep subconscious need in audiences who belong to a civilisation that Genet sees as 'increasingly marked by death and turned towards it', and they are expected to follow the characters in leaping through the paper screens of illusion into the limbo of the dead. Hence Blin's presentation of the play as a subjective vision – thus picking up on the significance of dreams in *The Balcony* and the visionary approach in *Deathwatch*, which 'unfolds as in a dream' – and his comparison of the effect to 'the street you see at night when you are drunk – you see it in a different way . . . This is true discovery. You are perceiving reality; for the first time all bonds and restrictions have been broken. Objective reality has been dislocated.'[65]

The means Genet envisaged for achieving this transformation of reality echo many of Artaud's characteristic staging devices although, if Blin is to be believed, Genet has read little of his work. He required gestures to be unnatural, having no relationship to those used in everyday life, heightened and 'hieratic' or 'visible'. Vocal tones were to be distorted, and organised into a complex, quasi-musical score, 'which ranges from murmurs to shouts. Sentences, a tempest of sentences, must be delivered like so many howls, others will be warbles.' He expected the actors to turn themselves into animals, and called for emotional states to be presented in absolute terms, so that even mere apprehension would become 'a painful vision of fear' in which the actors carried their trembling in every limb 'to trancelike lengths'. Exactly as in Artaud's design for *The Ghost Sonata*, Genet called for larger-than-life props, encircled by a black line or with their shadows outlined on the screens by an actor 'to lend the moment a certain density'; and the actors' make-up was not only mask-like and asymmetrical, but extended into a stylised tracery of tendons and veins comparable to the skeletal musculature of *The Cenci* costumes. The paintings on the screens were to be modelled on 'drawings done by madmen', and Genet even recommended Blin to search for examples specifically at Rodez, the asylum to which Artaud had been committed.[66]

This was the first production of his work in which Genet had been extensively involved and the stylised presentation of *The Screens* corresponded to the ideas that he had set out in a preface to *The Maids* twelve years earlier. Already here there were definite echoes of Artaud in his references to 'Japanese, Chinese and Balinese revels', his ideal of dramatic art as 'a profound web of active symbols', and his description of the actor as 'a sign charged with signs'. But instead of concentrating on the inner significance of this symbolism, Genet emphasised the external form. The conventional 'masquerade' is not rejected for an Artaudian 'true vision', but for 'ceremony', and the example chosen is the Mass, described as 'the loftiest modern drama' because 'the point of departure disappears beneath the profusion of ornaments and symbols'.[67] As a title like *The Screens* indicates in naming the play after its stage setting rather than its protagonist or theme, the centre of Genet's plays is the style, a reversal of normal values that limits significance to externals. Thus Saïd's trousers, standing empty on the stage, become the focus for Leila's passionate adoration, or in considering what 'a black' is, Genet asks, 'first of all, what's his colour?'

It has become almost a commonplace to refer to Genet's theatre as a black mass,[68] and this is not simply a figure of speech loosely based on Genet's constant allusions to the sacred or the presence of a priest as one of the major characters in each of his three full-length plays. In Genet's theatricalisation of reality, where pretence is overt and every action is presented as performance, all activities take on liturgical significance. Separated from function, they become rites, 'pure' images whose efficacy is in inverse proportion to their actual effectiveness, like the figures in *The Balcony* who aspire to 'be nothing, though reflected *ad infinitum* in these mirrors, nothing but my image'[69] and lose their power when they try to exert authority in the world of events. It is no accident that all Genet's plays except *Deathwatch* revolve around revolution, since, according to Frantz Fanon, 'revolution is the modern ritual' and its true aim is not an external change in the power structure, but the creation of a new identity for the oppressed by the violent exorcism of an alien presence that dominates them through spiritual possession.[70] So for Genet political revolution becomes a metaphor for spiritual transcendence and 'funeral symbols' are substituted for the equally symbolic clenched fists or red flags. This at least is the aim, but particularly in his later plays Genet's audiences have seemed incapable of making the imaginative leap from object to symbol. As the shocked outrage and accusations of racism that greeted the Paris production of *The Blacks*, or the riots, cries of 'traitor!' and protest from the Ex-Servicemen's League at *The Screens* indicated, political passions obliterated the metaphysical level instead of being subsumed in it. And Genet's overt theatricality, his emphasis on the false nature of the spectacle out of which 'true images' are created, is clearly an attempt to counter this.

But the stress on performance is also central to Genet's theme, and is itself given religious significance, since theatre as illusion is the opposite of reality or 'being': 'The Devil makes believe. That's how one recognises him. He's the great Actor. And that's why the Church has anathematised actors.' In Genet's Manichaean world of 'being' and 'nonbeing', the image of 'God' is associated with established order and hypocritical society, so that true faith becomes the mirror-opposite of Christianity, hate replaces love and shame is substituted for merit (hence the emphasis on the brothel as a sacred place and the priestly vestments or saint's robes worn by the whores – Warda's golden 'cope of the Blessed Sacrament' in *The Screens* or Carmen as the Madonna in *The Balcony* – since it is in the brothel that the greatest degradation is achieved). The religious aim of his plays thus becomes to abolish God. As ceremonies, their structure is loosely based on church ritual, and Genet specified that *The Balcony* was to be 'performed with the solemnity of a Mass in a cathedral'. In *The Screens* Saïd's apotheosis repeats Christ's Passion and Ascension in reverse, his family is ironically referred to as 'the Holy Family', the heart drawn on the screens in the orgy of destruction is 'the Sacred Heart of Jesus, with flames in place of the aorta', and when Saïd reaches the lowest point of his degradation it is the Missionary, presumably the expert in questions of faith, who perceives that they've just deified abjection... They're organising. That's the beginning of a ceremonial that's going to bind them together more firmly than anything else. (*He sniffs the air.*) I recognise a familiar smell...[71]

The Screens was written as a poem, not a drama, since Genet believed that the French authorities would never permit a production. This perhaps accounts for the abstraction of the inordinately long text as well as the over-obviousness of its thematic statement; and the ceremonies embedded in it have less direct relationship to the Mass, which Genet considers inherently theatrical, than those in a play like *The Maids*. In this earlier play, partly because of its shortness, the pattern comes out clearly. The action, explicitly described as 'the Ceremony', is performed three times (a number with definite religious connotations), and its function is the direct opposite of the Mass. The emotion focussed on the sacrificial saviour is a mixture of carnal lust and hatred, instead of spiritual love, and the celebrant achieves communion with the deity by destroying his image, not worshipping it. Madame's vanity table is referred to as 'the altar', the kitchen is 'the vestry', and in this symbolic context Solange's arrangement of the fall of Madame's dress on Claire is 'arranging [her] fall from grace'. Claire calls Madame 'a Lovelier Virgin', and the terms used to describe her 'Your... *ivory* bosom! Your... *golden* thighs! Your *amber* feet!' are drawn from the 'tower of ivory' and 'gate of gold' in the litany of the Virgin Mary. The first time the fragmentary ritual is performed it corresponds to the Elevation of the Host. The debasement of the symbolic maid is used to establish the distance between the worshipper and the divinity, while the symbolic mistress is deified:

SOLANGE: (*in ecstacy*): Madame's being carried away!
CLAIRE: By the devil! He's carrying me away in his fragrant arms. He's lifting me up, I leave the ground, I'm off...

The second time the ritual is repeated, in outline only, its focus is the real Madame and the act of worship is the act of murder, with the ultimate crime as a form of canonisation modelled on 'the story of Sister Holy Cross of the Blessed Valley who poisoned twenty-seven Arabs'. The third repetition transfers the crime to a metaphysical level, not the murder of a God-surrogate but of God himself – 'It's God who's listening to us. We know that it's for Him that the last act is to be performed, but we musn't forewarn Him'[72] – and Claire's suicide, willing her sister to give her the poison she drinks, is a perverted reflection of Christ knowingly allowing himself to be crucified. The consecration is a desecration, self-annihilation is achieved by destroying God.

Genet's problem is that blasphemy is only possible for a believer, and today's society is secularised. As the wife of one of the colonists comments in *The Screens*:

Betrayal's not what it used to be. In the old days, as my great-grandmother used to tell me, an engaged couple would marry on the eve of their wedding. The male would gash the female, and an invisible red spot under her white gown would prove that love was stronger than God. One had to believe in God, of course, and betray.[73]

Transformation, the 'unnameable operation' on reality, is one of the key words in Genet's drama, but without belief a communion wafer remains bread instead of the body of Christ, and Genet's false spectacle remains illusion, poetry without the force of a 'true image'.

The relationship he tries to create between stage and audience is exactly that of Claire and Solange as mistress and maid. As the Master of Ceremonies tells the audience in *The Blacks*, 'We shall increase the distance that separates us – a distance that is basic – by our pomp, our manners, our insolence – for we are also actors.'[74] This is one of the reasons why Genet has consistently refused permission for this play to be performed by white actors, and why he specifies that a black audience should wear white masks or be represented by 'a symbolic white', on whom a spotlight would be focussed throughout the performance. The white audience are society, 'being', the worshipper: the black stage is the image of negation, 'nonbeing', divinity. But in place of belief this opposition is designed to arouse extreme and irrational emotion, the hatred that is fundamental to Genet's religious sense, by playing on racial fears and antagonisms. Another reason for insisting on a black cast was that the theatricality of the stage image would be transposed into a heightened reality by the force of the emotions that could only be generated in Negro actors who, in acting out the fantasy of rape, massacre and revenge, would be shocked into recognising the truth of the 'gestures' the play required them to perform. The disguised hatred they then projected at the audience would evoke a corresponding emotion in them, creating a level of involvement on which the dialectic of opposites would merge precisely because they had been separated to such an extent. And this effect was apparently achieved to some degree in the Paris production where, according to Blin, although the actors were all 'assimilated Negroes who were shocked by Genet's language, they did not want to be taken for savages'. The two actresses from Martinique playing the

White and Black Queens were brought by their roles to a volcanic pitch of hatred for each other that spilled over into their personal lives and stripped away the veneer of civilisation, liberating a primitivism quite in keeping with the play: 'I discovered that the White Queen was burning this incense to ward off the evil spell she accused the Black Queen of casting upon her . . . willing her to forget her lines. The Black Queen's witchcraft was present in her on-stage acting, in her secret, symbolic and ritualistic gestures.'[75] This hatred, which is fundamental to all Genet's plays in the repeated duality of masters and slaves, possessors and dispossessed – and also inherent in his intensification of the duality between actor and audience – is inextricably linked with fascination for the hated object. Genet's relationship with the police or Hitler's Nazis is one of love/hate, and the same mixture of desire and repulsion characterises his drama in the juxtaposition of beauty with scatological obscenity, of brutal slang with poetry that has been compared to Claudel's in its baroque extravagance. It also represents the reaction his plays are designed to evoke, creating a complex emotional unity between the stage image and the spectator who, at least in theory, becomes a participant in a 'communion', since for Genet 'a performance that does not act upon my soul is in vain'.[76]

Jerzy Grotowski

Genet's ideal of theatre as a spiritual catalyst, performance as an act of 'communion', had already been around for some time. For example when Firman Gémier, the actor so closely associated with Jarry's iconoclastic Ubu, became the first director of the Théâtre National Populaire in 1920 he had described the effect he wanted as 'a communion' in mounting festivals that would 'dramatise the life of the people . . . performed by the people themselves' to gain the same degree of audience participation and religious involvement as in medieval mystery cycles.[1] In a sense it is logical that any theatre rejecting twentieth-century society for its materialism and rationalism should turn to the alternative value scale of religious faith, while continuing to reject organised religion as being associated with the *status quo*. And the most striking achievements in this line are those of Grotowski, whose simplest description of his aim is 'to cross the frontiers between you and me . . . To find a place where a communion becomes possible.'[2] The terms he uses to describe his work are characteristically religious – transgression, profanation, passion, incarnation, transfiguration, atonement, confession and, above all, communion – but although his productions specifically attack what is sacred in the form of organised Christianity, his choice of texts has always been within the 'great tradition'. The visual images created by his actors are derived from popular hagiography too, so that he has avoided the communication problems inherent in a return to the past, (like Brook's *Orghast*) or a search for oriental alternatives (like Artaud) which, however comprehensible as reactions against contemporary western society, are self-defeating to the extent that they cut the theatre off from the cultural context of its audience. Like Brook's Centre for International Theatre Research, Grotowski's Polish Laboratory Theatre (founded in 1960, though only given its research status in 1962) has concentrated on exploring the fundamental basis of theatrical communication, and even more radically than Barrault or Brook, his search led him to discard music, representative scenery and illusionistic lighting, make-up and any but the simplest costumes, eliminating all the external paraphernalia to expand the one essential element that distinguishes theatre from film or television and without which it would not exist: 'the actor–spectator relationship of perceptual, direct, "live" communion'.[3]

Such a communion requires the imaginative participation that can only come from providing spectators with a thematic function in the performance, not just the sort of external involvement produced by surrounding them physically with action. So one of the constant factors in Grotowski's experimentation is his attempt to impose a psychological orientation on the audience that would integrate them in a particular way with each play. But initially he concentrated on finding methods of turning a dramatic action into an emotional environment for the spectators by simple changes in physical placing. In the group's first production, Byron's *Cain* (1960), this was limited to reducing the physical distance from the actors by using the forestage and the centre aisle between the rows of spectators: a surprisingly tentative move towards breaking out of the frame of the stage already anticipated by Copeau, who removed the footlights and linked the auditorium to the stage by steps at the Vieux Colombier in the early twenties. Grotowski's following productions abandoned any formal delineation of the stage, and in *Ancestors* (1961) or Wyspianski's *Akropolis* (1962) the spectators were seated separately and apparently randomly throughout the hall, the whole of which was used as an acting area, 'removing all frontiers' to create a single 'living organism'. In the former this was fairly conventional, with the audience being sucked into the action by the patterns of movement woven among them and those willing to participate physically in the climax being led by an actor as the 'chorus' in a harvest ritual. But in *Akropolis*, transferred by Grotowski from its original setting in Cracow Cathedral to Auschwitz on the basis of a description of it as 'the cemetery of the tribes' in one of Wyspianski's letters, the fragmentation of the audience was used to isolate the spectators and the actors ignored them while moving through them, so that the physical proximity paradoxically emphasised distance. The actors were the dead, a community without individual characteristics 'initiated in the ultimate experience', the individualised audience the living. And this simultaneous effect of separateness and immediacy was intended to give the impression of a dream, setting the action on an interior subconscious plane. As Grotowski commented, physically mingling actors and spectators under the banner of 'direct participation' frequently only aroused psychological barriers, while 'experience proves that by putting a distance between the actors and the spectators in space, one often rediscovers a [psychic] proximity'.[4]

Kordian (1962) deliberately exploited the potential antagonism of enforced participation by casting the spectators, who were seated on two-tier iron beds ranged throughout the hall, as patients in the mental institution of the play, enlisting their sympathy for the martyrdom of the hero by having the 'doctor' treat them as mentally ill along with the actor–patients among them, while encouraging them to reject the national myths believed in by the mad hero in asserting their own sanity. This structural integration, in which the spectators' opposition becomes a motive force in the action, was used in a progressively subtler way in Grotowski's next two productions. For Marlowe's *Dr Faustus* (1963) the audience were seated on benches around three refectory tables which functioned as both stage, settings and props. As they entered Faustus, already seated in the centre of the head table, invited them to take their places as guests at what was specifically a Last Supper. The 'food' served up to them by Faustus was a montage of the scenes of his life, acted in front of them on the tables which at one point were even up-ended and demolished by a courtier trying to kill Faustus with a violence that was physically frightening because of its proximity. But at the same time as being participants in a metaphoric communion receiving the sacramental offering of Faustus' sacrificial damnation, they also found themselves representing the banality of everyday existence, since the servants' dialogue in the comic scenes, deflating and mocking Faustus' pretensions, was spoken by two actors seated among them, who had entered with them in modern clothes, bringing home the point that 'our daily platitudes are themselves arguments against God'.[5] The same overlap between the reality of the audience as spectators and their role imposed by the performance, between the modern world and the mythic archetype, was even stronger in *The Constant Prince* (1968). Here the framing metaphor also embraced the basis of drama as a spectacle of conflict as well as reflecting the experimental nature of the Polish Laboratory Theatre, so that the context of the performance duplicated the premises of the play in a way that made it difficult to distinguish life from imagination. The associations evoked as the audience peered down from the rectangular wooden barricades were simultaneously those of voyeurs (the conventional image of an audience in naturalistic theatre), of spectators at the barbaric ritual of a bullfight (one of the images presented in the play), of 'witnesses' in a religious sense to

Christ's apotheosis in martyrdom, and (since the stage arrangement was also modelled on Rembrandt's 'Anatomy of Dr Tulp') those of professionals observing the scientific dissection of a human being. In addition they were clearly identified with the inhuman society of the torturers by their passive fascination for the torture enacted beneath.

The second of the constant factors in Grotowski's experimentation is the search for authenticity in performance. The actor as 'priest', the other pole of this 'communion', must present a revelation that evokes belief if the circle is to be complete and the play is to have an intrinsic significance for the spectator that justifies his structural integration in the action. In terms of a secular religion, spirituality can only exist within man, so that for Grotowski 'body and blood . . . that's where "God" is'; and his training methods are designed to remove psychological blocks in the actor, to allow him to strip away the 'daily mask of lies' that is his external *persona*, leading to 'a liberation from complexes in much the same way as psychoanalytic theory'.[6] This enables him to reveal his essential being in performance, so that as Grotowski's theatre developed every production became simultaneously a celebration of the 'holiness' of man and an existential challenge to the audience in reversing normal behaviour patterns which are designed to cover and protect this private centre of personality: a 'self-penetration' which is even more provocative in that most public of forums, the theatre, where traditionally the actor dissembles and disguises his true face with masks. The aim is to achieve an extreme intimacy where 'this act of the total unveiling of one's being becomes a gift of the self which borders on the trangression of barriers and love' – which is one reason for the increasing restriction on the number of spectators from approximately sixty-five for *Kordian* to under fifty for *Dr Faustus*, between thirty and forty for *The Constant Prince* and only twenty-five for *Apocalypsis cum Figuris* (1968). And this breaking down of the barriers between individuals goes together with breaking down barriers within the individual. Looked at from another angle it is this that is 'the surpassing of limits', and performances are structured so that at the most intense moments of self-revelation the actor transcends his 'self' in an apotheosis of human spirituality, creating an effect of 'translumination' in which the soul literally shines through the flesh by 'the integration of all the actor's psychic and bodily powers which emerge from the most intimate layers of his being and his instinct'.[7]

On this level the individual is transfigured into an image of the universal, and the whole of Grotowski's approach assumes that personality is superficial, artificial, while at its 'roots' humanity is generic. Hence any true manifestation of unconscious psycho-physical reactions will automatically correspond to Jungian archetypes, in particular to those postures and groupings embodied in archaic or religious sculpture, and the achievement of such stereotypes becomes taken as a guarantee that the true expression of the subconscious has been reached, that the actor has become 'the living incarnation of myth'.[8] In fact however, as Eugenio Barba, one of Grotowski's collaborators, has implicitly confirmed, these symbolic physical attitudes taken up by the group, like the medieval procession of flagellants and pilgrims that recurred in *Akropolis* and *Apocalypsis cum Figuris*, or by the individual in the moment of 'translumination', like the classic poses of pietà and crucifixion repeated more explicitly in each production from *Kordian* to *The Constant Prince*, were consciously adopted. Gesture and intonation was developed to echo 'a definite image. For example, the actor stops in the middle of a race and takes the stance of a cavalry soldier charging, as in the old popular drawings. This method of acting evokes by association images deeply rooted in the collective imagination.'[9] The result was closely related to the expressionist acting style: an exaggerated definition in movements and the elimination of those that were merely functional or mimetic rather than expressive; the cutting of gestures defining individuality, and the transposition of conventional attitudes into expressions of 'pure' emotional states; the stiffening of facial muscles to transform individual features into a rigid mask.

There are also obvious similarities to Artaud's concepts, although Grotowski only read *The Theatre And Its Double* in 1964 after the basic elements of his style were already set, and subsequently distanced himself from Artaud, pointing out that the 'transcendental point of reference' for his work was 'man', not the 'cosmic trance' that Artaud speaks of. Since, as he indicates, citing similar ideas in Vakhtangov and Meyerhold or his native Polish tradition, Artaud was an integral part of the wider avant garde movement, it is in a sense immaterial from what sources Grotowski developed his approach. But the archetypal ideograms, that he creates to awaken latent emotions in the spectator through subconscious associations, are the equivalent of Artaud's 'hieroglyphs', while his use of 'masking' is precisely that which Artaud admired in the Balinese dancers: 'in this systematic depersonalisation, in these purely muscular facial expressions, applied to the features like masks, everything produces a significance, everything affords the maximum effect.'[10] Grotowski's continual references to primitive religious drama and his double use of mythology, focussing on the archetype of saviour–martyr while dismissing the conventional images of harmony, aspiration and spiritual nobility as the deceptive values of a false civilisation in 'the dialectic of mockery and apotheosis', also parallel Artaud's vision. There is a consistent emphasis on 'cruelty', too, in the form of torture and suffering – though this mortification of the body to achieve spiritual ecstasy is decisively different to Artaud's proposed sublimation of cruelty and violence in the spectators by liberating such instincts – and critics were quick to note that productions like *Dr Faustus* and *The Constant Prince* epitomised the Theatre of Cruelty that Artaud himself had been unable to realise.[11]

All Grotowski's productions can be seen as variations on the single theme of self-transcendence, and the way the various texts were interpreted created a remarkable unity between the thematic centre of the performances and the focus of his research into acting. Describing the basic principles of the *'exercises plastiques'* developed for his actors as relating the psychic to the physical, the exploration and liberation of the subconscious, he commented 'when I say "go beyond yourself" I am asking for an insupportable effort... there are certain points of fatigue which break the control of the mind, a control that blocks us... the limits we impose upon ourselves that block the creative process'.[12] And this was carried over into the performances themselves, where the actor playing the Christ-figure in *Ancestors* reached a point of exhaustion at which his physiological state overlapped with the archetype he represented and the blood Christ 'sweated' from his crown of thorns appeared as the sweat running down his brow, or Ryszard Cieslak literally drove himself to the limits of physical endurance in *The Constant Prince*. It was also echoed in the dramatic situation of each play, where physical action was translated into subconscious terms and external intrigue was stripped away to leave a structure of physical suffering leading to spiritual apotheosis. In *Kordian*, *Akropolis* and *Dr Faustus* the original plots of real-life events were internalised and projected as hallucination, dream or memory. Kordian's attempt to free Poland from Russian rule is presented as a madman's obsession with saving mankind – perhaps the only way such a theme could be staged in contemporary Poland – discrediting the image of Christ while emphasising the human reality of martyrdom. The slave labour of prisoners in the concentration camp, building 'an absurd civilisation' dedicated to death, is counterpointed by the classical Greek and biblical ideals that motivate them, acted out as daydreams which stand revealed as derisory and delusive in the cruel context of reality. The archetypes of love or spiritual aspiration, Paris and Helen, or Jacob's struggle with the Angel, are reduced to grotesque parody through being embodied by condemned prisoners in clumsy boots and ragged sacks, while the final procession that follows the image of 'the Saviour' leads only to ashes. The joyful certainty of faith and hope of salvation is built up into 'supreme ecstasy' by dancing and devout litanies, but the Christ-figure they follow is the headless, emaciated corpse of a fellow prisoner, and the Promised Land they reach is the box-like tomb of the gas ovens. 'The joyful delirium has found its fulfillment in the crematorium.'[13] In both plays the conventional images of transcendence that have defined western humanistic civilisation were discredited, while the degradation of the body resulted in an inner illumination expressed by an unearthly smile at the moment of total exhaustion. In *Akropolis* this might have seemed yet another self-deception, but the true value of 'translumination' for Grotowski becomes clear in *Dr Faustus*, where the dialectic was fully developed.

Again the accepted stereotypes of the sacred were violated, but here values were simply inverted, reversing good and evil in a way directly comparable to Genet, whose work Grotowski admired and had used for acting exercises. Faustus' revolt is motivated by a reading of the Bible –

> 'The reward of sin is death.' That's hard . . .
> 'If we say that we have no sin,
> We deceive ourselves, and there is no truth in us.'
> Why then, belike, we must sin,
> And so consequently die.
> Ay, we must die, an everlasting death.
> What doctrine call you this? (I. i. 40-7)

– which every member of Marlowe's audience would have recognised as sophistry since Faustus omits in each case the well-known second half of the sentence: 'but the gift of God is eternal life through Jesus Christ' (Romans 6:23) and 'if we confess our sins, he is faithful and just to forgive us our sins' (I John 1:9). And by simplifying Marlowe's viewpoint into that of Faustus, Grotowski's interpretation turns God into a demonic deity, whose 'laws . . . are traps contradicting morality and truth'. Mephistopheles became an *agent provocateur* of God, donning papal robes to carry Faustus to hell, while Faustus was presented as the archetype of a saint, saintliness being defined in human terms as 'an absolute desire for pure truth' which can only be realised by rebellion against God if God is assumed to be evil. The actor playing Faustus was selected because of his physical resemblance to the archetypal picture of St Sebastian, and the scenes were organised around a structure of symbolic images. There was an annunciation, with Mephistopheles stretching diagonally over Faustus as a 'soaring angel' whose words were accompanied by the chanting of 'an angelic choir', a baptism, a pietà with a female double of Mephistopheles as the Virgin, the absolution of Mary Magdalene (in the shape of the Seven Deadly Sins, each represented by Mephistopheles) and the cleansing of the temple (the assault on the Pope), the Garden of Gethsemane and the female Mephistopheles as 'the Mother of Sorrows following her son to Calvary' when Mephistopheles drags Faustus off upside-down to his inverted crucifixion. Again the moment of ecstasy comes at the moment when conscious control over the body is lost. The spirit is exalted as a man is reduced to his animal 'roots'. Faustus 'is in a rapture, his body is shaken by spasms. The ecstatic failure of his voice becomes at the moment of his Passion a series of inarticulate cries . . . no longer a man but a panting animal.'[14] In the dialectic of saintliness and damnation where spiritual potential is liberated by the mortification of the flesh, Faustus becomes a Saviour in human, as opposed to religious terms, since the actor's 'total unveiling of being' in divesting himself of all the defensive shells and props of personality is intended as a challenge and model for the spectator:

through excess, profanation and outrageous sacrilege [revealing] himself by casting off his everyday mask, he makes it possible for the spectator to undertake a similar process of self-penetration. If he does not exhibit his body, but annihilates it, burns it, frees it from every resistance to any psychic impulse . . . he repeats the atonement; he is close to holiness.[15]

This synthesis of opposites and the attempt to create 'a secular *sacrum* in the theatre' was extended in Grotowski's two subsequent productions by locating the action on a purely human rather than eschatological plane, particularly in *Apocalypsis cum Figuris*, which also acts as a good illustration of how texts were treated in the Theatre Laboratory. The title refers to the prophetic Revelation of St John of the Cross, which foretells Christ's Second Coming, and the action is set in a contemporary religious festival, among the touts and beggars camping out around the shrine, who play out the Second Coming as a brutal drunken game. One drunkard, whose name happens to be Simon Peter, persuades a simpleton – in Polish *ciemny*, literally 'the dark one' with satanic overtones, a man possessed and deformed as a mark of his contact with the supernatural, but also an idiot incapa-

ble of comprehending the world who traditionally represents child-
like holiness, a different value scale – that he is in fact Christ, telling
him he was born in Nazareth and died on the cross for men who fail
to recognise him as God. He then nominates others as Mary Magdalene, John, Judas, and they repeat archetypal scenes of Christ's
Passion and crucifixion through which they express their sadistic instincts, subconscious needs and resentments. For the audience the
effect is a testing of the Christian myth, challenging its validity
through argument and blasphemy. But although Simon Peter, the
Simpleton–Christ's antagonist, rejects the superhuman demands of
spirituality in the words of Dostoevsky's Grand Inquisitor and is only
answered by T. S. Eliot's despair of attaining spiritual grace from 'The
Waste Land', and even though he has the last word – yet the torment
still produces a moment of 'translumination'.

Simon Peter extinguishes the candles which have served to light
the barbaric 'entertainment', and commands the Simpleton, who
chants the liturgy from the darkness, to 'Go and come no more!' But
the production asserts the reality of the spirit in human terms and
implicitly affirms the potential existence of a sacrificial saviour, even
in the abused idiot, who acts as a catalyst to strip his everyman–
tormentors of social masks, facing them with a challenge that undermines all their preconceptions. The spectators are expected to go
through a comparable psychological process, but as a whole *Apocalypsis cum Figuris* can be seen as embodying a ritual vision of theatre
outlined three years earlier, which in fact could only be completely
effective for the closed community of the actors themselves: 'Primitive
rituals are the first form of drama . . . through their total participation,
primitive men were liberated from accumulated unconscious material. The rituals were repetitions of archetypal acts, a collective confession which sealed the solidarity of the tribe. Often ritual was the only
way to break a taboo.'[16]

In previous productions Grotowski's focus on the actor's self-
exploration, self-revelation and self-transcendence had automatically
conflicted with the characterisation required by conventional dramatic scripts. At the same time literary classics had a particular value
for Grotowski, since they exist as archetypes in the public mind,
reverberating with 'a generalising function very close to myths'.[17]
However, to treat the texts as such, and to present their characters as
images with a quasi-autonomous existence in people's imagination
and capable of motivating people's actions – as in *Kordian* or *Akropolis*
– was only a partial solution. To be credible it entailed constructing a

further fictional frame which, even though designed to incorporate the audience, had to be removed from normal experience because it was only in such extreme conditions as insanity or imprisonment that fantasy takes over. In *Dr Faustus* the characters were treated 'as a trampoline, an instrument with which to study what is hidden behind our everyday mask – the innermost core of our personality – in order to sacrifice it, expose it', and the result was to create a deliberate confrontation with the actor's own experience. The actors played against their roles, and the dialogue was limited to what each found personally relevant. As Grotowski admitted, 'We eliminate those parts of the text which have no importance for us.'[18] Consequently the textual montages and even the themes changed as the actors developed new insights into their own personalities, and a play like *Akropolis* went through five distinct versions from 1962 to 1967, while *The Constant Prince* went through three.

Apocalypsis cum Figuris was different in that it evolved out of acting exercises and improvisations that were specifically designed to facilitate the actors' self-exploration, and the structure of images that were finally pieced together and expanded reflected the preoccupations that had moulded the previous productions. So there was an organic relationship between the 'score' (the objective actions and relationships) and the inner process that these were designed to communicate to the spectator. The characterisation was built on archetypes that the actors had come to identify with through their earlier work, with individual traits based on their own personalities, and the dialogue was limited to quotations which were not only non-dramatic – that is, not expressing a particular character and situation – but so widely known that the words were no longer associated with their author and could be taken to represent the consciousness of mankind itself. As might be expected from the theme, this montage was derived primarily from the personal religious poetry of T. S. Eliot and Simone Weil, the existential questioning of *The Brothers Karamazov* and above all the Bible. But speech was limited to what was essential for bringing out the symbolic significance of the mimed action, and words were reduced to pure sound 'to bring spontaneous associations to the spectator's mind' – an expressionist technique that led to the use of incantation, liturgical chanting and the Kyrie eleison. Thus *Apocalypsis cum Figuris* came closest to Grotowski's ideal of 'autonomous theatre', which had only been realised indirectly in previous productions, where 'the "peripetia" of the plays (as we do them) do not correspond to the text. They are expressed through purely theatrical means.'[19]

19 Poster for the Theatre Laboratory. Religious imagery & archetypal experience.

However it was his version of *The Constant Prince* that had the most direct influence. The significance of this production for the avant garde was partly fortuitous, political circumstances having kept Grotowski's work unknown to the West until it was already fully developed. The performance of *The Constant Prince* at Barrault's Théâtre des Nations festival in 1966 therefore came as a revelation. At first glance Calderón's *El príncipe constante*, with its highly mannered and rhetorical verse, its extended plays on words and convoluted dialectics, its melodramatic action culminating in the ghost of the dead prince leading the Portuguese army to victory, and its complicated equation of heroic values in the conventional form of love versus duty, seems an unsuitable text for Grotowski's treatment. But beneath the surface plot glorifying Prince Fernando's historical invasion of Algiers and his refusal to be ransomed in exchange for the city of Ceuta, the play is an *auto sacramentale*, a study of how man achieves sainthood that symbolises the conflict between eternal and mundane values, the spiritual versus the physical, in the battle between Christian and pagan worlds. Its inner focus is on the protagonist's fortitude (which Aquinas had defined as the cardinal virtue) and on his ordeal of degradation and starvation, a realisation of spiritual potential through the mortification of the flesh that directly parallels the self-transcendence aimed at in Grotowski's acting techniques. In the Slowacki translation used for this production the play is also linked to the Polish romantic tradition of baroque revival that Grotowski had built on in his earlier work.

The text was altered even more radically than in *Dr Faustus*, with the number of lines cut by almost two-thirds and switched between characters or out of sequence, with the fourteen major roles plus slaves and courtiers reduced to seven and played by six actors, and with fragments from the Polish liturgy interpolated at key points. The centre of the action became an erotic relationship between Fénix, the Algerian princess, and Fernando, which was barely hinted at in the original, while almost all reference to Ceuta was cut, together with the battle scenes. At the same time the Moorish and Christian characters were united into a single group, freeing the action from its historical context and turning it into an archetypal conflict between an individual and a sadistic, spiritually castrating society. Instead of the conventional exposition, complication and resolution of the original three-act form, with each act divided into three scenes, Calderón's geometrical sequence of nine 'days' was collapsed into a single action focussed on three monologues, in each of which Cieslak as the Prince reached an ascending level of 'translumination', structured into seven musical 'movements'.

The 'Overture' is the First Prisoner's assimilation into the society of his persecutors, which is possible because his opposition to them is a form of collaboration, being on their own level. This sets the 'normal' pattern and establishes the negative pole of the conflict in its extreme form of perverse sexual domination:

THE KING MOUNTS HIS SLAVE...

KING: *Climbs over the body of Don Enrique. He gestures to the prisoner between his legs . . . grabs his left hand and holds it to his heart . . .*

> I chose myself a horse with an empty saddle . . .
> It suffered from this internal wound,
> From the consciousness of the conquered
> That the conqueror sits in his saddle . . .

Don Enrique's face is distorted with pain and his body twitches violently . . . The body of the King bows to one side and tenses. The rhythm of his speech carries over into Don Enrique's body, which jerks in ever shorter intervals . . . The King's voice rings ever shriller. He stares fixedly up. Both bodies are rigid – climax. [20]

After this spiritual 'death' in physical orgasm, the prisoner is symbolically castrated by Fénix and dressed in the quasi-military black cloak and boots of his torturers. When the same sequence is repeated with the Prince, the castration cannot be carried through because – in a myopically wishful distortion of political realities – he responds with 'only passivity and kindness, referring to a higher spiritual order. He seems to offer no opposition.'[21] The thematic significance of this 'Divertimento', which includes a *corrida* with the courtiers as bulls, is given by the sub-title to one of its sections: 'Don Fernando is called to Christ.' And it is followed by a 'Solo', the Prince's first monologue 'To die for the faith' in which he achieves a state of 'translumination and ecstasy' on the repeated lines

> So that all may see
> How constant my belief makes me.

Then a 'Rondo' made up of minuet and polka, simultaneously presented as a litany and the Agnus Dei, in which the court expresses its anger –

Fénix lashes Don Fernando with the red cloth, rolled into a whip. At each 'Pray for us' she strikes the Prince's reddening back. The court watches on its knees . . .

MINUET-CRY I: *After the whipping Don Fernando turns around, throws himself on the floor and cries like a small child in the marked rhythm of a polka . . . all except the Prince and Fénix dance a minuet to the Prince's 'polka' with different variations . . . with closed eyes he hits himself in the stomach with his bunched up shirt. He rubs his head on the floor, one hand tearing at his hair . . . He beats himself violently in the genitals and face . . . He lies flat on the floor and licks it at each sobbing cry . . . his sobbing cries change without a break into clear, vibrant, echoing voice* [ringing like that of a preacher in a cathedral]. *Fénix kneels and confesses softly to the Prince, who . . . answers in a melodic crystalline tone. The court stiffen into schemata. Fénix kneels weeping beside the seated Prince* [whose position is that of a popular image of Christ in Polish folklore].

After this comes the second monologue or 'Solo' on the theme of physical suffering and humiliation; an 'Allegro' which includes a communion, where each courtier approaches in turn and bites into the Prince's flesh while the others chant in prayer, and the 'Golgotha' of 'the Prince–Job'; then the final 'Solo'. A short coda follows over his body, glorifying his death and transforming his sacrifice into a cult that will allow others to be killed in his name.

The third and final monologue on the spiritual rewards and joy of martyrdom was punctuated by paroxysms of laughter from Cieslak at those points where the original prince would have been most sincere, undercutting the 'official' religious theme and internalising the dialectic of derision and apotheosis in a way that clearly distinguished the actor's personality from the dramatic character. The climax of 'translumination, ecstasy' was thus divorced from the divine stereotype while retaining the parallels to Christ, presenting the triumph of the spirit over physical existence as reality for Cieslak himself by undercutting the fictional situation and the ideological propaganda: a significant thematic shift that defined the focus of Grotowski's theatrical experimentation. Calderón's hero allows himself to be sacrificed for the spiritual welfare of his fellow men and his suffering – only one of various interlocking levels of constancy and honour – is treated with detachment. Grotowski's Prince had no objective beyond himself and appeared a self-willed martyr, controlling his own torture and *using* his persecutors to destroy his body in order to purify his spirit. This exclusive focus on the protagonist was reinforced both by his extreme emotion, his rage against the flesh that made much of the violence self-inflicted and the level of realism in which actual rather than pretended suffering was presented. Following Grotowski's principle that 'the actor must not *illustrate* but *accomplish* an "act of the soul" by means of his own organism',[22] Cieslak's body expressed his psychological state in physical reactions that are usually considered involuntary – sweating profusely while remaining still; a red flush spreading over all his skin; tears flooding from closed eyes – giving an effect of absolute authenticity to the experience presented. As a result however, the self-transcendence became an act of voluptuous masochism. This element of wilful perversion was actually emphasised by expanding the King's accusation in the original and making it more explicit:

> Who forces him to suffer?
> ... has he not sealed his own fate? ...
> For his faith he will suffer he says
> For that will open the doors of paradise to him.
> He seeks death ...
> It is not we who maltreat him
> It is only he who makes himself suffer.

The intention may have been to bring out the dubious aspects of Christ's sacrifice, in line with the concept of 'religion expressed

20 *Via negativa: The Constant Prince*, Minuet-Cry I. The stage as bull-ring, schemata & the triumph of the spirit through mortifying the flesh.

through blasphemy'[23] that also provided a rationale for the Prince's self-absorption, turning him into an anti-Christ whose own salvation is achieved through provoking the evil instincts in his fellow men, an apotheosis damning those who made it possible. But the effect was intellectually confusing, although the performance had an undeniable emotional power in the truth and intimacy of the actor's self-revelation. And this impact was heightened not only by the mesmeric ritualistic elements of the performance and the symbolic mythical associations, but by the audience's functional role as voyeurs watching something prohibited, as well as by the sense that deeply rooted taboos – relating to personal exposure as well as religious reverence – were being outrageously violated.

The production of *The Constant Prince*, and particularly Cieslak's inspired performance, was generally acknowledged as a complete realisation of Grotowski's approach: the most extreme example possible of the actor overcoming psychological blocks to self-transcendence, justifying such terms as 'purification', 'act of humility', 'secular holiness', which until then had been received with scepticism.[24] But this culmination of his technical search had brought Grotowski into a totally different territory, where the requirements of theatre no longer applied. Already the *'via negativa'*, his reduction of the theatrical performance to its essence by a process of 'distillation' and 'contradiction', had led to the virtual elimination of plot and character. Instead of an imaginary action, the play had become an experiment in laying bare the essential spiritual nature of man by sacrificing the body, a psychological dissection that in a very real sense could only proceed if the actors had generated sufficient spiritual intensity on each preceding level. Instead of conventional characterisation, each performer's role was developed from improvisations searching for the individual's basic impulses in reaction to the demands of the group situation, creating a personal 'score' rather than projecting himself as an actor into a fictional 'other'. And the principle of self-cancelling contradictions set dialogue, physical action, vocal expression and gesture each against the other, as when the King's accusation was sung as a litany, with the court echoing the ending of each sentence in a sing-song chant, or when the agony of the Prince was expressed in a dance rhythm while the court performed a minuet, played a grotesque masquerade, or stiffened into animalistic shapes. What remained was the actor as an example of spiritual potential and the cathartic 'communion' with the spectator.

At the stage of development represented by *The Constant Prince*, as Grotowski pointed out, 'the Theatre Laboratory seeks a spectator–

witness, but the spectator's testimony is only possible if the actor achieves an authentic act. If there is no authentic act, what is there to testify to?'[25]

But the new authenticity in performance revealed the intrinsic artificiality of the actor/audience relationship, even when they were functionally involved in the performance and given a role that overlapped reality. It imposed passivity on the spectator, and thus effectively created a division between thinking and acting which reflected the split between mind and body that Grotowski sees as *the* destructive characteristic of western civilisation — indeed that he had designed his techniques specifically to overcome in searching to liberate the individual spiritually through physical stress, an aim corresponding to Artaud's dictum about reintroducing metaphysics through the skin. In reaction Grotowski's subsequent development led to the gradual elimination of any distinction between actor and spectator – 'the very word "spectator" . . . is theatrical, dead. It excludes meeting, it excludes the relation: man–man' – and finally to the abandonment of performance itself. This was also motivated by Grotowski's perception that the ritual and myth, which he had believed were inherited through 'the collective subconscious' and had therefore made the basis of his productions, in fact had little validity in a fragmented society: 'After so many explorations, experiences and reflections, I still doubt the possibility of direct participation in today's theatre in an age when neither a communal faith exists, nor any liturgy rooted in the collective psyche as an axis for ritual.'[26]

The first steps in this process came during performances of *Apocalypsis cum Figuris*:

In the first version of *Apocalypsis* the spectators sat on benches placed in a certain space so that each person was to feel alone . . . Then we looked for different bridges between us and the people – a kind of answer to their presence, an answer that is almost invisible – totally open to their reactions . . . Then we asked at certain points for people who want to come within us and improvise with us during the performance.[27]

From this position, which is superficially similar to the approach of the Living Theatre, Grotowski developed a total concentration on the internal process of self-discovery in groups of the public as participants. In effect they were subjected to an extended session of psychotherapy based on the acting exercises developed by the Theatre Laboratory, that now had the aim of rediscovering primitive 'roots' and corresponded to the 'rites of passage' described by anthropologists like Van Gennep.

The concept of a 'meeting' lasting several days superseded the idea of performance. Even in his early work Grotowski had defined theatre as an 'elite' art, an 'elect moment' demanding a spectator 'who really wishes, through confrontation with the performance, to analyse himself', and limited to those aware of 'genuine spiritual needs'.[28] During the early seventies, performances of *Apocalypsis* were used to find self-selecting groups of participants for these 'para-theatrical projects', and in 1975 the Theatre Laboratory formed a 'research university' in Pittsburgh, where all the different forms of 'meeting' developed in the Theatre Laboratory since Grotowski's 1970 decision not to create any new productions were brought together. These ranged from physical exercises and 'acting therapy' to work-shops labelled 'meditations aloud' and 'song of myself', which were used as preparation for two 'special projects'. In one, a large group of between seventy-five and two hundred people were gathered in a dark confined space, lit only by a charcoal brazier and flambeaux carried by the actors. Here they participated in group improvisations or exposed themselves to basic tactile experiences, while an extem-pore musical accompaniment on guitar and primitive reed flute re-sponded to the moods of the moment and unified them – a direct extrapolation of the search for 'how to disarm ourselves step by step from our daily acts, how to free ourselves from this fear that divides human beings, how to find the simplest and most elementary rela-tionships' that Grotowski had outlined two years earlier.[29] The other, a 'narrow special project' designed to strip away individuality and the accretions of culture, to return participants to their physical roots and build a primal grouping based on the individual's awareness of a primitive relationship between man and the natural world, took place with a small group at night in open country. The first part of the experience corresponded to an initiation by ordeal, isolating indi-viduals, depriving them of light and requiring them to run barefoot through the woods. This direct contact with the environment, em-phasising the senses of touch and smell atrophied in modern civilisa-tion (which participants felt liberated them from 'mental habits' and returned them to the state of 'a wild animal'),[30] led to a 'baptism' in a stream, after which the sound of tomtoms guided individuals to a fire, around which they danced as a group for the rest of the night to the beat of the drums. The experience ended with a 'monastic' break-fast and relaxed games improvised by the group in sunlight.

Such 'special projects' have lasted a week (with symbolic connota-tions of the creation of the world) in Poland, or for ten days at Penn State University in 1978; and the details have varied, each participant being required to lie in a hole in the ground while the group throw dirt on his body in a symbolic burial of the previous socialised self in one session, or bread for the final breakfast being communally baked at sunrise in another. But the overall pattern with its strongly ritualistic overtones remained basically the same, and participants have commented on the hallucinatory effects of the initial sensory deprivation, the disorientation of physical exhaustion – while it is hardly coincidental that both the pattern and the effect closely parallel African and Melanesian initiation rites or the mysteries at Eleusis.[31] This progress from theatre to psychotherapy, from presenting ritualistic images of self-transcendence to creating rites in which participants are 'reborn', and the consequent rejection of stage performance as inseparable from 'concealment and shame', are logical extensions of Grotowski's '*via negativa*' and his stress on authenticity and unity. The method of what he now describes as 'the Theatre of Roots' corresponds to the psychological theory of 'positive disintegration' developed by Dabrowski, one of the lecturers at the 1975 'research university'; and the aim is to create a scale of alternative values based on 'openness' and the 'elemental roots' of human nature in opposition to the 'shame and fear, the need to hide oneself and, also, the need for continually playing a part which is not us' supposedly imposed by society. This is to be achieved through 'an experience that has no spectators. There is no separation between the creative process and the creative result. This is the experience of Active Culture. It comes from all the participants and is shared by all of them, and not the results of [previously worked out and artificially recreated] experience... Shared activity and not shared expression.'[32]

Disciples: Europe and America

Grotowski's approach aroused considerable interest among leading avant garde directors. Among those he has worked with are Barrault and Brook as well as Joe Chaikin and Luca Ronconi, all of whom also participated in his 1975 'research university'. Brook, who arrived at a parallel concept of theatre as 'the terrain of self-discovery' during his African tour, has held joint workshops with him; and his influence is directly responsible for the various 'theatre laboratories' that sprang up in the early seventies. Typical of these are the Théâtre Laboratoire Vicinal in Brussels, where discursive speech has been rejected for 'poor' language approaching 'the cry, the shout, the litany or the chant' and text-less plays are supposedly structured on 'certain fundamental rhythms that every man may feel' appealing 'to the unconscious of the spectator'.[33] Or the Atelier de Recherche Théâtrale Georges Baal in Paris, where a bare stage and the absence of costumes or pretence is united with themes from Artaud and an attempt to liberate the audiences by breaking taboos. Or Terayama's Tenjo Sajiki Laboratory, where extreme means are used to destroy the 'artificial frontiers' between drama and reality, leading to actors being physically assaulted, spectators being overcome with claustrophobia or even burnt (at the 1973 Shiraz festival: the actors exploited the audience's fears by continuing without a break and jabbing flaming torches toward their faces after people in the front rows had been badly singed by a fire-blowing circus act, although Terayama later tried to fend off criticism by claiming the 'incident' was accidental). Grotowski himself has rejected such direct audience participation as 'a new myth', pointing out that true intimacy is more likely to be achieved through physical distance; and he has attacked many of those who claim to be following him for lack of discipline, emphasising 'the presence of a consciousness ... structure, clarity, the precise line' in his work.[34] But he acknowledged the work of Eugenio Barba, who acted as Grotowski's assistant from 1959 up to the *Dr Faustus* production, as a continuation of his own.

Barba's Odin Teatret (full title: Nordisk Theater-Laboratorium för Skuespillerkunst), founded in 1964 and transferred from Oslo to Denmark in 1966, has remained within the circle of the stage while rhetorically announcing 'the death of the theatre' and condemning even experimental theatres as 'the blasphemous caricatures of a ghost'. His continuation of Grotowski's research into the psychophysiological basis of acting led to the formulation of a 'new theatrical language' – or so he claimed, although in fact it strongly resembled the iconographic style of early expressionist silent films in using archetypal gestures, postures and facial masking to transform 'spontaneous' emotions into 'pure' states of Fear, Pain, Desire – and to a drama rooted in myth. Barba's theatre is more directly political than Grotowski's could ever have been in the Polish context, and in productions like *Feraï* (1969) or *Kaspariana* (1967) myths are used as images of 'the worn-out stereotypes that make up our habitual social conduct' to reveal these as inherently primitive, repressive and violent. Against them are set 'ritual' behaviour patterns, 'biological reactions that spring up in extreme situations', where the socially conditioned gestures of everyday life are transformed into a 'natural physical language', a 'sacerdotal sign language' of hieratic attitudes.[35]

Feraï attempted to present a universal paradigm of social structures by combining the legend of King Fredegod, whose rule was so Draconian that valuables could be left on the open street and whose death was concealed for three years in order to preserve social discipline, with the myth of Alcestis, Pherai (the Thessalian town ruled by Admetus) with The Faeroes (in Latin, Ferai). The body of the dead king formed a rather crude symbol for the death of the spirit under dictatorship, and Fredegod's kingdom was emblematically represented by a blanket spread out on the stage and weighted down with stones at the edges. Admetus, who succeeds to this kingdom by winning a duel and marrying Fredegod's daughter Alcestis, is unable to introduce freedom by political reform. To the proto-fascist people liberty means only the destructive licence of a drunken orgy, and they disinter the corpse of the dead dictator in a parody of Christ's resurrection; but the play ends with Alcestis' suicide and apotheosis, which creates a 'mystical' transformation in the state. On another level the play is a conflict between male and female principles epitomised in the three props, which formed the only material or scenic aids in the production – the masculine symbol of a knife with leather thongs that was used as a whip, representing political repression, as a sabre for the duel, a royal sceptre and a flute; the feminine and passive symbol of a blanket, used to represent the subjugated kingdom, swaddling clothes, the dead body; and an ivory egg symbolising both life and death, a skull and the fertile womb. As even such a brief summary indicates, reliance on mystical reverberations and archetypal dualities can be both confusing and simplistic. But the intention was to present a complex of expressionistic images with multiple meanings which each spectator could decipher in terms of his own experience, though this was more effective in *Kaspariana* because the metaphors were more familiar.

The figure of Kaspar Hauser has almost become a hallmark indicating Grotowski's influence, being used as an image of 'natural man' versus society not only by Barba, but also by Joseph Chaikin (in *The Mutation Show*, 1971) and by Brook. When the 16-year-old boy, who had been kept totally isolated from all human contact since birth, appeared in Nuremberg in 1828, he immediately struck the public imagination as the epitome of ideal innocence. His murder shortly afterwards came to symbolise the death of the spirit under the pressures of social conditioning, and his story has since become a familiar literary archetype. The progressive deformation of this 'beautiful soul' by education had been the subject of a novel (Jacob Wasserman's *Kaspar Hauser, oder die Trägheit des Herzens*, 1908); his image as the holy fool, whose murder is a metaphor for the breaking of man's natural relation to the universe, was a familiar theme in expressionist poetry (Georg Trakl's 'Kaspar Hauser Lied', 1913, or Hans Arp's 'Kaspar ist tot', 1920); and Peter Handke has used the story to demonstrate the breakdown of personality under the impact of language as the basic tool of social integration in his play *Kaspar* (1968). Barba's version exactly parallels Handke's play in scenes where Kaspar learns to walk or where 'the community as educator makes its appearance. Knowledge inherited from the most distant cultures (a choir which mingles Hebrew, Sanskrit and Greek) must be passed to its new member. Kaspar is violated with words: a prayer, a false syllogism (Jews are bad, Christians are good; we are Christians, we are good)'.[36] But here Handke's social criticism is transposed into a religious perspective. Kaspar's 'social birth' is marked by a hymn: 'Behold in awe, my child, the true God.' His life is prefigured in a 'saga' of a king who sends his son out among his subjects, only to have him killed by them. And in the final scene Kaspar allows himself to be 'consecrated' to arms like a medieval knight on the Darwinian/capitalist grounds that struggle is the basis of existence, having sought an alternative in the Bible but found only the words 'I have not come to bring peace but the sword. I have come to divide a son from his father, to set brother against brother.' The final image is that of willing sacrifice as he is left to face his executioner. As the sacrificial knife is raised the lights go out, and the play ends with the heavy irony of a psalm: 'Beautiful is the earth, Beautiful is God's Heaven, Beautiful is the pilgrimage of the soul towards its celestial home.'

Like Grotowski's theatrical work, the main problem with a play like *Kaspariana*, which has also been referred to as an atheist mass, is that the challenge to religion presupposes a climate of belief that no longer exists. At the same time, although Barba's intention may be 'to force the audience to drop its social mask and face a world in which old values are destroyed, without offering in their place any metaphysical solutions', the spiritual pole of existence that is opposed to socially conditioned and destructive behaviour patterns can only be communicated in images derived from the very religion that has been rejected as dead. But the value of Barba's work lies in its synthesis of Grotowski's ritualistic transcendence with an uncompromising existentialism akin to Samuel Beckett, which leads him to compare the function of his actors to Hindu *Alvars*:

Alvars profess that divinity does not exist, that hope does not exist, that all is illusion. In the search for a truth beyond all this, they perform acts disapproved by all society, which make a scandal of them and isolate them. But they are the *fools of God* and their conflicting passions in search of a unity fall into a realm which society respects: religion.[37]

Another director to have explicitly labelled himself as Grotowski's disciple is Richard Schechner, whose Performance Group in New York achieved overnight notoriety with *Dionysus in 69* (1968). Some years earlier Schechner had analysed *The Bacchae* as an absurd drama in which the petty and all too human qualities of egoistic vanity and capriciousness revealed in Dionysus' vengeance represent a cosmic scheme impossible to comprehend or propitiate, arguing that Dionysus incites Pentheus to blasphemy, that his rationale for destroying Thebes is unconvincing, since those he kills are his worshippers, and that the image of Dionysus as an irrational, ungovernable, ecstatic life force given by the chorus is contradicted by Euripides' characterisation of the god as ironic, self-controlled and intellectualising: a death force.[38] This interpretation formed the basis of *Dionysus in 69*, where the ambivalence of the god was intended to represent the tendency to fascism inherent in the retreat of the 'new left' from political revolution to the introverted sexual liberation of the drug culture. But this theme was almost totally overlaid by the ritualistic structure of the action, the orgiastic emphasis on nudity and dancing, and the automatic association of the central conflict between the formally dressed Pentheus and the nude Dionysus (played at one point in the production by a woman) with the contemporary clash of the authoritarian social establishment versus 'hippy' freedom, sexual fulfilment and the student revolution.

This was Schechner's most overt attempt to recreate ritual drama – an aim which led *The Drama Review* under his editorship to explore modes of non-verbal communication, the connections between human and animal behaviour patterns in play and ritualised activity and the types of religious performance surviving in primitive cultures.[39] In his view the intrinsic structure of avant garde theatre corresponds to that of primitive ceremony (ignoring the fundamental differences between the avant garde tendency to improvisations, the value it places on spontaneity, or its opposition to contemporary society, and the rigidly fixed lines and delivery, or the integration of the actors in their cultural context that characterises archaic drama from the simple performances of New Guinea or Australian Aborigines to the highly developed Balinese theatres). Both are seen to share the same principles of 'wholeness', 'concreteness', 'transcendental experience' and the stress on performance as 'process' not product. However, the real link would seem to be in the notional ideal of 'community', which leads Schechner to describe archaic tribal culture as 'communal' rather than 'primitive', and explains his emphasis on audience involvement. Ritual is defined as an action in which all the members of a community actively participate (as opposed to a conventional play – an action presented by professionals to a separated and passive collection of individuals), one which symbolically or even actually transforms the status and identity of the group depending on the degree of participation. And both ritual and community are assumed to be incompatible with modern society so that – in a typical syllogism – persuading spectators to participate gives a performance the status of ritual by transforming them into a community, and is thus a political act demanding or representing and so indeed automatically achieving radical changes in the social order! Nakedness is also seen as 'a rejection of the system', as much in affirming 'the body' as in discarding the social conventions/uniform of clothing;[40] and the thematic meaning of *Dionysus*, as with the Living Theatre's *Paradise Now* (also 1968), therefore lay not so much in what was performed as in simply getting spectators to strip.

Euripides' play was restructured into an initiation rite. 'Opening ceremonies' were designed to create contact between actors and the audience, who were carried individually from the entrance to the performing area in explicit imitation of cermonial practices described by Van Gennep.[41] The whole cast formed the chorus, which became the dominant element of the play, with scenes and characters emerging from choral activity and dissolving back into it as 'initiation by example'. The dominant image, created out of the rhythmic writhing and groaning of the group, naked and in unison, the men stretched out flank to flank on the floor with the women standing above, legs straddling them from shoulder to buttock to form an arched tunnel of flesh, was that of the birth canal, adapted from a New Guinea rite of passage. This was repeated twice. At the beginning, when the actor playing Dionysus was 'reborn' as a god – being literally pushed through the 'passage' by pelvic thrusts – and again, reversed, at the death of Pentheus, who instead of being torn to pieces was symbolically reingested into the community that he had tried to dominate as an individual. Within this framing image Euripides' plot was reduced to its basic elements with the intention of making it easier for the audience to join in the story by keeping it simple. (For the same reason there was a deliberate avoidance of professional acting techniques that might set the performers apart from the man in the street – though Schechner later realised that the majority of the performers were just poor actors, a common factor in many of the groups that sprang up in the sixties, where the emphasis was on the community as an alternative life-style and on self-expression rather than skill or talent.)[42] A bacchanal, broken up by Pentheus, was followed by a confrontation between Dionysus and Pentheus, based on encounter-group psychotherapy. Then came Pentheus' search for a woman in the audience, his seduction by Dionysus and a 'total caress', during which tender embraces gradually intensified into animal violence in an 'erotic love-death'.

The spectators were invited to join the bacchanal:

DIONYSUS: ... Together we can make one community. We can celebrate together. Be joyous together. So join us in what we do next. It's a circle dance around the sacred spot of my birth...[43]

Indeed certain sections of the performance could not be completed without a pre-determined response from a specific number of spectators, while at the same time simple rules were laid down to increase

21 The Birth Ritual in *Dionysus in 69*. Initiation, nudity & communal acting.

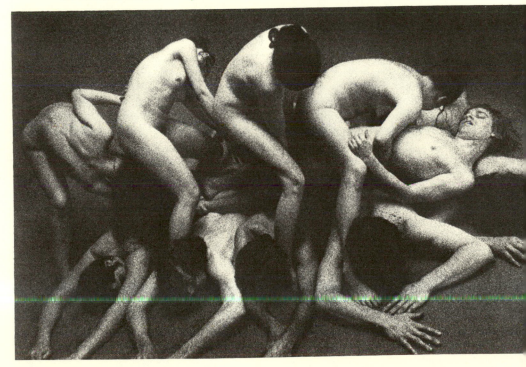

the degree of participation: only those who had taken off all their clothes being allowed into the 8 by 12 ft central acting area that was designated as 'the holy space'. The audiences were subjected to the same erotic embrace and attack as Pentheus in 'the caress', and almost every night some participated in the second birth sequence. This was taken as a tangible measure of success. But at the same time the nature of this involvement was both made over-explicit and left curiously unfocussed. As Dionysus repeatedly announced, 'it's a celebration, a ritual, an ordeal, an ecstasy'; and the audience were encouraged to join 'the community' by stripping and dancing with the performers as a positive act, even though by the time this level of participation was reached the group had a negative significance in terms of the play, mindlessly following a megalomaniac quasi-fascist leader in acts of violence. But when Schechner gave his audience a more specific function – as in *Commune* (1971), where fifteen randomly selected spectators were required to act as villagers in the My Lai massacre or find others from the audience to take their places – the actors' relationship to them was clearly one of intimidation, and the effect was discomforting because there was no way of signalling what their responses ought to be. In short, what the Performance Group approach demonstrates is that meaningful participation requires an established ritual familiar to all, not an alien rite where, however authentic the imitation, the performance is bound to be fake. And this is not only impossible in a society where cohesive religious belief has gone and its ritual forms have lost their validity, but doubly so given a political radicalism that rejects the social context, since whatever communal forms exist are there.

In addition, participation only becomes more than an illusionistic device if it can influence the tone or change the outcome of the performance. This possibility was built in to *Dionysus*, though in a way which effectively precluded it, by making the test of the god's power that Pentheus could not persuade any girl in the audience to allow him to copulate with her. However on one occasion the actor was successful, leaving Dionysus to announce, 'tonight for the first time since the play has been running, Pentheus, a man, has won over Dionysus, the god. The play is over.' Similarly in one performance of *Commune* some of the spectators selected refused to act as 'victims' and the play was broken off for over three hours while the cast and other spectators argued with them. At the very least then, participation disrupted the 'prepared rhythms' of the action: that is, diminished both the dramatic effectiveness of the structure and those qualities that made the performance ritualistic. Taken to its extreme it made performance of any kind impossible.

Schechner derived his term 'Environmental Theatre' from Kaprow's concept of the Happening, and tried to incorporate such disruptions by interspersing organised action with 'open' sections,

not improvised moments – where performers work freely from a set of objectives or rules – but truly open moments when all the people in the room acting either individually, in small groups, or in concert move the action forward. This 'action' is not necessarily known beforehand and may have nothing to do with the dramatic action of the play.[44]

But in his later work participation has been limited to physically following the action, playing scenes throughout the available area so spectators must change their position in order to see, or as a simultaneous montage so spectators are forced to be selective and each makes his own logical connections. In a sense this becomes subjective theatre, with each person perceiving a different play from changing perspectives that he himself determines – and that this is a logical extension of avant garde trends is indicated by Peter Stein's independent development of the same approach in Germany with productions like *Shakespeare's Memory* (1977) or *As You Like It* (1978).[45]

This movement through a complex arrangement of multi-level and sub-divided acting areas literally made the audience the environment of the play in Schechner's *Makbeth* (1969), where the performance was given focus by the way groupings of spectators gathered and dispersed. They became the soldiers, guests or crowds, powerless to intervene but compliant, watching a brutal power struggle with the same vicarious titillation as the modern man in the street crowding round an accident or the scene of a crime. At the same time spectators were set inside the environment of the play, as in a 1975 production of *Mother Courage*, where the whole of the Performance Garage was conceived as the wagon, with ropes and pulleys strung from walls and ceiling to represent harness or the tents of a military camp, and with the Performance Group itself presented as Mother Courage's 'small business'. There were also rather fake attempts to move the theatre out into the real environment with Dionysus leading bacchantes and audience through the opened garage doors in a triumphal procession up the street, or with Mother Courage's haggling played out on the pavement.

This merging of illusion and reality, and the stress on total involvement, together with the subjective nature of the dramatic event turned the Performance Group's early work into an undramatic form of psychotherapy – that was not so much for the audience as for the performers themselves – in a way that was all too typical of American avant garde theatre in the sixties. Each actor wrote his own dialogue for *Dionysus* and *Commune*, incorporating inflated personal experiences and trite life histories; and as one actor playing Dionysus only too revealingly commented: 'I am acting out my disease, the disease that plagues my inner being, that stops the flow . . . Dionysus is not a play to me. I do not act in Dionysus. Dionysus is my ritual.' When *Dionysus* opened almost half of the cast were under psychoanalysis, and group therapy sessions were held once a week, through which personal neuroses and resentments were brought to the surface. These fed into the theatrical work to such an extent that the tensions and conflicts within the 'community' became the real focus of *Makbeth*, leading to the break up of the original group, while the subject of *Commune* became the analysis of different kinds of group – Manson and his 'family', soldiers and their Vietnamese victims, the actors and their audience – and the play itself was conceived as 'a collective dream'.

The model was that of the Asian performer, whose training was seen as 'holistic' and 'the primary means of personal growth' (as opposed to western training, defined as an 'instrumental' and acquired skill), and the ideal was to recreate a shamanistic performance exorcising the 'disease' of the community in the form of taboos, hostilities, fears. But the effect was self-indulgent, the self-expression tended to cliché. Possibly the desired states of shamanistic 'trance and possession' could be achieved only by the total identification of performers with their roles. But the result was both naive and, as Schechner himself realised, narcissistic.[46] As with Grotowski, characterisation, the projection of the self into an 'other', was discarded, while texts became hypnotic structures of sound and the separation between spectator and actor was dissolved, with the aim of transforming theatre into psychotherapy. But here any demonstrable effect seems to have been limited to the acting group themselves, and could hardly be called therapeutic. As in Barba's work, the potential flaws in Grotowski's approach become clear, and some of the negative implications in this theatrical development are summed up by Schechner's description of the avant garde as 'more iconographic than iconoclastic . . . radical not in a political sense, but in the manner in which it attempts to go to the roots'. Indeed his claim that 'the locus of the essential theatre shifted from the page to somewhere between the navel and genitals of each performer'[47] – from his point of view a positive and progressive state of affairs – was unfortunately all too accurate.

The Living Theatre

Many of the same criticisms apply to the work of the Living Theatre, which – with an eclecticism that is itself typical of the avant garde – drew together almost all of the different trends so far discussed. When they founded their first (abortive) theatre in 1948, Julian Beck and Judith Malina concentrated on Nōh drama and medieval mystery plays, and their early productions included an adaptation of the *Oresteia* with masks and dances derived from Japanese theatre, Jarry's *Ubu roi*, Strindberg's *Ghost Sonata*, and the surrealism of Picasso and Gertrude Stein, while images from early expressionist films were used for their version of *Frankenstein* (1965). Artaud's theories inspired their production of *The Brig* (Kenneth Brown, 1963), with its emphasis on purgation through intensely felt actual emotions, and provided the dominant image of *Mysteries* (1964), which ended with a staging of Artaud's description of 'the Plague' as 'the very embodiment of his theatrical philosophy'.[48] Their development led naturally to the ritual of Genet's *The Maids*, which they performed with an all-male cast – almost the only production (apart from Lindsay Kemp's) faithful to this aspect of Genet's vision. Their notes for *Paradise Now* (1968) repeatedly refer to Grotowski's acting exercises and Cieslak's 'transluminations', which they saw as a model for removing psychological resistances, and translated into the 'flashouts' ('a transcendent moment in which [the actor] is released from all hangups of the present situation') that mark the end of each section of their play, while Grotowski's term *apokatastasis* ('the transformation of the demonic forces into the celestial')[49] was used as its central structuring principle. They repeatedly termed their political aim 'prophesying', described their theatre as 'performing a ceremony' and its intended effect as 'an absolute communion', referred to the actor as 'a priest' or 'shaman', and pointed out their 'concern with primitive and mystic rituals'.[50] Their performances replaced plot, characterisation and (in *Mysteries*, *Paradise Now* or their 1967 version of Brecht's *Antigone*) scenery by sequences of physical images, or 'hieroglyphs' formed solely from the posture and grouping of the actors. These drew on archetypes from Greek mythology – Icarus, Europa, the Minotaur – on Egyptian bas-reliefs, Amerindian totem-poles, the legend of Buddha and eschatological clichés – the pietà (of course) or the horsemen of the Apocalypse – while the overall structures of action were derived impartially from the Cabbala, from Tantric and Hassidic rituals, and from initiation rites such as the mysteries at Eleusis. From an ideal of theatre 'as a place of intense experience, half dream, half ritual, in which the spectator approaches something of a vision of self-understanding, going past the conscious to the unconscious', they developed an extreme form of audience participation where performance 'would no longer be enactment but would be the act itself'. Even their European exile was justified in exactly the same terms as Brook's African journey – 'to find ways of communicating with each other beyond those which involve speech. To find a way of communicating our feelings and our ideas through signs and being'[51] – while their recent development has taken them, like Grotowski, outside the theatre altogether. In short their career recapitulates the sources, aims and successive stages of the whole avant garde movement in microcosm.

The base root of all avant garde theatre is an uncompromising rejection of contemporary civilisation and existing social structures. Even if it has also led to the rejection of conventional modes of political action and accepted ideologies, it is this ultimately political position which has determined the almost universal appeal to irrationalism with its exploration of dream states and search for archetypal expression, as well as the return to primitive dramatic forms in ritual with its emphasis on religious experience and eastern mysticism. Nowhere is the link between politics and the apparently apolitical emphasis on the subconscious or mythology clearer than in the Living Theatre with its overt commitment to anarchism. Where this commitment was explicit it produced empty wish-fulfilment and simplistic equations – such as the assertion that 'the hippies' are 'reincarnations of the American Indian, aspiring to be the natural Man as represented by ... the great suppressed cultures' – or sophomoric slogans that were at best statements of conviction but had little relevance to the actual situation – such as 'Fuck the Jews. Fuck the Arabs. Fuck means peace', where 'universal intercourse' was proposed (without any sense of irony) as a solution to the problems of the Middle East, or the word 'Anarchism', spelt out by the bodies of the actors across the stage, was transformed into the word 'Paradise' with a shout of 'now!'[52] But to dismiss the Living Theatre's work as political naivety, as many critics have done, is beside the point. Their assumption was that individual spiritual change is the pre-condition for meaningful exterior political change, that dealing with a social issue on its own terms will only perpetuate the established cycle of violence and oppression of which it is a symptom; and their aim was therefore to create images that would act as an emotional inspiration, to challenge taboos and socially conditioned patterns of thought.

Perhaps unsurprisingly, the most powerful and convincing images were negative, representations of a dehumanising system of repression and exploitation, which were developed or reproduced from production to production and designed to cause an instinctive revulsion in the audience. One such image reproduced social relationships purely in terms of externals, ignoring philosophical 'content' to create a Kafkaesque structure of rigid and arbitrary rules, whose sole function was to reduce individuals to a Pavlovian state of obedience, cogs in a meaningless machine. This was derived from *The Brig*, where the dramatic action is contained solely in the 'regulations' of the US Marines prison:

No prisoner may speak at any time except to his guards. A prisoner must request permission to do any and everything in the following way: 'Sir, prisoner number – requests permission to speak, sir'. He must speak in a loud, clear, impersonal, and unaffected tone.
At each exit and entrance there is a white line. No prisoner may cross any white line without requesting to do so . . . No prisoner will sit down at any time unless it is necessary for the completion of his task.
Under no circumstances will a prisoner be permitted to walk from place to place. He must run . . .[53]

Under such conditions every normal daily activity can be used as an additional means of humiliation, and every form of contact between fellow prisoners is broken. Speech is forbidden, any expression of sympathy for another's suffering provokes immediate physical punishment. This isolation, together with the depersonalisation of being constantly forced to refer to oneself by number instead of name and in the third person is an intrinsic part of this particular play's logic, not to be confused with the similar expressionistic technique used for generalisation in a play like Elmer Rice's *The Adding Machine* (1923). It has the explicit function of 'rehabilitation', instilling an automatic response to orders in prisoners whose 'crimes' have been infringements of discipline. This frightening image of social conditioning as dehumanising brainwashing, with the military framework implying that the end result of deadening normal human emotions is killing, was reused in *Mysteries*, though it lost much of its significance out of its original context, clearly having more meaning to the actors than to European audiences who had not seen *The Brig*, and had to be given additional associations by a 'poem' composed of all the numbers and words on a dollar bill that was recited as an accompaniment. It was reused again in *Frankenstein*, where 'world action' was represented as a multi-storey prison structure through which the actors moved in a perpetual cycle: whistle, blackout, each prisoner moves to the next cell . . . lights, each freezes in a position expressing mental agony, becoming more mechanical and zombie-like as they progress through the structure . . . and at each whistle one leaves from the last cell (death) while another actor is dragged out of the audience to the first cell for fingerprinting and mug shot. A comparable image was 'the plague' – the groans, cries and distorted bodies of the dying, acting out repressed sexual desires in their death throes; survivors lining up the rigid bodies then laying them one on top of the other in a 'wood pile' with its connotations of cremation and the gas ovens – which was used unchanged in *Mysteries* and *Antigone*. What made such images effective was not their accuracy, certainly not any philosophical depth, but solely their simplicity and specificity: a point clearly demonstrated by the development from *Frankenstein* to *Paradise Now*. In the first cruelty was presented in the whole spectrum of execution from beheading and crucifixion to the firing squad and electric chair. In the second all across the stage paired-off actors took up the positions of the Saigon Police Chief and Vietcong prisoner in Edward Adams' award-winning photo of 1968, a graphic and immediately evocative image that was made unendurable for many spectators by its multiplication and reiteration: 'in unison . . . the victims rise, the executioners fire, the victims fall. This is repeated twenty times.'[54] A complex system had been reduced to a single, concrete and instantly comprehensive essential that – however superficial – carried conviction because the picture was already loaded with connotations.

By contrast the positive images intended as inspiration were all too often generalised to the point of abstraction or totally obscure, as in the static physical representation of Greek mythological situations or the use of incantation, yoga breathing exercises or Hindu mantras and ragas to symbolise hope, aspiration and 'revolutionary' action. In *Mysteries*, for example, scenes presenting the 'problem' of the present state of the world were set against 'solutions' in the form of an alternative life style suggested by 'ceremonies' celebrating the senses. 'Tableaux vivants' supposedly communicating 'that whatever posture our bodies assume it will always be beautiful'[55] were intended to exercise the eye; incense carried in procession through the auditorium in darkness stimulated the sense of smell; a 'chord', built up from the actors in a circle tuning in to the notes made by their neighbours, indulged the ear in a deliberate but ultimately meaningless confusion of categories: politics against aesthetics. In *Antigone* 'revolutionary' consciousness was to be transmitted, at least in theory, by creating a (purely visual) unity out of political polarities, with Polyneikes' rigid body stage centre throughout the performance as an unyielding 'No' to Kreon's activity in politics and war, or a bacchanal (lasting three-quarters of an hour) as an affirmation of life set against the conventional dramatic plot centring on death. Thematically at any rate the structure of *Paradise Now* was the most appropriate, being based on the principle of transformation, 'the demonic' qualities of 'rigidity' or 'hostility resulting from an unsatisfactory life' being 'exorcised' by the influence of 'movement' or 'the love force'. In the 'Vision of Apokatastasis', for instance, the executioners repeated the phrases shouted at the audience by the company in the opening 'rite' to represent the frustrations and repression of the social system – 'I am not allowed to travel without a passport... I'm not allowed to smoke marijuana... I'm not allowed to take my clothes off' – while the victims replied with words from the 'rite of prayer' that had been used to 'sanctify' the spectators – 'Holy eyes... Holy legs... Holy mouth' – continuing 'until the executioners are moved to respond, not with violence, but with love, and gently address the victims with the words of the Rite of Prayer. The 'Vision' ends with the embrace of victim and executioner. (Flashout)'[56] Again there is a confusion of categories, though here it is even more basic, stylised pretence being taken as a real event, vicarious emotion assumed to be objective actuality and not just subjective experience, theatre as life.

This attempt to merge theatrical performance and reality is characteristic of the avant garde approach, but the Living Theatre took it to extremes. In preparation for *The Brig* the actors voluntarily submitted themselves to 'Rehearsal Discipline Rules' paralleling the Marine regulations of the play, wore their costumes and continued the prescribed attitudes of sadism (on the part of those playing guards) or absolute obedience (the prisoners) off stage to create a real atmosphere of hostility, persecution and isolation. The production of *The Connection* (Jack Gelber, 1959) was a natural extension of this. The dialogue was largely devoted to establishing that the actors were in fact drug addicts, paid to come to the theatre to provide a sociological 'experience' for the audience. The actors were required to stay in character and mingle with the audience during intermission, and the theme asserted not only that 'straight' society was morally inferior to the counter-culture, but that the two were identical (pushers being 'business men' while business men were 'addicted' to money, sleeping pills, nicotine, etc.). Judith Malina described this as 'a very important advance for us ... from then on, the actors began *to play themselves'*. Costumes, make-up and characterisation were avoided, even in a fairly conventional play like *Antigone*, where she commented 'I don't want to be Antigone, I am and want to be Judith Malina.'[57] So it was quite logical to use Brecht's rehearsal device of having each actor preface his speeches with 'And then Kreon said... /Antigone said...' in the performance itself – not with the intention of creating a sense of alternate possibilities (Brecht's *Verfremdungseffekt*), but to transfer the level of imaginative reality from character to actor.

Naturally, with this value put on 'playing oneself' dramatic action was increasingly improvised, which led to a confusing lack of observable form even in such a highly structured play as *Paradise Now*. This was conceived as 'a spiritual voyage and a political voyage' charted in an ascending series of eight gradated 'Rungs', each of which was sub-divided into a 'Rite' establishing contact between actors and spectators, a cerebral 'Vision' performed solely by the actors and an 'Action' to be accomplished by the audience. Improvisation also resulted in the poor execution of what was often brilliantly conceived physical imagery, as well as limiting dialogue to a simplicity of the 'You Jane. Me Tarzan' variety, and reducing the action to a repetitive expression of extreme emotional states, hatred or passion being easier to communicate than nuances of sentiment. This led critics to condemn the Living Theatre, not unfairly, as converts rather than actors, self-indulgent and unskilled. But in a sense crude acting, unsustained characterisation and imperfect physical imagery was a logical, even obligatory expression of the group's anarchist ideology with its emphasis (however self-defeating) on essence or process and its total opposition to form or product. This was intentionally 'State of Being Acting as opposed to Enactment Acting... something between chance and free theatre'.[58] On another level the actors really did experience something of the emotions they presented, even the 'state of transcendent energy and transformation' defined as a 'flashout', through a form of self-hypnosis. Normal feelings could be heightened to a state of emotional intensity by using physical tension, by provoking hostility against themselves in the audience, by using communal rhythms or repeated movements. Drugs were also openly used 'to attain a state of inspiration, what we sometimes call a "trance"',[59]

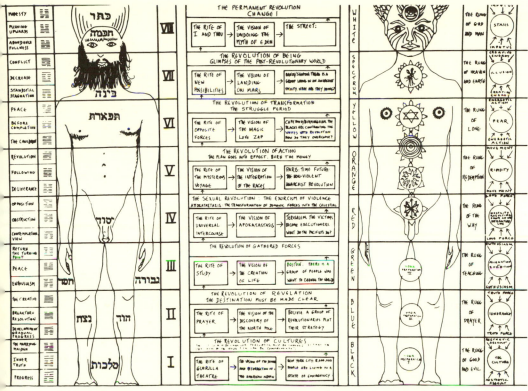

THIS CHART IS THE MAP   THE ESSENTIAL TRIP IS THE VOYAGE FROM THE MANY TO THE ONE   THE PLOT IS THE REVOLUTION

22 Programme-chart for the 'spiritual voyage' of *Paradise Now*. Symbolic
structures & eclectic imagery. (Compare the physiology of *Orghast*,
plate 17.)

which can have only impaired communication, substituting the performers' gratification for emotional impact on the audience.

In the last analysis, however, a performance could only be turned
into a real event by the total involvement of the audience. Initially this
was limited to an attempt to disorient the spectator, submerging
him in 'a dream', by painting the auditorium black, with 'narrower
and narrower stripes converging towards the stage, concentrating the
focus, as if one were inside an old-fashioned Kodak, looking out
through the lens, the eye of the dreamer in a dark room'.[60] But the
subliminal soon gave way to the physical. At first in *Mysteries* this
took the fairly conventional form of planting actors among the audience, who repeated the political slogans to induce the spectators to
join in. In *Frankenstein* the barrier of the footlights was broken,

though vicariously, with 'victims' of the system fleeing to the auditorium for refuge with teams of 'police' pursuing and dragging
them, plus other actors seated among the audience, back to torture
and imprisonment on the stage. Then in *Antigone* the audience were
involved thematically in the action. They stood for Argos, all the
actors on stage represented Thebans, and the battles were mimed
assaults on the auditorium, with the actor playing Megaros as a supposed spectator who was butchered in the aisle. Already in *Mysteries*
the Living Theatre had experimented with creating feelings of unease
in their audience by opening with a silent and motionless actor literally staring them down, and here the aim was to evoke fear and
hostility, like Genet in *The Blacks*. As the audience took their seats the
actors entered one by one, a counterforce, antagonistic and contemptuous, forming different groupings and moving slowly down stage 'to
spot each one and decide who you don't like' according to Beck's
directive,[61] then charging straight down into the audience in the attack on 'Argos' once sufficient hostility was thought to have been
established. At the end after the defeat of Thebes the pattern was
reversed, the actors lining up along the edge of the stage to receive
the judgement of their 'conquerors', then retreating and collapsing,
trembling and whimpering with terror at the applause.

This pattern of antagonism, with the same inherent confusion from
arbitrarily ignoring actual responses and treating even expressions of
approval or solidarity as hostility, characterised the opening of
Paradise Now, where the audience was approached as if it represented
the repressive forces of society. 'I'm not allowed to travel without a
passport... smoke marijuana... take my clothes off' was shouted in
spectators' faces with increasing urgency and hate, and each actor
used any response, however sympathetic, 'to increase his expression
of the frustration at the taboos and inhibitions imposed on him by the
structure of the world around him', with the dubious aim of evoking
in the audience a 'growing frustration at the sense of a lack of communication' with the actors.[62] The whole play that followed was designed to transform this alienation into its opposite, physical unity in
'the Rite of Universal Intercourse' with naked spectators and actors
embracing indiscriminately, even copulating – the ultimate extension
of the involvement and liberation of man's instinctive nature that
Barrault had aimed at metaphorically and Schechner counterfeited in
Dionysus – leading finally to the transformation of society outside the
theatre with love and nudity supposedly spreading contagiously as
the naked actors led the unclothed spectators in a pied-piper proces-

23 'Authenticity' instead of costume or character in *Antigone*, & symbols from physical grouping. Aggression as a substitute for audience involvement.

sion through the streets. The 'Rite' on each 'Rung' of the ladder leading to 'Permanent Revolution' was explicitly conceived as a 'rite of passage', and the overall structure corresponded to the primitive pattern described by Van Gennep: separation of the initiates from the social environment they were identified with through (in this case verbal) flagellation, purification and integration in a new group, which was frequently marked by sexual licence 'as a complete expression of that same idea of incorporation. It is the precise equivalent of a communal meal.'[63]

In terms of this ritual form audience participation was not just thematically required; in theory the spectators had to achieve particular states of consciousness at each stage before the performance could proceed. An awareness of 'the structures which make these prohibitions' and the alternative of 'Natural Man' had to be followed by the formation of groups of five on analogy to 'the elemental structure of the cell [biology being merged with Bakunin's revolutionary theories] as a pattern for social structure' and by 'PRACTICAL WORK... to rally those who are ready and to ready those who are open'. After (comm)union came 'a projection into time future', the visionary 'expansion of human potential. This could lead to flying' since 'freed from the constraint and injury brought down on us by the errors of past civilisation, we will be free to expand and to alter the nature of our being', and finally the actualisation of this image of the future: 'The theatre is in the street. The street belongs to the people. Free the theatre. Free the street. Begin.'[64]

Ignoring the ludicrousness of walking out naked into the sub-zero temperatures of a midwest American street in December or January, and quite apart from the syllogistic confusion of the biological with the political, the physical with the spiritual, the ideal with the possible and the image with actuality, which epitomised the sub-intellectual radicalism of the sixties, this level of total audience commitment was almost impossible to achieve. Significantly, the most effective part of this programme was a symbolic act, not a real action: the flying. One person at a time, members of the audience as well as actors, launched himself, as if diving upwards, off a high platform to be caught in the interlaced arms of the others standing in a double line below. And this corresponded so closely to the symbolism behind shamanistic folklore and shamanistic performances that it can hardly be a coincidence:

Shamans are able, here on earth and as often as they wish, to accomplish 'coming out of the body', that is, the death that alone has power to transform the rest of mankind into 'birds'...
Magical flight is the expression both of the soul's autonomy and of ecstasy... The breaking of the plane effected by the 'flight' signifies an act of transcendence...

Strictly speaking, what is in question is not a 'flight' but a dizzy trajectory, mostly in a horizontal direction [representing] the desperate effort to be rid of a monstrous presence, to free oneself . . .[65]

Even if this magical tradition was unknown to the audience, all the major symbolic associations were immediately obvious, and participation was so effective that 'flying' almost became the trade mark for the Living Theatre and was taken up by others, like Schechner.

But aside from such an isolated ritual, where only a small number of spectators were expected to perform and the form was already familiar to initiates from previous productions, physical involvement only occurred on the most basic level. Unlike Grotowski, who cast his audiences in well-defined roles that corresponded to their function as spectators and reinforced their passive receptivity, the Living Theatre demanded a degree of participation that transformed the spectator into the protagonist, but without giving anything more than an abstract 'map' or generalised slogans to indicate exactly what action was required. The resulting response was only too often cheap humour (animal noises, shouts of 'louder!' or 'begin!' directed at the silent actor in the prologue to *Mysteries*), self-indulgence (sexual gratification) or the provocation of precisely those instincts the performance was intended to eradicate (as in 'the Plague' scene, where although normally one or two spectators did 'die' with the actors or comforted the 'dying', the actors were frequently tickled, kicked or abused to try to get the 'corpses' to move, and once Malina's hair was even set on fire). There were comparable problems even when preaching to the converted, as the Living Theatre increasingly did once their work became associated with the student revolution that culminated in the events of May 1968 in Paris, where it was Malina and Beck who led the takeover of Barrault's Théâtre de France. From Brooklyn all the way to Berkeley in their 1968–9 American tour, whenever the actors announced they were not allowed to smoke marijuana the audience lit up joints and filled the house with the pungent smell of hashish while, as they were claiming they were not allowed to strip, clothes were being flung off all over the theatre. And in at least one performance the injunction to 'free the theatre' swamped the stage with naked spectators – and the play was brought to an abrupt end by a public discussion on the political relevance of the Living Theatre.

In an attempt to cope with this, explicit stage directions were included in the dialogue of *Paradise Now*, though these tended to the abstract, like:

– In the schools, the hospitals, the universities, psychosexual repression is
impeding the Revolution. Who dares form cells to help break down these
taboos?
– Stop the fear.
– Stop the punishment.
– Make it real.
– Do it Now.

or the inflated, like

– Be the heart. Act. Find the pain. Feel it. Make the sound of it.
– The heart of Africa.
– The sacred heart.
– Enact the impulses of the collective unconscious.[66]

The actors also provided examples for the audience and tried to guide
whatever actions they initiated, while the performance was left as
open as possible, with only about one-third of the time scripted and
the actual content of the 'Rites' and images kept generalised almost to
the point of meaninglessness in order to allow the most diverse spontaneous material to be incorporated. But the Becks were also prepared
to short-circuit the structure of the play, nullifying both the ritual
progression and the philosophical premise 'that if one were to
traverse all of the rungs one would unify heaven and earth' by asserting that the revolutionary paradise could be achieved 'at any
point. . . If the audience became so incensed at these prohibitions that
it – without our saying another word consummated a revolution –
whatever we mean by that – that's perfect, just as in the levitation
at the start of *Frankenstein*, we say: "If she levitates, the play is consummated."'[67] And in claiming this, the Living Theatre implicitly acknowledged the impossibility of controlling the level of participation
they required. Beck tended to put this down to the unregenerate
nature of society, so that failure became an additional justification for
their work, but the real problem could be more accurately described
as their failure to distinguish between theatre and reality, sex and
politics, and the vagueness of their idealism. (Note their use of the
term 'consummate' and the admission that they have no definition of
revolutionary achievement in the quotation above.)

In addition there was an intellectual dishonesty in the concept of
Paradise Now, which highlights the incompatibility of improvisation
and art, direct physical audience involvement and the aesthetic imaginary basis of theatrical performance. At every 'Rung' on the 'verti-
cal ascent' the audience were exhorted to 'free' the theatre as a
paradigm of revolutionary action:

- Free theatre. The theatre is yours. Act. Speak. Do whatever you want.
- Free theatre. Because in the society we envisage, everyone is free.
- Free theatre. Free being. Free life. Do anything. Do nothing. Be.
- Breathe.
- Expand consciousness.[68]

This became the theme note through reiteration, and if the play was to succeed in its own terms it had to be accomplished. Yet the only 'free theatre' up to that point, the original conclusion of *Mysteries*, had been abandoned after only one attempt as abortive, counter-productive, even 'disgusting', and Malina's conclusion, after a whole year of discussions among the company, was 'I don't think . . . that it is possible to obtain a satisfactory response from a whole audience under actual conditions.' Both as artists and as political activists the Becks were concerned with creating a shaped imaginative and emotional experience, but calling for 'spontaneous' actions from the public effectively abdicated their control: 'Some of [the audience] performed "choices" that were really beautiful and absorbing, although some were sort of extravagant, more foolish and horrible. But when you do "free theatre", you cannot say that this is bad and this is good.' At best the ordinary person will resort to repetitive clichés when required to express his 'consciousness' or 'being' and, as Beck himself realised, 'there's something wrong with a play that keeps reducing an audience to that low level'.[69] But when an extended cooperative action of any subtlety or coherence did occur during *Paradise Now* this was because the performance had been infiltrated by professional agitprop (agitation and propaganda) groups who staged their own pre-rehearsed, alternative play.

With *Paradise Now* the limits of this line in the Living Theatre's development were reached, and in 1970 the group split up. Since then the Becks' rhetoric has been more ideological and their work has been based on the agitprop drama that characterised communist theatre in the 1920s and 1930s, although it still retains a distinct ritualistic and mythical emphasis. Agitprop elements were already present in the naive use of slogans, the characterisation of Kreon as a cardboard figure implying that the social structure will dissolve of its own accord as soon as pressure is applied, the stress on moving theatre out into the street and the aim of uniting the audience with the actors in a real-life revolutionary action at the conclusion of a performance. (There is little essential difference between the procession through the streets at the culmination of *Paradise Now* and the final stage directions to a 1920s' agitprop piece like J. R. Becher's 'Sketch for a revolutionary battle-play', *Workers, Peasants, Soldiers*, which called for machine guns to be 'distributed on the stage and... handed down from the stage among the spectators' and for the actors to lead the audience out of the theatre 'to take the police headquarters by storm'.)[70]

At the same time the Becks' concept of 'Guerilla Theatre' – elaborated into 150 miniature playlets to be performed in procession in front of appropriate buildings in any city – is still based on myth and contains many scenes lifted from their earlier work. Where the subtitle of *Paradise Now* was 'Undoing the myth of Eden', the overall title of this mammoth street spectacle is *The Legacy of Cain*, and its intention is the 'exorcism' of slavery by presenting images of enslavement in everyday activities. The different sections that have been performed at various times include 'the Plague' and a 'Prison dream play' (staged in gaol after the group were arrested in Brazil); 'The money tower', performed outside a steel works in Pittsburgh – and presenting the economic system as a multi-storey structure comparable to the 'prison' of *Frankenstein*, in which men live an existence of 'Visions' and 'Nightmares', 'the visions of the poor' being 'the nightmares of the rich'; 'Seven meditations on political sado-masochism'; 'Six public acts', in which the actors 'go to the sources of institutionalised murder' and create simple images to 'reverse public consciousness', for example the actors pricked their fingers and encouraged spectators to do the same, mingling their blood in a ritual of brotherhood and smearing it on a flagpole (designated 'the House of State' at Ann Arbor) as a symbol of the deaths caused by wars, the police, the national guard, etc., with the repeated chant of 'this is the blood of us all'; and 'Turning the earth: a ceremony for spring planting in five ritual acts.'[71]

The Living Theatre Action Declaration of January 1970 had announced the breakup of the original group with the call to 'Abandon the theatres... Create circumstances that will lead to Action... Smash the art barrier': aims which are reflected in their move to Brazil as a country in the initial stages of revolution, then to the US industrial centre of Pittsburgh, as well as in the strong agitprop focus of their later work. And this rejection of the theatre and art in favour of direct intervention in reality is the logical end position of twentieth-century avant garde developments, one already inherent in the expressionist attempt to create an immediate and therapeutic transference of emotion to the audience or in Jarry's and Artaud's equally self-destructive acting out of their dramatic principles in their lives.

But the Living Theatre's continuing definition of action as provoking a shift in consciousness, an interior change in the nature of the spectator, also epitomises the avant garde. And the logical means to achieve this end are subliminal or spiritual, a return to the idealised conditions of archaic drama to achieve the cathartic effect associated with tragedy. This explains the Living Theatre's continuing emphasis on performance as a religious and ritual event, ceremonies of exorcism, initiation and communion, the projection of dream states, even 'meditations', all designed 'to transmute violence into concord' (the rationale appended to the title of 'Six public acts'). It is also this adaptation of primitive rites, the concept of a 'holy' actor as shaman, the formalised audio-visual structures of archetypal images and hypnotically repetitive incantation, which distinguishes this dominant line of theatrical exploration from the experiments in straight political theatre on the one hand, and the Happening or Russian formalism on the other. However, as in much of the Living Theatre's work, these qualities have an inherent tendency towards arcane or facile exoticism, and 'Turning the earth' is a good example. As scenery a large mandala of the birth of the earth was reproduced from Jung's *Mandala Symbolism* (quite incomprehensible to anyone who had not read the book) and set up in an uncultivated city lot. The action consisted of a series of rites, 'Retching the Past' – suggested by an obscure ceremony from the Omaha Indians, in which the actors put pebbles symbolising 'dead earth', the crippling effect of 'the heritage of violence', etc., in their mouths and spat them out – followed by celebrations of 'Rebirth' and 'Community':

When all the people in the circle have completed their ritual [giving each other symbolic names to indicate that they have been 'reborn'] they rise and form a circle, arms around each other and create a chordal sound together, beginning with a low hum. The low hum rises rapidly and gives birth to choral musical notes of throats opened in unity and ecstasy.

This culminates in a token planting of trees and flowers, and although 'the intention of the play is to stimulate a fresh relationship in the community towards the earth, towards land, towards the question of property', the only discernible effect of the ritual is to make a simple activity unnecessarily pretentious.

Ionesco and Beckett

Initially, of course, 'avant garde' was synonymous for 'esoteric' or 'incomprehensible'. But gradually its approach filtered through into public consciousness, and works that have become accepted as modern classics began to reflect its principles. These plays – many of them associated with 'the Theatre of the Absurd' following Martin Esslin's influential study, which has effectually determined a whole generation's concept of modern drama – tended to use mythical images, ritual patterning and techniques of subliminal communication for equally legitimate but often quite different dramatic purposes. The forms became divorced from their original aims. This process was all the easier, since to a large extent they had been developed by directors rather than dramatists, and so were not inextricably associated with any particular writer's unique vision. Beginning in the fifties, they were applied to plays concerned with philosophical statements, even political theses. They were used to create new interpretations of traditional masterpieces, particularly Shakespeare, and more recently proved an effective formula for conventional popular theatre.

In some cases authors essentially within the avant garde movement gained recognition because other, more fashionable aspects of their work were emphasised, Eugène Ionesco being a case in point. Ionesco is normally interpreted in terms of the 'philosophy of the absurd' outlined by Camus in *The Myth of Sisyphus*. His theme is said to be a statement of the impossibility of communication and the futility of life in the face of inevitable death, illustrating Sartre's proposition that the consciousness of existence leads to an awareness of 'the nothingness of being'. This is used to explain what is seen as a rejection of the whole concept of personality in the transferable or transforming characters of plays like *The Bald Primadonna* (*La Cantatrice chauve*, 1948, produced 1950) or *Victims of Duty* (*Les Victimes du devoir*, 1953), the reduction of social reality to clichés and empty formulas, and an attempt to create an 'abstract' theatre where the primary function of a play is to reveal and express the formal principles of the theatrical art form.[1] Such analyses of Ionesco's work as dramatic statements of a philosophical position, 'pure' theatre, or anti-theatre in the sense of parody drama – and given his assertion of the identity of contraries in an early essay with the title of 'No!', it would be perfectly legitimate to interpret his plays as simultaneous expressions of all three – all have a certain validity, and can be clearly derived from some of Ionesco's own theoretical statements or from selected comments about drama put into the mouths of characters in his plays. But there is a mythical, even mystical aspect to his work that is frequently overlooked, as is his relationship to the whole avant garde movement from Jarry to the surrealists. Ionesco's appreciation of *grand guignol* puppet theatre and his position as a 'Grand Satrap' of the Collège de Pataphysique link him to Jarry. His post-graduate thesis on Baudelaire indicates his interest in the symbolists. Surrealists like Phillipe Soupault and André Breton have hailed his work as a natural extension of their own. A play like *Hunger and Thirst* (*La Soif et la faim*, 1966), originally titled 'Life in the dream', is on one level a reworking of Strindbergian themes, with not only a structure derived from *To Damascus*, and disgust at existence symbolised as in *A Dream Play* by dirt covering the walls of a family home, but also a hero – simultaneously a Christ-figure and a projection of the author – whose pilgrimage in search of an elusive ideal in female form ends in a 'monastery–barracks–prison' where inmates are brainwashed into believing themselves to be poisoned by thoughts of freedom. And even though Ionesco rejects Artaud's theory of cruelty, he acknowledges his work to be following Artaud in his aim of creating a 'metaphysical' theatre, 'to change the metaphysical condition of man, to change life, but from within out and not the reverse, from the personal towards the collective', as well as in his attack on 'petit-bourgeois' attitudes as a 'false culture' that 'separates us from everything and from ourselves'. For Ionesco 'it is precisely the process of this devitalised culture, imprisoning us in an inauthentic reality which Artaud perceived' that defines one pole of his work, and his solution also parallels Artaud in the consequent 'necessity of breaking language in order to reconstitute it, in order to "touch life", to put man back in contact with the absolute'.[2]

From this perspective Ionesco's attack on the banality of social behaviour and the meaningless clichés of everyday language in parodies of family life like *The Bald Primadonna* and *Jack, or The Submission* (*Jacques, ou la soumission*, 1950, produced 1955) take on new meaning. The pressures of conformity that have produced carbon-copy characters, whose activities and relationships are therefore arbitrary and nonsensical, are not exaggerated to reveal human existence itself as absurd, but only the forms of social conditioning that destroy individuality. 'Inauthenticity' is only contingent, not necessary. What is being attacked is the contemporary emphasis on rationality, with its accompanying materialism and devaluing of the subconscious or spiritual levels of the mind; a dualism which either produces a zombie-like vacuity, or perverts one half of the psyche into inhuman violence, as in *The Lesson* (*La Leçon*, 1951) where a professor is shown gaining total ascendency over the thirty-ninth in an endless series of pupils, which in each case leads to the rape and murder of an unresisting girl. This clearly relates to the sexual nature of power or the negation of individuality by the educational system, but on a more basic level it is an image for the domination of the intellect (in the rather over-obvious symbol of the professor) over the instinctive and physical side of human nature (the student being finally reduced to an awareness of herself solely as a body). In this symbiotic couple the Professor can only establish his dominance by repressing the Pupil's natural vitality, and the result is insanity. The point is even more explicit in *Rhinocéros* (1959), where the surface reference is political, the metaphor for men turning into rhinoceroses coming from Ionesco's personal journal of 1940 where it is specifically used to describe the dehumanising effect of Nazi propaganda. But for Ionesco politics as such is only a symptom, and he defined the play as 'mainly an attack on collective hysteria and the epidemics that work beneath the surface of reason and ideas but are none the less serious collective diseases passed off as ideologies... concealing beneath a mask of cold objectivity the most irrational and violent pressures'.[3]

In this light the proliferation of objects in his early plays, mounting piles of coffee cups, multiplying furniture that entombs one character, or the fungoid growth of a corpse that pushes others off the sides of the stage as it expands are not intended to represent the human condition *per se*, but only the effect of materialistic rationalism. The power of Ionesco's images may have made it appear that they embody an irremediable existential state, but in fact they are supposed to be a challenge to the audience, an exaggeration revealing what we commonly define as existence to be unnatural in order to provoke rejection as well as recognition, to make us aware that we are *more* than the empty figures representing us on stage, that there is a more authentic level of existence available to us. Hence the overt travesty in *The Bald Primadonna*, where the Martins meet as strangers and only discover that they are husband and wife by learning that they live in the same house and sleep in the same bed – yet the genesis of this situation (a game played by Ionesco and his wife on the subway) demonstrates the very capacity to care and share that the play categorically states to be non-existent – or the provocation of the original ending, where the author was to come forward and shake his fist at the audience, crying 'You bastards, I'll skin you alive.'

This challenge is both subtler and more explicit in the final image of *The Chairs* (*Les Chaises*, 1952), where the whole of an invisible fashion-able society is ushered in, seated in serried ranks of chairs, sold pro-grammes and refreshments to hear 'a message for all men, for all mankind', so forming an on-stage mirror of the real audience. The Orator, as a man who rhetorically presents another's words, is the actor; and the impossibility of communicating anything meaningful rationally, since he turns out to be a deaf mute, though as an image his 'performance' contains a great deal of meaning, repeats Ionesco's own dramatic approach in microcosm. This non-existent on-stage 'audience', described only in superficial and social terms by profes-sion or dress, reacts in a purely rational manner once the Orator leaves – 'snatches of laughter, whisperings, a "Ssh!" or two little sarcastic coughs',[4] sound effects clearly designed to duplicate the probable response of the real audience – and we are left with a vision of ourselves as a void. The intention of this ending was specifically to block rational psychological interpretations of the play that could lead *The Chairs* to be seen as a *folie à deux*. Dramatically, the old couple and their dialogue, which comprises the 'action' in a conventional sense, is no more than a prologue. The whole weight is on that final stage picture: on the audience as 'an absence of people', on 'the unreality of the world, metaphysical emptiness'. Yet obviously the real audience cannot be actually made to feel that they do not exist. To claim that what we are accustomed to accept as 'reality' (which after all is only a concept – as Ionesco agrees 'the world is a subjective and arbitrary creation of our own minds') is illusory, presupposes that other levels or alternative definitions of reality, represented by the Orator's 'ANGEPAIN . . . ADIEU' (Angelbread . . . God), are at least as valid. And if anything the spectator is being made aware that he does indeed exist, though only in very different terms to the 'nothingness' by which his social and material being is represented on the stage. For Ionesco the conceptual structure of reality is on the point of collapse, and his plays are 'helping to accelerate this process of disintegration', by reproducing in the spectator those states of awareness 'that could set the world ablaze, that could transfigure it' for him, and which he describes in his personal memoir:

first of all, every notion, every reality was emptied of its content. After this emptiness, after this dizzy spell, it was as if I found myself at the centre of pure, ineffable existence... I became one with the essential reality... Thus my mind could find its centre again, reunited, assembled out of the matrixes and limits [i.e., material objects, social organisations, grammatical structures, logical connections] within which it had been dispersed.[5]

In his early work the emphasis is on creating the pre-condition for this 'transcendence'. And it is this that explains the breakdown of language and the reduction of those logical concepts, like time, by which we structure our lives, not just to farcical absurdity, but to arbitrariness (as in *The Bald Primadonna*, where a clock strikes the hours out of sequence and irrelevantly). In the same way the menacing magnification and proliferation of objects in a human vacuum, where characters are literally 'dispersed' by reduplication and therefore lack inner being, and even the characteristic rhythm of his plays, with their mad mathematics of 'dizzying' geometrical progression and acceleration that he compares to Feydeau's farce, are designed to drain all social and material existence of meaning, while simultaneously accentuating its external qualities to the point where it becomes unendurable. But the purpose of this apparent negation is to persuade the audience to affirm the (carefully unstated) opposite:

The universe, encumbered with matter, is then empty of presence: 'too much' links up with 'not enough' and objects are the materialisation of solitude, of the victory of the anti-spiritual forces, of everything we are struggling against. But... to feel the absurdity or improbability of everyday life and language is already to have transcended it; in order to transcend it, you must first saturate yourself in it.[6]

As he noted with reference to Kafka, it is 'when man is cut off from... his religious or metaphysical roots' that activity becomes senseless, and this is his real criticism of society. Ionesco's vision is essentially a religious one, even if it stands outside 'official' theologies, and it is here that his apparently 'Absurd' work links up with the preoccupations of Brook or Grotowski. The motive force behind this transcendence, what makes it possible for man to escape from the 'stereotype' to which he has been reduced by society is 'God', defined as 'the universal energy that we partake of and participate in... a universal consciousness';[7] and in a play like *Victims of Duty* both poles of his vision are presented, the 'forgotten archetypes' as well as the stereotypes.

On one level this is the 'pseudo-drama' its sub-title calls it, with the same emphasis on the inauthenticity of socially defined existence. There are the expected transferable identities and confusions between different people with similar names (Madeleine changes from dull housewife to siren, to old woman, to the detective's mistress; the anarchist who murders the detective takes his place; the 'problem' of the play is whether the previous tenant of the Chouberts' apartment spelt his name 'Mallot' with a 'd' or a 't'), and the usual multiplying objects (by the end the whole stage is piled with the coffee cups of social convention), plus the theme of repressive conformity. On this level the play is also a parody of all the traditional dramatic assumptions about intellectually analysable meanings, logical motivation, or cause-and-effect plot, since, according to Choubert, 'All the plays that have ever been written, from Ancient Greece to the present day, have never been anything but thrillers. Drama's always been realistic and there's always been a detective about. Every play's an investigation brought to a successful solution.' Against this is set the anarchist's ideal of drama, which is specifically identified with Ionesco's work:

D'EU: The theatre of my dreams would be irrationalist... Inspiring me with a different logic and a different psychology, I should introduce contradiction where there is no contradiction... We'll get rid of the principle of identity and unity of character and let movement and dynamic psychology take its place... The characters lose their form in the formlessness of becoming.[8]

And this, with its almost explicit echoes of Strindberg's preface to *A Dream Play*, is also an accurate description of the play itself, where the detective's 'investigation' becomes a search into the Chouberts' subconscious and the banality of the Chouberts' bourgeois sitting-room dissolves into the protagonist's psyche. The empty reality of material objects and socialised people becomes dreamlike, while dreams become real.

In Ionesco's own production of *Victims of Duty* in 1968 in Zürich, it was this level of the play that he emphasised. Outlining his motive for writing as 'spontaneous research' into 'the unconscious', he stated that the scenes were transcriptions of his own dreams – in particular the central sequence where the protagonist, entangled in a wood, sinks down into a bottomless pit of mud, reappears as a child and climbs up a ladder to fly in a strong blue light – and noted that these were dreams which Jung had classified, thus linking his subjective experience with archetypes. The social surface was only to be considered as the catalyst for this transcendence. Conventional identity, already empty on that level, dissolved into projections of the psyche, affirming the awareness of 'true' personality on a fundamental, universal plane, and Ionesco explained to the actors that

the main theme . . . is the revolt against the Super-ego and the defeat of this Super-ego. The policeman – that is censorship, the conscience of society, which is also the father, that is the incarnation of society – is killed by the anarchist . . . Like all new, revolutionary tyrannies this tyranny too sets Choubert back in the social order and imposes on him the behaviour of a child, that is of a repressed person . . . a Super-ego with the beard of an anarchist.[9]

From this perspective Choubert becomes the ego, 'the inner I', Madeleine the id and the stage a mindscape, with Madeleine and the detective acting as twining creeper and tree in the forest. 'In my original vision . . .' was repeatedly used by Ionesco, prefacing his directives to the actors. Their portrayal of the roles had to correspond to his original dream, and the figures were not to be presented in psychological terms as individuals. Their changes in age, relationship or attitude were sudden switches intended to reproduce the startling transformations, arbitrary contrasts and irrationality of dreams, and the actors were forbidden to search for personal motivations. At the same time the dream sequences were acted with as much physical realism as possible. The descent was illusionistic with Choubert, lit by a green light from beneath, gradually sinking through a trap downstage centre, while for the flight a ladder was lowered from the flies and the actor's climb was real, not mimed. This followed Ionesco's principle that 'authentic realism only exists in concrete images', which is the only way 'essences' can be represented in art.[10]

It is on this surrealistic, Jungian level that Ionesco sees his drama as myth, a point he makes repeatedly in calling for a universal and 'primitive . . . drama of myth' springing 'from the soul of the people' (by extension his own, a subjective problem at its most fundamental expressing 'the problems and fears of literally everyone'), or drawing an explicit parallel: 'truth lies in our dreams . . . there is nothing truer than myth'. Almost all of his later plays are interpretable as dreams; in *Exit the King* (*Le Roi se meurt*, 1962) the stage is literally the consciousness of Bérenger, Ionesco's self-projection, whose castle is the inside of his head which disintegrates in death as he and the figures representing the different elements of his psyche dissolve into the neutral gray light of nothingness; while transcendence in the image of flying recurs in *Amédée* (1954) and *A Stroll in the Air* (*Le Piéton de l'air*, 1963), though in none of his plays can this state of integrated and liberated awareness of being be maintained, reflecting Ionesco's personal experience of its transitoriness. Myth therefore exists more as a potential in his plays than an actuality, though his consistent dramatic aim has been to create a 'drama that is not symbolist, but symbolic; not allegorical, but mythical; that springs from our everlasting anguish'.[11]

It may be largely the association of Ionesco with 'the Theatre of the Absurd' that has given his work its popularity by setting it within a comprehensible intellectual framework, but this has led to a misleading emphasis on such themes as the isolation of the individual, the meaninglessness of human activity and the attack on a mechanical civilisation. In other words the negative preliminary part of his visionary process is taken as the whole, and the mythic and metaphysical dimension of his plays, with its return to 'primitive roots' in the subconscious, tends to be overlooked, despite such explicit statements as

For me, the theatre is the projection onto the stage of the world within . . . As I am not alone in the world, as each one of us, in the depths of his being, is at the same time everyone else, my dreams and desires, my anguish and my obsessions do not belong to myself alone; they are part of the heritage of my ancestors, a very ancient deposit to which all mankind may lay claim.[12]

As with Grotowski and Brook, one aspect of Ionesco's approach is concerned with stripping theatre to its essentials, and at an early stage of his career he had defined his aim as rediscovering the 'basic principles' of theatre and reproducing them 'in pure scenic movement'. In practice, however, for all his comparisons of theatre to abstract arts like architecture and music, this has mainly meant a deliberate naivety and led to instructions that in staging a play like *The Chairs* 'everything should be exaggerated, excessive, painful, childish, a caricature, without finesse'.[13] But in a dramatist like Samuel Beckett this stripping away of worn-out idiom has become the keynote of his development. The initial reaction to *Waiting for Godot* (1953) was that here drama had reached its minimal limits, and several critics summed up the apparent absence of dramatic action by quoting from the play: 'Nothing happens, nobody comes, nobody goes, it's awful.'[14] His following plays then progressively pared away activity as well as action. Of the four figures in *Endgame* (1957) only one can move, of the couple in *Happy Days* (1961) one is buried first to her waist then to the neck in a heap of sand while the other can only crawl with painful slowness, in *Come and Go* (1963) the characters sit almost motionless, and in *Play* (1964) only their heads protrude from the urns that contain the ashes of their bodies. W. B. Yeats may have once expressed the wish to rehearse his actors in barrels so that nothing should distract from the power of language; by contrast Beckett's progress into stasis is accompanied by increasing silence. Not only does dialogue become monologue, so that in *Happy Days* one of the two characters says only 53 words, of which 52 are in the first Act; but drama is reduced to 'a dramaticule', and *Come and Go* has only 121 words *in toto*, of which over half are repetitions with minimal variation. Until in *Breath* (1969), which lasts under two minutes, there are no characters, no dialogue, and the complete stage directions read:

Black. Then
1   Faint light on stage littered with miscellaneous unidentifiable rubbish. Hold about 5 seconds.
2   Faint cry and immediately inspiration and slow increase of light together reaching maximum in about 10 seconds. Silence and hold about 5 seconds.
3   Expiration and slow decrease of light together reaching minimum together (light as in 1) in about 10 seconds. Silence and hold about 5 seconds. Then
Black.

Rubbish: no verticals, all scattered and lying.
Cry: instant of recorded vagitus. Important that two cries be identical.
Switching on and off strictly synchronised light and breath.
Breath: amplified recording.[15]

So much critical writing has been generated on Beckett's work that all a study like this can add is a brief footnote to the readily available interpretations, which range from Christian or existentialist to Nietzschean or nihilist and from the tragic to the comic, since Beckett consistently refuses to limit the connotations of his plays by elucidating them except in gnostic ambiguities, such as 'No symbols where none intended.' All Beckett's plays present variations on the same bleak image of existence, increasingly refined to its essentials. *Breath*, for instance, is clearly a restatement of Pozzo's final insight in *Waiting for Godot* – 'They give birth astride of a grave, the light gleams an instant, then it's night once more'[16] – and this vision is quite distinct from that implied by the avant garde return to myth and ritual with its positive stress on liberating the primitive and rediscovering the 'roots' of human existence.

But there are various elements derived from the avant garde that do appear in his work, in particular the use of biblical echoes to gain mythic resonance, the ritualisation of action through geometrical movement and repetition or the stress on 'play', as well as the use of conventions associated with expressionist monodrama that has led to interpretations of *Endgame, Play* or *Not I* (1972) as interior monologues in which the characters represent different aspects of a single psyche. The basic avant garde quality of transcendence may be absent in Beckett, but there are parallels with both Strindberg and the surrealists. In particular thematic details of *A Dream Play* (one of Strindberg's draft titles was *Väntan – Waiting*) recur in *Waiting for Godot.* The tramps' inability to recognise Pozzo on his re-entry mirrors the officer's ignorance of Agnes' identity when he meets her the second time, the single stunted tree in the alley blossoms overnight just as Beckett's tree sprouts 'four or five leaves', while Estragon's name, almost but not quite an anagram of 'strange', may reflect The Stranger of *To Damascus,* and it was Blin's production of a Strindberg play that caused Beckett to send him the script of *Godot.*[17] At the same time Beckett showed an early interest in dada and surrealism, translating pieces by André Breton and Paul Eluard for a 1932 issue of *This Quarter,* in which a selection of Tristan Tzara's poems and the Dali/Buñuel script of *Un Chien Andalou* were also published. And *Not I* with its division of characters between a mouth and a silent auditor (representing 'ear' in this trilogy of perception where the audience is cast as 'eye') is reminiscent of Tzara's *Gas Heart* (*Coeur à gaz,* 1920) which has Eye, Mouth, Nose, Ear, Neck and Eyebrow as characters and a similar dialogue of *non-sequiturs* that have an initial but deceptive appearance of logical relationships. *Not I* indeed is an interior drama, with its source in a silent and motionless figure, whom Beckett observed waiting on a Tunisian street, enveloped in a djellaba and apparently listening intently, though to an inner voice since there was no other person near; and the high speed monotone delivery required for the play, punctuated by silences and screams, was intended to have a subliminal effect. As Beckett told Jessica Tandy, 'I am not unduly concerned with intelligibility. I hope the piece may work on the nerves of an audience, not its intellect.'[18]

The way Beckett uses mythic resonances is clearest in *Waiting for Godot,* where the cyclical pattern is both the eternal recurrence of human life in its deadening sameness – 'The essential doesn't change /Nothing to be done' . . . 'The tears of the world are a constant quantity. For each one who begins to weep somewhere else another stops' – and the annual vegetation cycle of primitive religion, here reduced to a near-final state of entropy. Beckett has agreed that his plays deal with the same range of human experience as religion, and explained to Jack MacGowran that the key to *Godot* was St Augustine's paradoxical doctrine of grace given and grace withheld: 'Do not despair; one of the thieves was saved. Do not presume; one of the thieves was damned.' Even though Beckett has quite rightly resisted the simplistic suggestion that 'Godot' might be equated with God, the play clearly contains this interpretation as one of its levels of ambiguity, and it does indeed end with a revelation, though at first glance this seems merely a parodistic epiphany refusing illumination since it consists of Estragon's trousers falling down around his ankles. It is hardly accidental that the dialogue is filled with fragmentary biblical allusions, while a misquotation sets the opening tone with 'Hope deferred maketh the something sick' (Proverbs, 13:12 'Hope deferred maketh the heart sick; but when the desire cometh it is a tree of life'). And as with Marlowe's use of biblical quotation in *Dr Faustus*, Beckett obviously hopes (and vainly, given today's decline in Bible-reading, thus mirroring the proverb on yet another, internal level) that his audience might supply the missing phrase, since it is what gives symbolic relevance to the single tree on stage, apparently dead and useful only for hanging oneself on, but proving to contain living sap: the cross as the 'tree of life'. The effect, of course, is ironic and depends on the almost certainty that we – like the tramps – have only a nodding acquaintance with the quotation, are unable to complete it and will therefore be teased by the possibility of a deeper and spiritual meaning, which our own ignorance alone negates. And other allusions extend the tone by setting up even vaguer echoes in the audience's mind, as in the rejection of a sound mistakenly taken for Godot's voice with 'Pah! The wind in the reeds', which plays on Christ's question about John the Baptist: 'What went ye out in the wilderness to see? A reed shaken by the wind?' As for the final revelation of Estragon's bare shanks, it is simultaneously a classic piece of music-hall farce and a real epiphany, the invisible indeed being made manifest: Behold the man! (a double image already used by Joyce, whose work Beckett knew well having helped him as an amanuensis: 'I am sorry to have to tell you, hullo and evoe, they were coming down from off him – How cullious an epiphany').[19]

The play clearly exists on two distinct but simultaneously superimposed levels, perceptions of life taken deliberately from opposite extremes of the philosophical spectrum, yet constantly interpenetrating in the action. Further evidence of this intention exists at those points where the double images fail to merge, and one contradicts the premises of the other, as with the tangible letter of the original French version, which indicates the real existence of 'Godot'. The tramps as 'all humanity' are not only subsisting in a desert of despair and mocked by delusive aspirations, but at the same time are standing on their own calvary and at the foot of the cross (mound and tree, with the road in the original French version leading to 'Holy Saviour'). The world presented is either one without God, in which actions are meaningless, and the only authentic response is to treat life as a cruel joke; or one where salvation is an ever-present possibility with passive suffering and patient waiting (both of which have the same root in Latin) as the proper spiritual preparation for grace. And although the usual interpretation explains that religious belief itself is the hope deferred – eternally being non-existent – and that any imagery of salvation is only there to be denied, its persuasiveness says more about the critics' own agnosticism (and perhaps about the pervasiveness of the theory of 'Absurd theatre') than about the play itself, which Beckett is careful to leave open. What the relative weighting is, even what is actually perceived, depends on the perspective of the individual spectator, and like the farcical epiphany the play seems designed to challenge the audience's perception, with the surface image of uncompromising bleakness and the mythic dimension offering a spiritual alternative.

As for the ritualisation of action, its function can best be indicated by Beckett's own productions of his plays. His direction of both *Godot* and *Happy Days* (Berlin 1975 and 1971) stressed situation at the expense of content, giving shape to the plays through exactly repeated moves and gestures that echoed the repetitions in the dialogue, while in *Endgame* (Berlin, 1967) his primary concern was to create a symmetrical geometry of visual patterns. Hamm's chair had to be dead centre on stage, his posture at the end identical to the opening, and in the prayer sequence the three pairs of hands and bowed heads had to form exact equilateral triangles. On one level the play is a reversal of the myth of creation, with the progress of the action – 'There are no more bicycle-wheels . . . There's no more nature . . . There's no more tide . . . no light . . . There is nothing to say' – and Clov's reaction of 'Nothing . . . nothing . . . good . . . good . . . nothing'[20] to viewing the void outside (Beckett cut all reference to the small boy seen in the landscape in his 1964 Paris production) being an almost word-for-word reversal of Genesis plus the first sentence of St John's Gospel: 'In the beginning was the word' / 'the earth was without form and void . . . And God said, Let there be light . . . Let the waters

under the heaven be gathered together... Let the earth bring forth
living creatures after his kind, cattle and creeping things... and God
saw that it was good'. Applied to this disintegrating universe, the
precise patterning which Beckett specifically referred to as 'Pythago-
rean' representing ideals of harmony and proportion, are bitterly
ironic. This effect of negative artifice, which extended to the dialogue
too, with Beckett enforcing a total separation of word and gesture,
question and reply, as well as a colourless staccato delivery, also
reduces the action to the level of 'play', and the production underlined the chess image of the title. Hamm and Clov's red faces contrasted with the white of Nagg and Nell, Clov was made to move in
zigzags, the knight's two squares forward and one to the side, while
Hamm's role was explained to the actor as 'the king in this chess
game that was lost from the beginning. He knows from the start that
he has made nothing but senseless moves.'[21] (In an end position
where only knight and king are left checkmate is impossible.)

Beckett's ritualisation has little in common with the avant garde in
its purpose, although there is a clear overlap in form. Unlike the use
of primitive quasi-religious ritual forms for hypnotic or subliminal
effects by Schechner or the Living Theatre, Beckett's geometric shap-
ing stresses artificiality rather than 'noble artifice' and consistently
threatens to reduce his themes to plays on the double meaning of the
word 'play' – hence too the self-conscious music-hall jokes that re-
mind us this is only theatre: 'I see a multitude... in transports of joy'
(Clov, with his telescope trained on the audience), 'End of the cor-
ridor on the left' (Estragon to Vladimir as he hastens into the wings to
relieve himself). Sociologists have compared games to ritual re-
enactions of combat, but the primary significance of games for Beckett
is that playing becomes its own justification, having no relevance to
real action or exterior purpose, a refusal of 'significance' being the
only significant statement possible in the meaningless world – and
this is extended to include the theatre, which is why the double
meaning of 'play' is given such weight in Beckett's drama. The
dramatist has put himself in the position of Vladimir and Estragon,
whose actions are 'sport of all sorts' to 'pass the time', and in *Endgame*
the stage literally became the board it had been (rhetorically) compared to in *Waiting For Godot*. Throughout rehearsals Beckett referred
to *Endgame* as 'simply a basis for acting', and in an unusually frank
moment he commented:

the link between individuals and things no longer exists... There are so
many things. The eye is as unable to grasp them as the intelligence to

understand them. Therefore one creates one's own world, *un univers à part* in order to withdraw ... to escape from chaos into an ever simpler world ... I have progressively simplified situations and people, *toujours plus simples* ... The value of the theatre lies for me in this. One can set up a small world with its own rules, order the game as if on a chessboard – Indeed, even the game of chess is too complicated.[22]

Adamov, Arrabal and Weiss

Where Beckett used mythic resonances and ritualistic formulisation for his own ends, others adapted the expressionist dream play or presented drama as ceremony. Arthur Adamov's early plays are an example of the first, Fernando Arrabal of the second. Both took their starting-point from Strindberg, acknowledging him as 'the master of us all' because of the central 'element of madness, of obsession' in his work (Arrabal), or admitting that it was *'A Dream Play* which incited me to write for the theatre' (Adamov);[23] and the circular structure of Arrabal's *The Grand Ceremonial* (1965) was modelled on *To Damascus*, while Adamov's *The Rediscoveries* (*Les Retrouvailles*, 1955) mirrors the final situation in *The Father* with the male protagonist reverting to infancy under a dominating mother-figure.

Adamov began as a minor member of the surrealist circle around Paul Eluard and knew Artaud well – though any Artaudian theatrical influence is indirect, coming through Blin who acted the principal role in *The Great and the Small Manoeuvre* (1950) and directed *The Parody* (1952). And the way he uses the stage to project dreams, or bases his plays on subjective neuroses is straight in the surrealist mainstream with its location of reality in the subconscious. While the structure of short, non-sequential scenes separated by momentary blackouts in a play like *The Parody* is typically expressionistic, as is the juxtaposition of public and interior scenes, and the way 'tableaux should succeed each other almost instantaneously. Quasi-cinematographic sequence'.[24] But however expressionistic this may be as a technique to slip images through under the threshold of rational thought in a way that could be compared to subliminal advertising, the image it initially evokes is one of human existence as dislocated and absurd, of life reduced to a 'parody' by the absence of the spiritual dimension. In Adamov's paradoxical drama, absence is the most oppressive form of presence – a direct reversal of Ionesco's terms of reference, yet one that indicates shared concerns – so that the meaningless and self-defeating activities of his empty, puppet-like characters is not only a bitter vision of the contemporary human condition, in which 'degenerated concepts, dried-up abstractions' are all that remain of 'the old sacred names', the word 'God' having been 'so long degraded by usage that it no longer means anything', but simultaneously a challenge to affirm the existence of what is missing: 'the unfathomable wisdom of the myths and rites of the dead old world'.[25] This is clearest in a play like *The Invasion* (1950), where a scholar searches for a transcendental meaning in the jumbled mass of fading and indecipherable papers left by a dead author. The obvious interpretation is that existence is without meaning or redemption, a random (and sordid) entanglement. But on another level the 'invasion' is the awareness of the possibility that there may indeed be meaning to existence. And the overwhelming need for such a meaning, which becomes an obsession that drives the scholar into isolation and suicide, could equally be seen as ultimate proof of its value. It is only by taking the surface statement of his early plays as containing the whole of their content that Adamov can be labelled as belonging to the 'Theatre of the Absurd', and it is partly this misapprehension which has led to the general assumption that there is a radical split between these and his later plays. But the difference is more a shift in tactics than a change in theme, and the belief in a potential meaning for existence, which is not so much absent as provocatively omitted from his early work, led naturally to his later political commitment.

Adamov's early plays are, as it were, a negative transposition of avant garde principles. As with Ionesco, personal vision is taken as representative of everyone's experience on the subconscious level (Adamov's enthusiasm for Jung led him to translate *The Ego and the Subconscious* into French). But Adamov's dream projections are used to reveal the repressive psycho-social blocks that cut man off from the spirit, rather than the potential for transcendence, and so concentrate on the neurotic: 'since the particular is always a symbolic expression of the universal, it follows that the universal is most effectively symbolised by the extreme of the particular, so that the neurosis which exaggerates a man's particularity of vision defines its universal significance that much more completely.[26] In these early plays the police-state society of victimisation and repression is a materialisation of man's psychological condition in the contemporary world. *The Great* [subconscious] *and the Small* [social] *Manoeuvre* defines the parallel, and there is no essential difference between the interior voices its crippled protagonist is compelled to obey, as a result of which he becomes progressively mutilated, and the impersonal voice over the radio at the beginning of each scene in *Each Against All* (*Tous contre tous*, 1953), which determines the treacherous pattern of reciprocal persecution.

Like *The Great and the Small Manoeuvre*, the autobiographical *Professor Taranne* (1951), singled out by Adamov as the most significant of his early plays, is the 'direct transcription of a dream without seeking to give it a general meaning, to prove anything'. Both plays centre on masochistic self-destruction, but here the professor's loss of identity does not seem as purely negative as it is usually said to be, since the personality that is stripped from him is defined solely by an academic reputation based on plagiarism. Here the neurosis, an obsession with identity and the corresponding fear that one has no real existence, was clearly an expression of Adamov's own psychological state, the only difference between his dream and the play being that he shouted out 'I am the author of *The Parody*' instead of 'I am Professor Taranne';[27] but the actual implications of the action have a positive aspect. The fake attributes that are stripped away epitomise a materialistic and intellectualising civilisation, and the image of the professor removing all his clothes on the beach – the 'crime' for which he is arrested at the beginning and the tableau we are left with at the end, when he disrobes in front of a blank seating-plan that was to have placed him at 'the table of honour on an ocean liner' – is surely not so much an image signifying the helpless loss of identity as one of a man divesting himself of his social *persona* (by definition false) and returning to the natural condition symbolised by nakedness. As for the seating-plan, 'a huge grey surface, uniform, absolutely void': this is usually taken to represent his complete loss of any authentic being or existence.[28] But it would seem much more logical to see it as standing instead for the emptiness of the society rejected.

Adamov has gained a considerable reputation in France, which has helped to popularise the avant garde approach, culminating in a mammoth collage of his early plays and autobiographical writing by Roger Planchon at the Théâtre National Populaire in 1975 – although what this production effectively, if unintentionally, demonstrated were the flaws inherent in his 'world of archetypes'. The effect of staging several plays together underlined their undramatic stasis, the repetitiveness of the images, and the two-dimensional allegorical nature of the characters: flaws that Adamov himself was aware of, admitting that he 'suffered from the limitation imposed on me by the vagueness of the place, the schematisation of the characters, the symbolism of the situations'.[29]

Similar failings, without the same capacity for objective self-evaluation, recur in the work of Arrabal, who has translated some of

Adamov's plays into Spanish and perhaps even over-emphasises Adamov's influence – as well as admiring Grotowski, Brook and the Living Theatre, all of whom he classifies with himself as 'Seneca's descendants'. Following Adamov, Arrabal has described most of his plays as dramatised nightmares: 'direct manifestations of my inner world as revealed through my dreams . . . The visual – the dream – is my starting point.' But his emphasis on 'ceremony' (the external and formalised surface of his plays) together with the provocative extremism of his themes, his scatological obscenity, blasphemy and sado-masochistic eroticism, gives an impression of willed fantasy rather than true subconscious experience. This overt intention to shock, however, is more than simply *épater les bourgeois*. It is central to his aim of creating a 'panic theatre', which would arouse the same irrational and primitive terror in the presence of nature as the god Pan, though he also uses the term 'pan' in the sense of 'all-encompassing': 'For me the theatre remains a ceremony; it's a feast both sacrilegious and sacred, erotic and mystic, which would encompass all facets of life, including death . . .'[30]

Arrabal associates excess with poetry, but in practice his extremism limits his vision to private caprice rather than expanding it to the universal. The hunchbacks and cripples in his plays reflect the horrified fascination that he claims is his reaction to the physical side of existence 'particularly during those moments when I feel myself assailed by a sterile lucidity'. Where he depicts lovers, they whip their women, who beg to be chained to beds or children's prams. They caress passionately, but always prove incapable of consummating their relationships, preserving their 'purity' by killing instead of coitus, or by choosing life-size dolls and dead, or almost-dead bodies as objects of their lust – again quite explicitly and consciously reflecting neurotic obsessions: 'the temptations inherent in purity', which according to Arrabal 'fascinate me even to the point of nausea', and his apparent belief that any erotic gratification except masturbation would defile his poetic inspiration.[31] Most strikingly his strong Catholic upbringing is perverted into a deliberately blasphemous evocation of the sacred in plays like *The Solemn Communion* (*La Communion Solennelle*, 1965), where a young girl, ceremoniously attired in an 'unbelievably baroque dress', is 'initiated' by killing a necrophiliac, who copulates in a coffin, or *The Automobile Graveyard* (*Le Cimetière des*

---

24 Arrabal's costume designs for *The Solemn Communion*: ceremonials, eroticism & perversion.

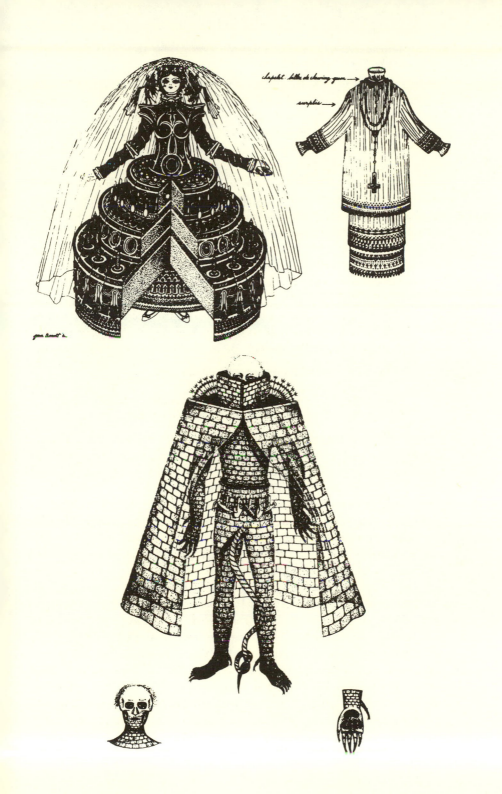

voitures, 1957), where the protagonist Emanou (Emmanual) – who steals, lies, is hypocritical and promiscuous and admits to killing a Jew – repeats Christ's Passion in the parody setting of a vast scrap-heap: born in a stable, betrayed to the police by a kiss from one of his group of musicians while the other denies knowing him, crucified on the handle-bars of a bicycle.

Perhaps the most interesting variant on this theme is *The Architect and the Emperor of Assyria* (*L'Architecte et l'Empereur d'Assyrie*, 1967), where the very vehemence of the denial of God becomes a paradoxical way of asserting his existence. The make-believe 'emperor', the sole survivor of an air crash who lands on a desert island inhabited by a single savage, has three interrelated obsessions. Having failed to prove the existence of God on a pin-ball machine by achieving the 'impossible' score of 1,000 with a single ball (a drunk 'tilted' the table at 999), he attempts to provoke God to turn him into a pillar of salt by moving as he relieves himself so that his faeces trace the words 'God is a son of a bitch' on the beach. He also plays out a mock Passion:

> How can I redeem humanity singlehanded?
> *He mimes the crucifixion . . .*
> The feet, yes. I can nail them better than the centurion but . . .
> *His gestures show that nailing the hands is a problem.*

His second obsession, power, is linked to this through the figure of the emperor he dreams of being: Nebuchadnezzar, whom God punished for pride by making him believe himself an animal 'till thou know that the most High ruleth in the kingdom of men' (Daniel 4:25). And in the fantasies acted out during the play he not only pretends to be a horse, cow, dog and sacred elephant, but at one point finds a pair of horns really growing on his forehead. The action is solely composed of these fragmentary ritualised games of domination, strongly reminiscent of the 'ceremonies' of the *cérébraux* in Genet's 'grand balcony'. The 'emperor' and the savage he has dominated and drawn into his sexual fantasies play out the roles of tyrant and slave, corpse and sexton, priest and penitent nun, woman–mother and lover–son (as in Arrabal's other plays, passion is represented by flagellation) and finally judge and accused. In the trial, where the 'emperor' acts not only as the criminal – himself – but as all the witnesses, including his mother whom his evidence reveals as his victim, the game becomes reality because it embodies the third obsession, which also incorporates the other two. He has murdered and eaten his mother (he claims to have fed her to his dog, linking her with the biblical

Jezebel, but his games have already shown him in the role of his dog), and as expiation demands to be killed and eaten by his judge – the savage – dressed in his mother's clothes. His body is laid on an altar-like table and this cannibalism is presented as a blasphemous mass; but one in which God is finally manifested, though in a typically perverted form. Water miraculously turns into Jeyes' fluid, instead of the expected wine, proving that 'there is an afterlife . . . beyond'; and there is a real transubstantiation: 'the ARCHITECT assumes the voice, tone, features and expressions of the EMPEROR' as he digests his body, finally becoming him (the actors switch roles) when he eats his brain. Typically too this is performed in a way designed to arouse visceral revulsion:

Thanks to your nucleic acid I shall be master of your memory, your dreams . . . and your thoughts. *He taps on the chisel placed behind the* EMPEROR'S *ear. He makes a hole: he sticks the straw in: he sucks out the brain, a substance like yoghourt trickles down his cheeks. He licks it.* Ooh![32]

Like most of Arrabal's work, this is presented as a dream, though in a rather self-conscious way that is perhaps intended to make it possible for the audience to subliminate their probable feelings of disgust, which might lead them simply to reject the play, by interpreting the action on a metaphoric rather than actual level, as images from the subconscious rather than representations of real events. Even the scatological blasphemy of the 'emperor's' defecating habits is illusory, since he is permanently constipated, and it is specifically stated that the characters are 'not in the real world'. To wake out of the dream they only have to clap their hands, which the 'emperor' ostentatiously refuses to do, while the visionary nature of the fantasy is underlined by comparing it to Hieronymus Bosch's painting of the 'Garden of Delights'.[33] At the same time this is a monodrama. Both characters are opposing facets of the same universalised personality, as the ending clearly demonstrates when the savage-transformed-to-emperor, once more alone on the island, hears a plane crash and the 'architect' enters as a sole survivor to repeat the opening of the play with reversed roles. The savage represents the primitive side of man, with magical powers that enable him to speak to animals, move mountains, turn day to night – all of which he loses as he takes on the emperor's attributes. The dominating intruder represents the civilising intellect, flattering himself on a cultural heritage and proud of a philosophy that has produced only death (war games) and sexual repression. The action is endlessly repeated both because on the religious level ritual sacrifice leads to resurrection, and because on the psychological level any element of the personality that is repressed reappears in a new form.

In Arrabal's plays, which he claims are written 'spontaneously', the avant garde exploration of dream states, primitivism and ritual has become prostituted by an all too literal attempt to realise Artaud's call for 'a new idea of eroticism and cruelty'. Even the so-called innocence of Arrabal's retarded characters, whose incest and murder, sadism and suicide are performed with child-like unconsciousness of the consequences, appears as a further perversion; and he was apparently flattered by a description of his work as 'midway between de Sade and St Theresa of Avila'. As one of his characters says: 'Why am I presenting you with this catalogue of horrors? . . . I want to dazzle you.'[34] Indeed it is only a quality of crude simplicity in presentation that saves his fantasies from pornography. At the same time similar shock effects are characteristic of contemporary drama, and the same image of cannibalism as simultaneously a religious mass and a quasi-sexual comm-union, reused by Arrabal in *The Young Barbarians of Today* (*Jeunes barbares d'aujourd'hui*, 1975), recurs in plays like Heiner Müller's *Slaughter* (*Die Schlacht*, 1976) or Edward Bond's *Early Morning* (where it is given an additional rationale as a metaphor for capitalist competition).

But the mythic dimension is not limited to existential or psycho-sexual drama, which has obvious thematic links with the avant garde and might be called its natural extension. It also appears in a strictly political documentary such as *The Investigation* (*Die Ermittlung*, 1965) or *Vietnam-Discourse* (1968). Peter Weiss began his career with sur-realist films. Like Adamov and Arrabal he was strongly influenced by Kafka, and an early play like *Night Visitors* (*Nacht mit Gästen*, 1962) has similar child-like characters who act with murderous violence in an irrational dream atmosphere.

The Investigation was Weiss' response to a public challenge to German authors to use Auschwitz as artistic material, and on the surface it is a straight duplication of the trial transcript published in the *Frankfurter Allgemeine Zeitung*. Immediacy and authenticity seem to be the criteria, and the text has an apparently objective, neutral tone. The only 'plot' is the historical progress of prisoners from the concentration camp gates to the crematorium, and the audience's abhorrence at the recitation of appalling conditions and inhuman actions is intensified by the substitution of clinical, quasi-scientific terms for emotive words in the original transcript. This gives the impression that the events described are not only real but horrifyingly normal, since Weiss' aim is to create revulsion against the present social system, which is seen as containing exactly the same seeds as fascism, and the state-approved extermination of Auschwitz is not presented as an aberration but as the 'logical and ultimate consequence' of economic exploitation.[35] The functional language, presenting genocide in terms of production and consumption, like the consistent transfer of active tenses into passive, focusses on the system rather than individual responsibility, and there are no 'characters' as such. The witnesses are referred to as 'anonymous ... mouthpieces', while the accused are only superficially personalised to indicate the spuriousness (from a Marxist perspective) of bourgeois concepts of individuality, having names but reacting in protest or approbation as a group. The staccato and irregular free-verse lines are designed to inhibit emotional expression, and the culminative effect of lists and repetitions is substituted for conventionally dramatic climaxes. In production *The Investigation* was presented as nearly as possible as an actual trial. The audience were either associated with the witnesses or the accused by having the actors seated among them, and one performance opened with the announcement 'court in session: Please rise', while others – in sharp contrast to normal theatre – displayed placards pointing out that applause was inappropriate.

At first glance nothing could be further from the avant garde approach. Indeed the impression of factuality is so dominant that Bernd Naumann (whose newspaper reports of the trials Weiss listed as his primary source) claimed that Weiss' 'falsification' of evidence in introducing interpretation as if it were testimony or altering the sequence of speeches invalidated the play as a drama. But the reportage conceals a mythical structure, indicated by the sub-title of 'Oratorio in 11 Cantos'; and it is this which carries the real theme of the play on a subliminal level – so much so that the first production of the play was conceived, with Weiss' approval, as a 'Third Testament': 'Here the theatre re-enters the realm of religious ritual, which it had left. It turns back from the regions of the purely aesthetic ... and becomes the ritual exorcism of an incomprehensible fate; the most moving and meaningless Passion in world history.'[36]

While writing *The Investigation*, Weiss published two articles in which he discussed Dante's 'comprehensive allegory', claiming to 'have something of this totality in eye',[37] and the eleven sections of his play are each sub-divided into three scenes so that their total corresponds to the thirty-three cantos of *The Divine Comedy*. The 'perfect number' three with its religious connotations recurs in its prime form or in multiplications throughout the play. There are three judges, nine witnesses, eighteen accused, and the third witness is the key figure who spells out the political significance of the facts. On one level this symbolic numerology seems in bitterly ironic contrast to the realities expressed within it. But if the camp is seen as literally 'the inferno', this structure has a utopian function that shifts the weight of the play decisively from the past to the future. Unlike Dante's metaphysical vision, this is a secularised reality. If hell exists here and now, paradise is also a material possibility, and political revolution replaces spiritual purification (purgatory). This interpretation is backed up by Weiss' choice of words in one of his Dante essays, where he refers to exploring social situations on the stage so as to provoke the sort of political action that would be 'an absolution' through changing existing conditions. It is also reinforced by the concept of the play as an oratorio (in musical terms a *celebration* of the Passion) and not a requiem, since the significance of the crucifixion lies in the resurrection – in Weiss' terms the social ascendency of the masses to a heaven on earth – and the ending of the play is therefore left open, no judgement being given.

This use of a subliminal structure for giving a perspective to what appears at first glance a documentary compilation of facts has been largely overlooked by Weiss' critics. But he obviously found it of value, even it it was not consciously perceived by audiences, and he reused the pattern more overtly in *Discourse on Vietnam*. Here not one but two 'phases' are given, though the numerology is left deliberately incomplete, with only two acts of eleven scenes each – twenty-two out of the 'perfect' thirty-three. Act I presents Vietnamese history as a repeated pattern of oppression and exploitation corresponding to the 'inferno' of Auschwitz: 'All that changed in thousands of years / The names of the rulers.' Act II deals with the struggle against the Americans, representing the revolutionary purgatory, and the final speech points to the missing third 'phase' – the communist ideal of triumphant world revolution, the paradise that will complete the numerical structure:

> What we have shown
> is the beginning
> The fight goes on.[38]

Again it is the patterning with its mythical connotations that carries the real meaning, not the historical analysis or the conventional elements of dialogue and dramatic situation.

Shakespearean adaptations

As Ruby Cohn has pointed out, the most obvious reason for adapting Shakespeare's plays is to modernise them.[39] In the past this usually meant rewriting scenes and altering endings to correspond to the ethos of the age, the classic example being Nahum Tate's notorious version of *King Lear* with its rationalisation of the plot, giving Cordelia and Edgar a motive for their actions by introducing a romance between them, and its final rescue of Lear and Cordelia, which accurately reflected the so-called Age of Reason's ideals of sentiment, logic and poetic justice. This is still generally the case. Brecht's version of *Coriolanus* (1952) or Edward Bond's *Lear* (1972) reflect current political issues – class warfare and the triumph of a people's democracy over the military aristocracy, or the self-defeating necessities of power and the self-sacrificing activism that may eventually succeed in dismantling the structures of fear and repression – while Stoppard's *Rosencrantz and Guildenstern Are Dead* (1966) expresses the existential philosophy fashionable in the early sixties. It should also be noted that all of these three examples seem to use Shakespeare's play, or their audiences' awareness of it, as alien imaginative material, and either present an action so different that it only bears a paradigmatic relation to the original, or decisively alter the perspective, to create a dialectical oposition between their themes and Shakespeare's vision. This is partly because adapters from Bernard Shaw to Bond have been motivated by a reaction against the general romanticisation of Shakespeare: 'as a society we use the play [*King Lear*] in a wrong way. And it's for that reason I would like to rewrite it so that we now have to use the play for ourselves, for our society, for our time, for our problems.'[40] However, from the end of the sixties on there have been a whole series of adaptations that these general observations do not apply to, since instead of modernising their Shakespearean material they emphasise primitive or mythic elements, and instead of attacking the popular images of Shakespeare they use these as subliminal echoes to evoke pre-intellectual responses. In a sense the whole avant garde movement began by adapting Shakespeare in the parody of *Ubu roi*. But these new adaptations are serious (sometimes to the point of pretentiousness) and must be seen as an attempt to align the avant garde approach with the cultural mainstream, although they were still treated by critics as experimental theatre. So it is hardly accidental that many of them dealt with *Macbeth*, the play Jan Kott had picked out as the archetypal modern tragedy in *Shakespeare Our Contemporary* (1961).

The two 'collages' that reached the stage in 1969, Marowitz's *A Macbeth* and Schechner's *Makbeth*, are representative. Even the earliest adaptation of the play (William Davenant, 1674) had enlarged the role of the witches. But in these versions the supernatural became totally predominant. For Marowitz the killing of Duncan represented 'the murder of God' and Macbeth kills 'not for kingship but to experience the ecstasy of such an action'. While in Schechner's interpretation Duncan is 'the Primal Father' with Cawdor, Malcolm, Macduff and Banquo as his sons, all of whom share the impulse to kill him, so that Macbeth's murder of Duncan is a form of titanic rebellion embodying an archetypal psychological conflict. In both the witches are omnipresent and omnipotent. As 'Dark Powers' in *Makbeth* they played the roles of all the common people – soldiers, messengers, servants – as well as representing 'female energy', which according to Schechner was repressed in 'this patriarchal world' and so forced to operate 'behind the scenes, from underneath, in the guise of Lady Macbeth and . . . the energy and anger of the masses, the workers, the exploited'. As voodoo spirits in *A Macbeth* they 'infiltrate' Lady Macbeth's body 'as the spirit of the dead occupies the frame of a human being designated as a medium', and they not only initiate the action but determine every detail by homeopathic magic. Taking Macbeth's line 'To crown my thoughts with acts / Be it thought and done' literally, they 'don the costumes of Lady Macduff and child, and act out the murder Macbeth has envisaged. In the world of black magic it is possible to destroy an enemy by simulating his death . . . it follows "naturally" that Macduff learns his wife and children have been slain.'[41]

Although this focus was clearly derived from Orson Welles' 'Voodoo *Macbeth*' of 1936, there is an essential difference which marks the atavistic avant garde influence. Welles set the play in nineteenth-century Haiti, where primitive superstition might be more credible; and although voodoo drumming and chants formed an insistent background to the murders of Duncan, Banquo and Macduff's family, Hecate was a flesh-and-blood priest – the leader of the voodoo chorus – Banquo's ghost was a death mask, and the supernatural was only present as an atmosphere, a belief of the uneducated characters that the premise of the production demonstrated to be unreal. By contrast Marowitz's version presupposed that 'diabolical intention, devoutly held and fastidiously practised, unquestionably produces tangible results', and he claimed that by 'tackling the play in terms of pre-Christian belief, in terms of spells and hexes, I have found a diabolical centre... in restoring the play to its proper "religious" setting, it begins to operate more organically'. At the same time this supernatural 'reality' was located in the subconscious as a hallucination imposed on Macbeth by the witchcraft of his 'possessed' wife: 'What we see on stage is only a reflection of what Macbeth sees, and so all questions of reality have to be referred back to the psychotic protagonist through whose distorted vision we view the play.' Actions are doubled and characters multiplied as in the Strindbergian dreamplay convention – the murders of Duncan and Banquo are performed twice, at one point there are three identically dressed Macbeths on stage – and as in Marowitz's earlier Collage *Hamlet*, the simultaneous and discontinuous scenes were intended to mirror 'the broken and fragmentary way in which most people experience contemporary reality', involving the spectators subliminally through structure as well as by using 'a stream of images' (Shakespeare's original play) that were assumed to be dormant in their minds.[42]

Similarly in Schechner's *Makbeth* the major image was 'totemistic cannibal feasting', and the final script was arrived at by threading together 'association exercises' (in which random fragments of Shakespeare's text were used to evoke the personal fantasies of the performers), while all the formal elements of the production were designed to liberate a corresponding level of subconscious activity in the spectators. Narrative and character were replaced by spatial and sonic structures. The performance area, which encompassed the audience, was divided into distinct 'territories' for each group of 'archetypal characters' ('Doers', Macbeth and Lady Macbeth; 'Victims/ Founders', Duncan and Banquo; 'Avengers', Malcolm and Macduff; and 'Dark Powers'), while a central 'table' was the 'no-man's-land' each group struggled to control. And a vocal score was composed by Paul Epstein 'to replace dramatic (linear) text with choral (simultaneous) textures', distorting the form of words to create tonal patterns, and 'layering' speeches by dividing them between different voices or having them spoken as 'rounds' in which themes were repeated and varied as descants. In many ways the production was unsuccessful, but the intention was well illustrated by the 'maze' that the audience had to find their way through before entering the performance area. Life-size photographs from previous (traditional) *Macbeth*s, placards bearing well-known lines from the play and mirrors formed the irregular walls of a twisting passage with dim lighting imitated from Madame Tussaud's Chamber of Horrors, where it makes spectators seem to merge with exhibits and tableaux apparently come to life. As the designer commented, the result was 'frankly disorienting. Walls turn into mirrors. and mirrors into walls. Spectators bump into each other and excuse themselves for having jostled what turn out to be only reflections, and the audience begins to be joined with the distorted and reorganised fragments of the Macbeth legend.'[43]

Ionesco's *Macbett* shares the same dream quality of doubling action and multiplying characters, though his play is more open to political interpretation and Macbett's dying word, 'Merde' is a deliberate echo of Ubu's opening statement. Every figure carries the personalities of others as potentials within them. The same actress plays Lady Macbett and a (beautiful and naked) witch who transforms herself into Lady Duncan – in Ionesco's version Duncan is given a wife, and since this pair assassinated the previous ruler to gain his position, murder becomes simply the established means of transferring power. Macbett and Banco are indistinguishable, wearing identical costumes and beards, speaking the same long monologue on bloodshed with the same gestures and repeating the rebellious speeches of Candor and Glamiss word for word, while the witches' call to Macbett is '*alter ego surge!*' Again the witches not only represent subconscious urges in the characters but also supernatural forces who control every detail of the action – though the characters tend, mistakenly, to explain them away as simply the logic of events:

MACBETT: We are not masters of the happenings we provoke... Everything that occurs is the opposite of what one wished to come to pass... It is not man who rules events, but events that rule mankind.

As a result of this break in the causal link between will and consequence there is no question of guilt. What is presented (in Macbett's words) is a 'senseless world, where the best of men are far worse than the wicked', and the play with its circular structure is an image of existence as surrealistic cruelty. The vision of future kings is a line-up of historical and mythical monsters from Genghis Khan to man-eating giants and Jarry's King Ubu. The keynote is struck by the twice-repeated description of life in death:

MACBETT/BANCO: ... Millions died of terror or committed suicide. Tens of millions of others died of anger, apoplexy or grief. Not enough land left to bury them all. The bloated bodies of the drowned have soaked up all the water of the lakes... Not enough vultures to rid us of all this carrion flesh. And to think there are some left who go on fighting!

And the ending intensifies the opening picture of unrelieved tyranny, epitomised by the serried ranks of guillotines filling the rear of the stage, as the originally deceptive speech in which Malcolm tests Macduff's loyalty becomes a proclamation of official policy:

MACOL: ... My poor country shall have more vices than it ever had before; more suffer, and more sundry ways than ever, by him that shall succeed. *While* MACOL *is making his declaration murmurs of despair and stupefaction can be heard. At the end of this speech no one at all will be left around* MACOL. ... Confound all unity on earth! Let us, to start with, make this Archduchy a Kingdom – of which I am King. An Empire, of which I am Emperor. A Super-Highness, Super-Sire, Super-Majesty, Emperor of all the emperors...
He disappears into the mist. [44]

The exaggeration of this 'jeu de massacre' may be intended as farcical – for Ionesco *'Macbett* is a comedy nonetheless. I hope that people will laugh'[45] – but Heiner Müller uses much the same extremism to form an unambiguous image of Artaudian cruelty in his version of *Macbeth* (also 1972). Müller claims to be working within Brecht's 'epic' form of theatre, and his latest work is a rewriting of Brecht's 'teaching play', *The Measures Taken*, but his aim is 'to swamp' his audience instead of imposing a distanced, objective attitude. He interprets Brecht's scientific theatre as a 'laboratory for social fantasy', stresses the concept of 'drama as process' (rather than product) by 'fragmenting the action', and sees it as 'only effective when the audience are swept into the action from the start'. The result is an openly irrational and mythic drama intended to create an image that the spectator will both identify with subliminally and find unendurable: 'the time for intervening to alter something is always less. Consequently there is really no more time for discursive dramaturgy, for a calm presentation of factual content.'[46]

Müller cuts Shakespeare's verse to the bone and transforms every incident into a perspective of horror illustrating the theme that

> The world has no exit but the knacker
> With knives to the knife is life's course.

Macduff's sword nails the porter to the door he was slow to open, Banquo's murderers castrate him and take his genitals to Macbeth to prove that he is dead, a lord is skinned alive on stage, and the irrationality of human nature is stressed in the witches. They end the play by hailing Malcolm with their opening greeting to Macbeth, and their dominant role is epitomised by their degrading power over Macbeth: 'tearing his hair out and his clothes to shreds, farting in his face, etc. Finally they leave him lying half naked, screeching they throw the crown to one another until one of them puts it on.' This accentuation of violence may indeed be intended as a response to the urgency of political action, and the undertones are full of repressed class conflict – as when the peasant soldiers, ordered to execute a landowner, flay him alive to learn 'how a lord looks underneath his skin'. One perceives his flesh to be the same as a peasant's and Macbeth orders the other soldiers to kill him too to prevent the formation of any revolutionary solidarity.

Macbeth quotes Ovid while watching the lord being skinned, echoing the classical string quartets outside the gas chambers in Nazi concentration camps, and this is made a keynote for the play, challenging the audience's conventional aesthetic response to theatre by contrasting the brutality on stage with a frame of pictures – Michelangelo, Botticelli, Rubens – which line the proscenium. But the visceral impact of Müller's presentation overpowers any political interpretation. Despite references to fascism, the Artaudian 'cruelty' transforms history into a nightmare, and the verbal compression together with the completeness of Müller's condemnation of the world he presents, which effectively denies any possibility of an evil political system reforming itself, gives an impression of determinism. Thus a peasant, threatened with execution by both his Scots oppressors and his English 'deliverers', hangs himself as the only release from fear, while Macbeth's death 'makes the world no better', and Malcolm's first act as king is to show what he has 'learnt from his example' by having Macduff murdered.[47] Müller's image of society has mythic dimensions, being both feudal and futuristic as well as fascist, and the negative parable is so forceful that the final impression is of cruelty as a universal, unchanging human condition. Indeed the violence is so extreme as to be surreal, so that the sadism becomes a seductive fantasy of fear, which has led East German critics to attack the play as pornographic.

Popularisation and public acceptance

The bleakness of Müller's vision may preserve it from pornography, but such an accusation could be levelled with justice at certain attempts to exploit the avant garde approach in other Shakespearean adaptations, such as Marowitz's *An Othello* (1972), where Othello's

epileptic fit was turned into a paranoiac vision of an adulterous Des-
demona indulging in an orgy, with blocking and movements lifted
directly from *Oh Calcutta!* And even as the avant garde movement
was reaching new peaks of intensity with Grotowski's influential
productions or pushing against its limits in the Living Theatre and
Schechner's work, which already contained popularising elements,
its techniques were also being adopted by otherwise purely conventional dramatists.

Initially the influence was primarily thematic, resulting in plays like
David Rudkin's *Afore Night Come* (1962), where the action centres on
ritual sacrifice in an atmosphere of primitive rustic menace but the
presentation is extremely naturalistic; and the contrast between ordinary, if stupid and routinely brutal seasonal workers and their incoherent hints about 'the Blood' and 'the Lamb' that lead to the decapi-
tation of a scapegoat/outsider, his body slashed with the sign of the
cross, has an unintentional effect of parody. Alternatively atavistic
themes were treated in historical costume dramas, like John Whiting's
study of demonic possession in *The Devils* (1961) or Peter Shaffer's
quasi-mythical *Royal Hunt of the Sun* (1964). Where avant garde techniques were taken over lock, stock and barrel together with the
themes, the effect was all too often confused and tended to farce, as in
Ann Jellicoe's *The Sport of My Mad Mother* (1958).

Jellicoe made her début as a conventional naturalistic playwright of
wry comedy. She then came under the influence of Artaud, and
plunged enthusiastically into mythical subjects and ritual forms in a
play defined as 'anti-intellect . . . not only because it is about irrational
forces and urges but because one hopes it will reach the audience
directly through rhythm, noise and music and their reaction to basic
stimuli'.[48] The context of juvenile gang warfare in the back streets and
waste lots of industrial slums is never fully developed and the characters are openly allegorical. The leader of the gang is a grotesque girl
with long red hair falling from her brow like a Japanese lion wig and a
heavily made up, dead-white face. She is the catalyst that liberates
repressed instincts of violence:

Everyone's got something inside and she makes it grow and grow and come
bursting out . . . It'll start with one fight and then the whole street – all
exploding and growing and exploding, and every bit of every explosion
makes everything round it explode. The whole street's fighting – the whole
block – the whole country – the sea – the air – all the planets. And she stands
there, her eyes glittering and sparkling and laughing the whole time. Bearing
it.[49]

She is, rather over-obviously, the death goddess of the title – 'All creation is the sport of my mad mother Kali' – who can drink poison and survive. As such she is an incarnation of atavistic urges, and her antagonist is an outsider (an American), who represents the scientific approach, rationalism and intellectual control. But the normal valuations are confusingly reversed or over-simplified. The anarchic death instinct turns out to be a life-force as the girl gives birth on stage at the end of the play, while the intellectual is emotionally sterile. As myth the play is intended to appeal to the subconscious, and the archetypal pattern of a man who castrates himself after being rejected by his mother, linked by Jellicoe to the primal psychological anxiety that comes with expulsion from the womb, is never made explicit. It is designed as an image that the audience will 'invest... with their own fantasies and desires, emotional fears, anxieties and drives', and the appeal is therefore 'to the senses, emotions and instincts. So we have colour, movement, rhythmical and musical sounds... symbols, myths and rituals.' Consequently there is no plot, and the rhythmical action is structured into a series of rites in which everyday activities or dialogues are heightened and formalised, since ritual is seen as something purely external: a significant mode of expression that gains a 'magical' efficacy through hypnotic effects, quite independent of religion or belief. 'A ritual generally takes the form of repeating a pattern of words and gestures which tend to excite us above a normal state of mind. Once this state of mind is induced we are receptive and suggestible and ready for the climax of the rite. At the climax the essential nature of something is changed.'[50]

Although the rhythmic use of language is highly effective, applying ritual patterning to everyday banality tends to self-parody, as in a sequence where the use of a common-or-garden hair rinse is built up into a rite and the climax produces a real change indeed, but hardly an essential one – the hair turns green. And the action, for all its assault on the senses, is incapable of being developed because there is no coherent philosophy behind it. Consequently the potentially apocalyptic vision of the play never rises above unconvincing make-believe and deteriorates into misconceived theatricality with the 'birth', which is followed by the mock breaking up of the theatre itself (in lieu of an ending):

GRETA: O bloody organic confusion... Oh you! Oh you! Oh... Oh...
    Oh... just here... (*Pause*)... (*Pause*)... (*A long pause.*)... Now I let
    this child into life... Now I thrust this bird into air... (*Machine-gun fire*

off. Enter FAK carrying a large white sheet and PATTY *sketchily dressed up
as a nurse and carrying a large book entitled 'How To Deliver A Baby'.* STEVE
[The musician who has been accompanying the action downstage with
drums and percussion] *rams a wig on his head, picks up a banjo, which
he holds like a tommy-gun, and comes on raking the auditorium with his 'gun'.)*
STEVE: *(to audience)*. Stay where you are. This is a stick-up. O.K. where is
she . . . *(to audience)*. O.K. you lot, clear out. I'm blowing this place up.
We'll have a bonfire: bring your own axes.

This is supposedly the climax of the myth. But since it is presented as
farce the only actual effect is to deprive what went before of any
sincerity, which was hardly countered by warning the audience in a
programme note not to expect a story or an argument or even a
coherent structure, but only a 'poetic' vision 'strung together with the
inconsequence of real life'.[51]

The confusion of styles and lack of imaginative integrity in such a
climax provide an object lesson in the potential problems of adopting
theatrical forms without the principles they were designed to express.
But the adaptation of carefully diluted avant garde techniques has
produced some strikingly successful commercial theatre, notably in
the work of Peter Shaffer. And even Ann Jellicoe's attempt to use
overt theatricality as a challenge to the audience's belief, that can
create a high level of involvement if they can surmount it to suspend
their disbelief, a raising of the imaginative stakes as it were, has
proved effective in an example like Lindsay Kemp's dance–drama.

Kemp's work, despite its remarkable theatrical power, has been
almost totally ignored by serious criticism, perhaps because instead of
formulating clearly defined original ideas his contribution has been to
synthesise established experimental forms with the most popular
kinds of art – rock concerts (Kemp has choreographed David Bowie's
shows), cabaret, circus, even strip-tease – although it has attracted
disproportionate attention from the police. His work is in some ways
an extension of Diaghilev's *Ballets Russes* and his company includes
Anton Dolin, but it was specifically from reading Artaud that Kemp
developed his approach. His most characteristic production is *Flowers*
(1966), an adaptation of Genet's autobiographical novel *Our Lady of
the Flowers*, and it was Artaud's emphasis on myth, ritual and trance
states that made him realize how Genet's vision could be actualised
on the stage. Opening with a scene of mass masturbation, orgasm
and crucifixion, performed to pulsating lights and musical rhythms,
the play assaults the senses, sensibilities and preconceptions of the
audience, overwhelming the spectator with audio-visual effects and

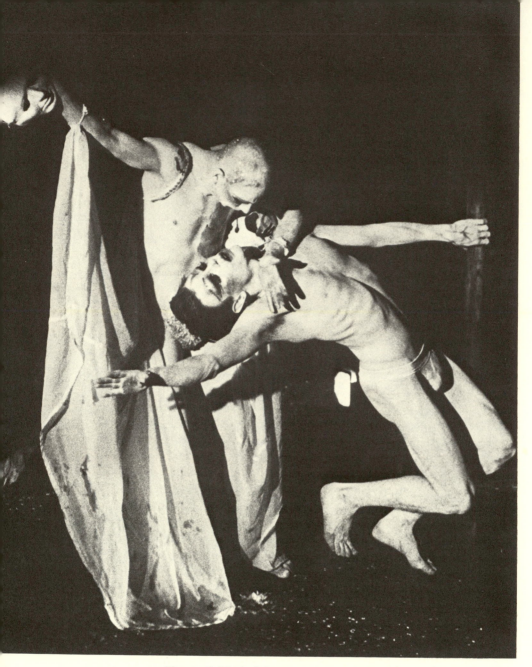

25 *Flowers*. Subliminal dances & erotic archetypes.

images of perverse tenderness, sexual violence, spiritual cruelty. The opening is explicitly designed to induce a trance in the actors, in which 'the subconscious will take over the body' and liberate it 'to follow the subtle direction of the dance within us', and the performance – mimed and danced without words – is improvised around the fixed structure provided by a complex score of sound effects, taped and live music, out of a body of rehearsed material over three times the length. This means that performances, which are in a continual state of development (*Flowers* is still in Kemp's repertoire as of 1979), can change every night to reflect the actors' personal emotions or to relate directly to different responses in the audience; and the rhythms are deliberately kept 'very basic, organic. It's absolutely essential to adapt oneself to the breathing of the audience, the heartbeat of the audience for a performance to become a communion, a shared ritual.'[52]

The central image is that of an inverted religious ceremony, a black mass celebrating sexuality – specifically homosexuality – and 'the idea was to create a mythological background to the particular images . . . to bring in themes that resonated'. This was even more obvious in *Salome* (1974), where Oscar Wilde's text was preceded by a prologue of primitive dancing, lit by flames from incense bowls and culminating in orgiastic rape. This led to symbolic scenes of a snake destroying a dove, of John the Baptist as an angelic Dionysus whose wings were torn apart and the feathers scattered through the theatre in a poetic analogy to the dismemberment of the god's body, then to theatrical images from *Hamlet* reflecting the incest motif. Kemp's work contains no characterisation in a normal sense. The actors in theory express their own personality on a subconscious level, heavy make-up is used to transform their faces into masks that accentuate their own features, emotions are exaggerated towards the simplicity of universal psychological states, and a highly formalised slowness and grace of movement successfully merges the individual and the archetype. But where specific characterisation and dialogue is called for, as in Wilde's play, the effect verges on caricature, and transvestite acting (Kemp's company is assertively male apart from one token girl) inevitably tends to high camp, which indicates the limitations of Kemp's approach. However this falsity even becomes a source of strength when the audio-visual rhythms are effective in drawing the audience into the action, and the theatricality is accentuated deliberately. Herodias is given a pair of huge rubber breasts; Dolin as Herod strips off his wig to reveal the old tired *actor* beneath; Salome's seduction is accompanied by a grandiose musical cliché like the *Liebestod* theme from *Tristan and Isolde;* in *Flowers* the homosexual fantasy breaks into popular lyrics such as 'Somewhere Over the Rainbow' or 'Blackbird Bye Bye' with cathartic comic release; and the presence of a real girl serves to underline the falsity of the men in drag – but this paradoxically transposes them to a higher level of imaginative reality. In Genet's terms, it is a demonstration of a true image being formed precisely because the spectacle is fake. If it works, the challenge to the imagination involves the audience more deeply in the action than any conventionally illusionistic presentation could, but Kemp realizes the dangers involved in relying so extensively on the subconscious and in the overt incongruity of a 40-year-old man playing a 12-year-old girl: 'working with extreme images is *Grand guignol,* melodramatic, which brings in an element of parody. You are on a tightrope of belief. We balance on a knife edge between the serious and the ridiculous.'[53]

Lindsay Kemp's aim is basically psychological, and his assault on the audience, simultaneously sensual, emotional, moral and perceptual, is intended to challenge the repressive norms of social behaviour, 'to liberate . . . who we are, releasing the bird, or the angel, or the natural dance which is in all of us, enabling us to fly'. And even if the explicit celebration of homosexuality is perhaps self-indulgent, or the fantasy dream world conjured up too special for many of the public to project their fears and desires into, with its *fin de siècle* images derived from Beardsley and Gustav Moreau, as theatre it is spectacular. It is also popular, and has appealed sufficiently to audiences in Poland, Holland, Spain, as well as in England and America over the last fifteen years, for Kemp's company to survive without any form of subsidy.

By contrast Peter Shaffer succeeds by avoiding any ethical or psychological challenge to the public. After writing detective stories, naturalistic plays and farce, Shaffer turned deliberately to avant garde conventions, and *The Royal Hunt of the Sun* was specifically intended as '"total" theatre, involving not only words but rites, mimes, masks and magic'.[54] His most effective moments were striking visual and aural images: the mime of the great massacre, in which a wave of Indians with barbaric feather headdresses rise to be cut down by the *conquistadores* again and again to 'savage music' and violent drumming, a geometric dance of slaughter ending with a vast bloodstained cloth, dragged out from the centre piece of a gigantic golden sun representing the Inca empire and bellying out over the stage to the sound of screams; or the graphic symbol for the rape of Peru when the Spanish soldiers tear the gold from the sun, leaving it a blackened, disfigured and empty circle; or the final tableau as Pizarro kneels by the strangled Inca, believing desperately in his resurrection and waiting through the night for the sunlight to strike his body, surrounded by Indians in huge funeral masks intoning 'a strange chant... punctuated by hollow beats on the drums and by long, long silences in which they turn their immense triangular eyes enquiringly up to the sky'.[55] But these vivid theatrical moments are set in a conventional dramatic context of character development and the conflict of opposing moral principles. As a result they remain mere spectacle, separate from the theme of the play, which is carried by the dialogue. And although the characters seem to raise important philosophical issues – the loss of faith and the search for meaning in life in the contrasts between the cynical

26 *The Royal Hunt of the Sun.* Masks & magic as spectacle.

narrator and the romantic boy he was when he took part in the
Spanish expedition, between the nihilistic Christian Pizarro and the
pagan Inca who believes himself to be god; or capitalism versus communism in the contrast of the active principle of Spain, with its emphasis on individual struggle, freedom and personal will, against the
passive regimentation, material contentment and mass spiritual slavery of the Inca empire – these issues are never developed. There is no
true dialectic because in the final analysis the answers given are the
easy ones that confirm popular preconceptions. The good qualities of
both civilisations are one-sided, so materialism and individualism are
equally destructive. Spiritual needs can never be met by institutions:
and so on. In the National Theatre production the visual imagery of
the Inca's garotting was specifically that of crucifixion and pietà,
which turned his death into an agonised rejection of Christianity. But
then the play had already substituted a humanistic 'joy' for religious
experience, effectively making questions of God irrelevant. Theatrical
excitement is a valuable and all too rare quality, but here, as in other
more conventionally well-made plays like Terence Rattigan's or Fritz
Hochwälder's 'unpretentious anti-anti-theatre', excitement has become an end in itself.

The same basic criticism applies to Shaffer's most popular play to
date, *Equus* (1973), which combines the psychological thriller and
self-discovery on a psychiatrist's couch with the exploration of myth,
atavistic religious belief and magic. Technically it borrows eclectically
from the avant garde – a bare stage, part of the audience seated
behind the acting area to intensify the response by allowing spectators to observe the reactions of others, an actor seated among the
audience, sound effects from speakers placed throughout the auditorium, dream sequences and a scenic structure that cuts across the
logic of time and cause and effect following the irrational associations
of the subconscious, ritual chanting, stylised masks and mythic archetypes: Apollo versus Dionysus. In addition the terms describing
the audience/stage relationship exactly echo the details of Grotowski's
setting for *The Constant Prince*, with the spectators as 'voyeurs' and
'witnesses' on 'tiers of seats in the fashion of a dissecting theatre'
surrounding a square inner stage that 'resembles a railed boxing
ring'.[56] As in *The Royal Hunt of the Sun*, it is this avant garde stylistic
level that generates emotional involvement. The visual imagery is
totally compelling, with the stylised centaur–horses formed from
sombrely clad actors wearing skeletal silver horses' heads and hooves
creating an effect of magical transformation, while the boy's nightride

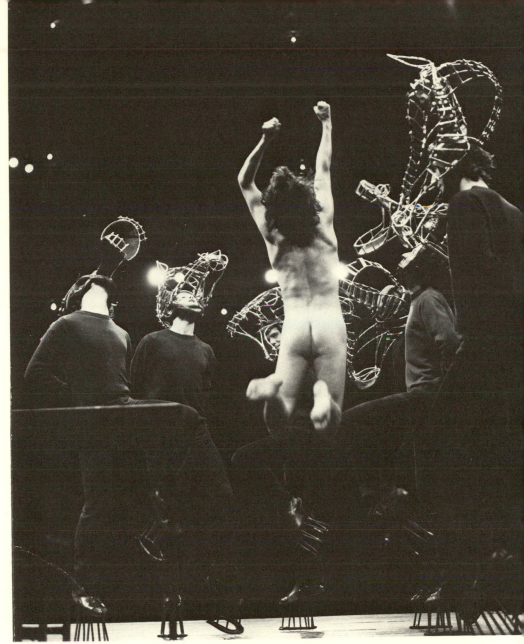

27 Pop-myth in *Equus*. Nudity, stylised theatricality & a bare stage.

on a revolve whirled around by 'horses' standing at the perimeter suggests an ancient and uncompromising force come to life. The images are more closely integrated with the theme than in the previous play, but the weight of the overall statement discredits their imaginative reality, partly as a result of the play's genesis.

The starting-point was a true story of a stable-boy who blinded twenty-six horses, the dramatic value of which was that it 'set up all sorts of reverberations', and the first draft focussed on the boy.[57] In the final version the interest shifted to the effect of the boy's experience on his analyst and, although the programme notes contained excerpts from Frazer's *Golden Bough*, the dialogue presented an explanation in Freudian clichés. Sexual experience is the test of normality. But a repressive upbringing leads to perversion, and this results in impotence and guilt feelings, which can only be resolved by an act of violent sacrilege. The myth that the boy creates and his orgiastic ceremonies with his private god, incarnate in the horses, which both satisfies the fundamental need for worship and liberates natural instincts (symbolised in the cliché image of nakedness), becomes a mere flight from repressive reality that can be dismissed as personal fantasy. At the same time the analyst is brought to recognise that the 'normal' is sterile and passionless, that his own detachment disguises sexual frustration, and that 'curing' the boy of his obsession means destroying the spiritual intensity and individuality which give life value. Again significant issues have been raised, but only as a form of intellectual titillation, and the audience's desire for archetypal significance – itself perhaps an indication of avant garde interests filtering through into public consciousness, or the same reaction against contemporary materialism that has motivated the avant garde exploration of the primitive – has been satisfied without disturbing them on any fundamental level.

Equus was a world-wide success. The avant garde approach had, as it were, arrived – but in a watered-down and conventional form, with Shaffer unabashedly defending his play as 'well made' and reacting to accusations of artifice and glibness with the claim that 'if those are the qualities [critics] detect, then the play isn't well made *enough*'.[58] The dilution of their principles and the adulteration of their techniques is perhaps an inevitable corollary to public acceptance of the avant garde. But association of their approach with the commercial theatre and social approval removes the essential quality of protest, and presents an apparently insuperable problem. Where does an avant garde movement go to retain its integrity?

New directions and conclusions

It is the fate of every successful avant garde to be adopted by the society they despise or oppose, to be taught by universities, used as name-dropping reference points by art critics in the daily newspapers and analysed in such studies as this – a process of emasculation through which radical ideas do act as leaven in the public consciousness, but only at the expense of having their original explosive force defused. This is particularly true of drama where the effective agent is performance, transitory and unrecoverable, while public notice is almost always retrospective. The irrational becomes a subject for intellectual discussion, aesthetic notions expand to embrace anti-art, and it is this process of osmosis that has destroyed the avant garde, not the star-status of any single representative. Almost by definition, the leading dramatists or directors are those who win public acceptance, but this is largely irrelevant for the movement as a whole. For instance, by the time Jarry's work was fashionable the cutting edge of the avant garde had moved on into surrealism, expressionism or dada; by the time Barrault became the guardian of official culture as director of the Théâtre de France, new initiatives were already leading to Genet and Ionesco, the Living Theatre and Grotowski. But the avant garde process is also one of entropy. Continually overstepping each new limit reached in preceding work, either to outstrip acceptance or in following a logical line of exploration, ultimately leads to the negation of the art form that makes creation possible, as in Grotowski's decision to create no new productions or Beckett's progress from *Waiting for Godot* (considered to be an extreme of minimal theatre when first staged in 1953) to the shortness, stasis and finally silence of 'dramaticules' like *Come and Go* or *Breath*. At the same time, as more aspects of the movement become accepted the point is eventually reached where the premises and principles, by which the avant garde defined themselves, become the basis for work that is obviously in the mainstream of modern drama, and then for popular theatre by thoroughly conventional playwrights.

Despising popular art, or dismissing it as ersatz art because of its entertainment or profit motive, is a self-defeating form of cultural snobbery, since the only art that has ever had any lasting influence is art that was vulgar enough to entertain – and it is one the avant garde is particularly prone to. Yet the distinction between vulgarity and vulgarisation is a real one, and Ezra Pound's definition of artistic integrity and vision as 'a brief gasp between one cliché and another' is all too accurate. So that when experimental forms become fashionable then further work on the same lines tends to deteriorate into eclectic recapitulations of earlier avant garde achievements without the imaginative integrity of the original. Alternatively it becomes either a meaningless exercise in extremism, or self-indulgent exoticism.

A group like John Juliani's Savage God theatre, which claims to represent 'that direction of the theatre that extols participation and process . . . above observation and product',[1] is an example of the first tendency, interchangeable with almost any number of other mediocre pseudo-avant garde groups. Juliani's title, taken from Yeats' comment on *Ubu roi*, refers back to Jarry, but his work lacks any real focus or originality. A 1971 'laboratory' season of fifty-one mini-productions in Vancouver (under the inflated acronym of PACET – Pilot investigation in an Alternative Complement to the Existing Theatre) ranged from 'consciousness raising exercises', to 'explorations in sensory deprivation'. At one extreme there were unannounced performances in public places, Strindberg's *The Stronger* for instance being presented just once in a crowded downtown café by actors pretending to be ordinary members of the public and making no attempt to draw attention to the piece. At the other extreme audiences were guided through a series of darkened rooms to the accompaniment of disorienting sounds and lights. Aiming to obliterate what was seen as a false distinction between art and life, PACET abandoned technical expertise and even rehearsal, together with the concept of a stage; but the artificiality of the exercise was clearly revealed by the pretentiousness of *An Evening of Arrabal*, when Juliani in the role of the author answered questions put by three of the actors in a semi-improvised 'interview', with excerpts from Arrabal's plays presented to illustrate his points leading up to an enactment of *Erotic Bestiality*, where balloons and confetti were distributed to the public at the point of orgasm in the performance, while 'Arrabal' stripped to reveal a bra and garterbelt beneath his everyday clothes, announcing 'I think, as a playwright, I am greatly overrated.'

A fair example of the second type of response is a performance like

Ralph Ortiz's *The Sky is Falling* (Temple University, 1970), where extremism took the cheap form of physical violence that was not only tasteless (taste being a legitimate object of avant garde attack), but pointless. Again the title harks back to an avant garde precursor, this time Artaud. But now that the symbolic images of violence Artaud advocated have become a form of aesthetic titillation through familiarity, the desired shock effect can only be achieved by real atrocities. Thus the scenario called for 'one hundred live mice in a wire screen and two gallons of blood in plastic bags' to be placed inside a piano, which was then ceremonially smashed, spraying the audience with blood and mangled or half-dead mice.[2] The actors stripped and burnt their clothes, dismembered live chickens, and systematically brutalised one of their members, who acted the part of an epileptic so convincingly that some spectators called for a doctor. At the opening the audience were 'interrogated', they were subjected to verbal abuse if they refused to participate at any point, and at the end insults were screamed at them as 'a bunch of fucking voyeurs'. In treating Artaud's concept of 'cruelty' all too literally, any sense of a metaphysical plane was lost, and purely visceral reactions replaced subliminal responses (at least one member of the audience vomited). Designating two of the actors as 'shamans' and the spectators plus the rest of the cast as 'initiates', or describing the actions as 'destruction rites' – like the attempt to give the orgiastic sadism a political extension in referring to the chickens as Vietnamese babies, smashing eggs with cries of 'enemy foetuses', and identifying Lieutenant Calley of the My Lai massacre with Kali, the Hindu goddess of destruction – was simply gratuitous.

The third possibility, a facile retreat into exoticism, is epitomised in a performance like *Bliss Apocalypse* (1970) by a group called 'the Floating Lotus Magic Opera Company'. Again one of the major figures was Kali, though here the action transformed the death goddess into 'simple naked Woman, clean as primal earth, and Mother', and other characters included the Minotaur, the Phoenix, a 'Sun-Dancer Prophet', a 'Shaman' and 'Vairocana', a figure combining Tibetan Buddhist iconography with an American Indian totem. This awesome confusion of mythological archetypes never rose above the level of pretentious cliché: 'The whole vision was designed', according to its author, 'to be performed outside in the raw air of IT, on a hillside after civilisations all blow their plugs' and 'conceived as an initiation ceremony opening areas of sound and image, guiding them with the chanted sound of vocal AUM'.[3] And it was presented in a wild mixture of contradictory styles, the only common factor seemingly being that all were highly conventionalised and alien to western culture. 'Gagaku No-drama' and 'Kabuki sounds' (defined as 'wheezing wailing... high-pitched microtonal sound' and 'high pitched singing notes') accompanied 'battles of forces... as in Javanese dance-battles, angular', a 'ritual hieroglyph dance' and movements supposedly 'as in Tai Chi', while what little dialogue there was substituted rhetorical inflation for sense:

> O Face to Face with the Spirit of Enlightenment
> AWAKE! AWAKE! LIGHT FLOWS UP THROUGH OUR SPINES!

None of these examples would be worth mentioning but for the amount of attention paid to them. *The Sky is Falling* was sponsored by a university, Juliani's 'laboratory' season even received governmental funding, and all three were extensively reported in journals like *Theatre Quarterly* and *The Drama Review* as imaginatively exciting and potentially productive new directions. But if the avant garde line from Jarry and Strindberg is still viable, it is in developments like the 'autistic' drama of Robert Wilson or certain facets of contemporary dance.

Robert Wilson's work, which has acknowledged affinities with Gertrude Stein and has been proclaimed as 'heir to the surrealists' by Louis Aragon, takes its approach from two of his collaborators, a deaf mute and a man with severe brain damage. Working with them in a form of dramatic therapy, Wilson discovered that their disabilities had given them radically different forms of perception, which allowed them to understand things that escaped normal people who were primarily concerned with words. He noted that the deaf mute picked up sounds in the form of vibrations or 'interior impressions' and seemed to think in terms of pictorial images, while the other created a 'graphic' logic from the aural shape of words independent of conventional sense: 'the word Katmhandu [sic]. Later it would be Cat; then Cat-man-ru. Later it would be Fat-man-ru, and then it would be Fat man... The words were really alive. They were always growing and changing... like molecules bursting apart into all directions all the time – three dimensional.'[4] Wilson's plays, like *Deafman Glance* which formed the basis of *KA MOUNTAIN AND GUARDenia Terrace*, are created to express this more sensitive and physical perception of the world, as opposed to the conventional intellectualised perception. Their structure is musical in the sense that the action is an architectural arrangement of sounds, words and movement, in which images are restated or varied to form thematic motifs. On one level the pacing and choice of images is a direct reflection of autistic thought patterns.

On another level the presentation is designed to sensitise the spectator to the same subliminal range of nuances as a brain-damaged deaf mute. The stage becomes a projection of 'abnormal' inner states, which gain imaginative power to the extent that they evoke the unconscious fantasies of the spectator – and Wilson sees autism as an increasingly common psychological response to the pressures of contemporary life: 'More and more people are turning into themselves... You can see it in the subways, where everyone is bunched together, and nobody is looking at anybody. What they are doing is signing off. They have to because there's so much overload... It's actually a means of survival.'[5]

The aim is therapeutic, to open the audience to 'interior impressions', and the result is an audio-visual collage of dream-like and seemingly disconnected images in which words and events are deliberately presented with obsessive repetitiveness and painful slowness. In *KA MOUNTAIN AND GUARDenia Terrace*, for example, the performance at the 1972 Shiraz festival took 268 hours spread over seven days and moved from a small picture-frame stage, open at the rear to show a mountain through the proscenium, out to cover the whole of the mountain face. Actions were performed in slow motion, both to gain a dream quality and to intensify the audience's awareness, to focus their attention – at one point the only movement was that of a live turtle crossing the empty stage, which took almost an hour – while the mountain was dotted with unrelated visual images in the form of two-dimensional cardboard cut-outs: Noah's ark, a dinosaur, flamingoes, the Acropolis surrounded by a ring of ICBM rockets, Jonah's whale, a graveyard, and the Manhattan skyline on the summit, which was burnt to the ground on the last day of the performance and replaced by a Chinese pagoda with the Lamb of God inside (the original plan, vetoed by the festival authorities, had been to blow up the mountain top or paint it entirely white). There was no intellectual sense to be made out of this apocalyptic collage, despite readings from the Book of Jonah and *Moby Dick* in one section of the performance. Actions stood in an oblique relationship to the dialogue, as when the words of Melville and the Bible were 'answered' arbitrarily by an enthroned Wilson either with falsetto whimpers and cries, or with a deep bass echo of what had just been read; and where the dialogue was in character it resembled automatic writing or dadaist free association:

The journey. The old man. The body. The old man. The stories. The old man leaves. Birth. Ocean. Birth. Ocean. The beginning of movement. The beginning of sound. Branch. Bench. Horizontal zone. Spring... Winter. Burial. White mountain. Green garden. The old man returns. The body. The old man. Thatit cotet quantet yeatet. As you, an earthfather geetly childed, gatet, greetet, growtet, gaitet, because that is how it is. Take this basket to the riverbank and fill it follet, fotet fountet, fatet. As you, an old man, mother, mourning, morning, morn, for it can be no other way. Whalet whartet woetet wantet waitet upon the bank of yonder river and thy basket shall be there abundant filled. Birth. Broken earth. Black. Day. A whale in the cube room... There are seven days. There are seven levels... Seven fires light the day dies dancing six times unto the last a seventh day, a SUNDAY, a SUN CITY... [6]

The mythical connotations, Moses in the basket, Jonah, the creation of the world corresponding to the seven-day performance of the play, 'ka' representing the soul, the seasonal birth–death–resurrection pattern, all are obvious. But unlike Grotowski or Artaud these fit into no coherent concept. Each spectator has to make his own 'sense' out of this stream of consciousness, and this can only be achieved on the level of subliminal association since the random form, the repetitions and even the inertia make intellectual, 'exterior' connections impossible.

KA MOUNTAIN was on an epic scale, with more than fifty actors plus a small zoo of live animals, but 'chamber' pieces like *A Letter for Queen Victoria*, presented at the Spoleto festival in 1974 and on Broadway in 1975, have exactly the same qualities, except that here the dream images are drawn from social rather than religious archetypes. Queen Victoria appears, in full regalia, to be read a long and totally incomprehensible letter, couples in white sit at café tables gesticulating frenetically and all speaking the same lines – 'chitter-chatter, chitter-chatter' – simultaneously. But the effect is disorienting rather than satiric, with two ballet dancers slowly spinning either side of the stage throughout the performance, complex choreography in slow motion, and somnambulistic characters talking in endless *non-sequiturs*. Again there are apocalyptic overtones: a sniper shoots the couples who collapse one by one across their tables, and the performance ends with a long-drawn-out scream. Such inconsequential violence is psychologically disturbing, not dramatic, and rather more obviously than in *KA MOUNTAIN* the images focus on perception itself rather than what is perceived: four aviators/Lindberghs stand with their backs to the audience looking at a changing land/cloudscape through a huge window; a Chinaman stands behind another enormous window-frame staring out at the audience through a continually opening and closing Venetian blind.

The danger is that the audience's awareness will be deadened instead of sensitised by the stasis, that they will be confused instead of illuminated by the undefined connotations, and that the only thing perceived will be tedium. But Robert Wilson is not alone in his approach. A playwright like Jean Vauthier also reduces exterior action to a minimum, forming his dialogue by random association, noting words on separate pieces of paper then grouping these 'according to the melodic lines'; and his work has found an appropriate interpreter in Jorge Lavelli, who defines his aim as 'forcing language to explode on stage . . . Once language has been freed from its various limitations – stereotyped definitions – it can arouse [altogether new and unexpected] feelings within the spectator's being.' What this meant specifically in staging Vauthier's version of *Medea* was treating it 'like a musical score' and finding 'an *immoderate* vocal attitude: sounds which would force word explosions on stage' together with stylised gestures to 'create a whole new inner atmosphere, a world through which the senses can flow forth freely'.[7]

The equivalent to Wilson in contemporary dance is Meredith Monk. Just as Wilson calls his quasi-balletic, multi-media dramatic spectacles 'operas', so Monk has described her performances as 'theatre cantatas' or 'dance–music–theatre pieces', and defined her aim as developing 'a form that could accommodate each side of that triangle: music, dance *and* theatre . . . for my own integration'. It is this therapeutic level of her work and its relation to the subconscious that distinguishes it for her from dance proper: 'Dance problems have to do with space, time and motion. I kept space and time, but the motion part was not part of my work. My impulse is initially emotional or psychic. It comes from the subconscious.'[8] So Monk's work functions on a double level where the physical exploration of a spatial area like the Guggenheim Museum (*Juice*, 1969) or spatial relationships (*Tour 4: Lounge*, 1969, or later *Tours* where the audience are encouraged to move among relatively static performers) is simultaneously a journey through an inner space of symbols representing historical, psychological or even self-reflexive artistic development. Starting from an expressionist standpoint with her initial training in Dalcroze eurythmics, Monk's early work was strongly reminiscent of surrealism, as in *16 Millimeter Earrings* (1966). Here film and tape were combined with live dance and song to present emotional states in a direct form or evoke pre-rational responses through distortions of the body and violent juxtapositions of images: a film of Monk's face was projected, enlarged, onto a sphere suspended above her head;

Wilhelm Reich's clinical account of orgasm (on tape) was accompanied by Monk rising nude from a black box surrounded by deliberately fake flames created by blowing red streamers upwards, while a film of a doll burning was projected onto a screen behind her dancing figure.

As imagery this is banal, and wherever Monk's pieces are explicit her meanings turn out to be clichés. The weak point of her work is where it derives from sixties' romanticism, indicated by the presentation of her group as an 'ideal community', or the use of the performers' personal experiences as material for their scenes. If this sounds reminiscent of the Performance Group, it is because the links are indeed there, with several of her earlier pieces staged in Schechner's Performing Garage, and the programme for *Tour 4* picking up on some of the most interesting of his 'environmental' concepts:

Section III . . . six simultaneous events distributed in different areas of the lounge. Each event contains changes, progressions and permutations. There are no climaxes, beginnings and endings. Within each event it is to the advantage of the spectator to move freely from event to event. It is expected that the audience will wish to observe the changes in the various events and to go back and forth among them.[9]

Where this remained a largely arbitrary technical device in Schechner's work, here it is filled with thematic significance as a way of expressing one of Monk's primary concerns – perception – since the focus is (as in Peter Stein's work) on shifting perspectives, and not on integrating the audience physically in a dramatic action. In *Quarry* (1978), for example, the Holocaust was presented simultaneously on different planes through the use of regressive frames. A film of people and stones brought out the geological/victim ambiguity of the title, making gigantic rocks look like tiny pebbles as a key to the displacements of scale, in which the horrifying realities are distanced by choral stylisation, by the juxtapositioning of twentieth-century and Old Testament Jewish family groups, and by their presentation as the feverish distortions of a child's highly subjective and egocentric imagination conjured up by the opening chant:

I don't feel well. I don't feel well. I don't feel well. It's my eyes. It's my eyes. It's my eyes. It's my hand, it's my hand, it's my hand. It's my skin, it's my skin, it's my skin.[10]

The same displacements of perspective and focus on perception, together with the presentation of a subconscious world of archetypes, can be even more clearly seen in 'an opera epic' like *Vessel* (1971), where the transformations were sequential not simultaneous. The

'Overture' took place in Monk's loft, a miniaturised performance where small-scale gestures evoked whole scenes – a woman representing a waterfall by letting her long hair unroll – or single figures stood for whole armies, and where performers dressed in black formed subtly changing tableaux against a black background. The action was that of a passion play with the main figure representing Joan of Arc, everywoman, and Monk herself as the artist–creator. It was orchestrated by progressions in scale – from the loft, to the Performing Garage, to the vacant space of a parking lot – and by contrasts in style and scope. In part II black was replaced by silver-costumed dancers and a silver-painted Joan on a silver mountain of scaffolding. The subtle symbolism of minimal gestures became either the theatricality of paper-crowned kings and clown-faced queens, or the magnification of details normally beneath our threshold of consciousness, as when the only noise in the Performing Garage was the (amplified) sound of lettuce tearing as a chorus performed a background of everyday actions like mixing salad. Instead of one figure as a whole group, the accusing Bishop Cochon was acted simultaneously by a symbiotic/schizophrenic pair of performers. Part III ('Existent Lot') was a mixture of the representational and the abstract, with children in court costume and Joan disappearing into the night behind the sparks from a welder's torch, while other details came straight out of Jarry's *Ubu roi*, with a musical battle between a troop of kazoos and a troop of pennywhistles, or an impossible number of 'cuckoos' climbing out of a Volkswagen bus in a never-ending line.

Pieces like these are mosaics of images which Monk likes to compare with Cocteau's concept of concrete theatrical peotry. As mosaics, the ordinary and everyday is transposed into the symbolic by moving it out of context or presenting it in abstract movement, emphasising posture and 'still' gestures. In the same way recognisable words, for instance dialogue from Shaw's *St Joan* in part I of *Vessel*, modulate into chants, speech without sense, and a 'sung' structure of sound that tends to be described by reviewers in terms of Indian music, animals and even 'primal cry'. There is no causal connection between the images, no story line or characterisation in terms of psychology and situation, but only 'a musical and choreographically structured continuity' designed to evoke 'timeless' ideograms for the spectators: 'Mother or a Father; Murderer or Murderess... Madman or Madwoman; or themselves as a God or a Goddess.'[11] The key point here is the ambiguity. By making positive use of the fact that archetypes have no fixed or specific meaning (where even Grotowski had tended to reduce them to single-level stereotypes) Monk creates a structure of transfigurations and transformations that can only be grasped as dreamwork and is designed to evoke instinctive resonances from the pre-rational levels of the spectator's mind, though the dangers are exactly the same as those inherent in Robert Wilson's performances.

Another American dancer more overtly concerned with the use of mythic material and the return to the primitive through ritual is Ann Halprin, who has also defined her approach as 'the blowing up of details, every feeling and reaction becoming a significant event'.[12] It was Halprin who created the 'flying' sequence for the Living Theatre, which became an integral part of both *Mysteries* and *Paradise Now* and was taken up by Schechner in *Commune* as the ideal physical image for both aspiration and community. (An actor or spectator climbs to a high platform while the others form a line with interlaced arms below to catch him when, on the rhythmic chant of 'BREATHE... BREATHE... BREATHE... FLY', he leaps as if diving upwards into the air.) Her early work, like *Parades and Changes* (1965) 'a Journey into Body Consciousness', was based on Gestalt therapy and convinced her that a performer could only essentially play himself, leading to the Grotowskian demand that performance should be 'living a real authentic situation, not playacting at it. Being authentic in each moment.' Like Brook or Grotowski her aim became to explore the creative process itself as distinct from creating autonomous 'scores' for performance, and dance was used to find a 'common language' through involving the audience in 'movement experience'. In *Animal Ritual* (1971), for instance, the dance–mime was improvised within a symbolic framework of patterned movement across the performance area and in response to verbal instructions designed to evoke 'our long buried and half-forgotten selves', which opened with the demand to make the mind blank, to 'see' an animal come into a naked landscape and to 'be' that animal, and ended with the audience 'initiated' into communal action. Similarly *Trance Dance* (1973) was an attempt to 'exorcise' the socially imposed mental image of the self that is reflected in behaviour patterns and conventional gestures through hypnotically repetitive rhythms and movements:

Objective: To create a communal rhythm to flow between everyone, performers, and audience. Abolition of resistance through moving into a trance-like state. Separating the 'mind' (intellect, attention) from the 'body' (feelings, awareness).
Score: Adopt and repeat basic step with up-down rhythm. Use drumming as unifying element. Flow with other's movements... Vocalise breathing... Merge with others' sounds... Allow 'myth' to happen when audience enters

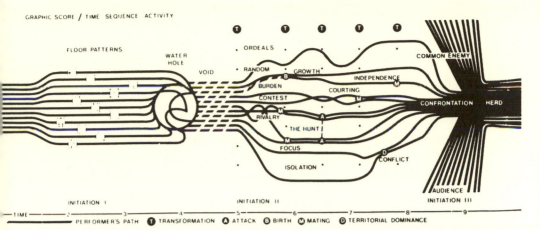

28 Spatial 'score' for *Animal Ritual* (from above). 'Paths' are thematic
guidelines within which each performer improvises independently.
Note that the public are assumed to participate spontaneously at
'initiation III' (which was signalled by a 'chant': 'Bo'u'lu . . . Boici . . .
Bo'ee – thank the gods for giving us the power to invoke the
supernatural').

and takes Trance Dance over as *its* group creation as a moving
community . . . A group consciousness and a MYTH (tribal happening)
emerges . . . The MYTH symbolises the spirit of the collective psyche of the
group.[13]

The difficulty here is that much of the free association called for was
painfully obvious, and a virtue becomes made of simplicity so that in
a performance like *Animal Ritual* 'interaction' was reduced to aggression versus sexual union, as in the Living Theatre.

But the shared emphasis on myth as psychological archetype rather
than culturally transmitted image, and on ritual form as a therapeutic
element rather than a stylised expression of mysticism marks the
work of these artists as a new development which is at the same time
a return to the earlier principles of the avant garde in different terms.
Their work is in many ways imperfect, although that is perhaps inherent in artistic experimentation. But what may eventually turn out
to be most productive is the return to 'roots' in exploring the nature of
perception itself, and the attempt to extend the range of communication onto an instinctual and subconscious level, which leads us back
to the original avant garde appeal to the pre-social and 'primitive'
levels of man, and to a cathartic level of theatrical experience that
qualifies as a valid contemporary form of tragedy.

This might sound contradictory, and 'tragedy' should certainly not
be confused with the avant garde attempts to resuscitate Dionysian

rites or the mysteries at Eleusis, nor with borrowings from archaic survivals like the Balinese trance dancing. The real significance of primitive forms is as theatrical models containing alternative values; and this relates to the two defining characteristics of avant garde theatre. The first is the fundamental opposition to society, along with the rejection of established political structures as an agent for change (as well as conventional theatre) on the grounds that as products of society these automatically distort anything within their scope, moulding even opposition into their own image; and following from this, the avant garde aim to change the world by changing the consciousness of individuals. The danger, inherent as much in the symbolist retreat behind gauzes, or the expressionist location of reality in the mind, as in Wilson's autism, is introversion. If the function of theatre is in any sense to initiate spiritual revolution, the actor must become an example for the audience. The work of the expressionists or Grotowski therefore presupposes the absolute authenticity of the emotional or spiritual states that the actor projects, and this has led some avant garde groups to the self-defeating assumption that performance can only be improvisation, that theatre can only be 'sincere' as a form of therapy for the actors themselves. Where the focus remains on the audience, these criteria of spiritual change and sincerity are responsible for the attempts to involve spectators directly in stage action, which can be seen as the second defining characteristic of avant garde theatre. The emphasis being on real experience, total participation replaces the traditional level of vicarious imaginative involvement. This of course is also a facet of the return to primitive dramatic models, as an attempt to regain the unity of performers and observers in tribal rituals, particularly rites of initiation – however idealised and unreproducible these may have turned out to be in practice. As we have seen, the at-first-glance nihilistic avant garde regression into formalism, the subconscious, the distant past or even the deliberate childishness of dada (OED, 'infantile sound') is not only political in its destructive aspect, but places positive value on the irrational, instinctive and emotional side of human nature. Thus Peter Brook is representative when he claims that since 'in the total sickness of the society we're living in, the possibility of affirmation through the [conventional] theatre is virtually excluded' it is therefore essential to rediscover the 'roots' both of theatre and of human experience, specifically the 'root' within 'the human body . . . because the human body, in all its aspects, organically, is common ground for all mankind'.[14] And it is on this level that avant garde theatre should be seen as a form of contemporary tragedy.

Almost all definitions of tragedy follow Aristotle, and even now our perceptions of what it might be are still preconditioned by a critical vocabulary of words like hamartia, peripeteia, anagnorisis. But Aristotle was clearly deriving his theory empirically from an analysis of Greek drama, and arguably his concept of tragedy only applies fully to Sophocles' *Oedipus*. Unfortunately what was originally descriptive has been interpreted as prescriptive, with the result that attention is usually focussed on external qualities – the unities, reversal and recognition, the nature of the hero – instead of seeing these as simply means to an end. Aristotle himself explicitly presents tragic structures and forms, even themes, as preferred techniques for manipulating audience responses in specific ways, and judges their appropriateness solely by the kind of emotion they evoke. So even for Aristotle (though not for some of his neo-classical or nineteenth-century interpreters) the primary condition for tragedy is catharsis: the empathy that unites spectator and actor, creating a degree of emotional participation which is made possible by the use of archetypal situations and has a specifically therapeutic effect, transcending suffering – the purging of intensely felt pity and terror – to reaffirm man's spiritual potential in the face of a hostile universe. The forms of avant garde theatre may seem a far cry from classical drama, but the differences should be seen merely as a measure of the gap between the ancient Greek and post-industrial social contexts in which very different means are required to gain comparable effects.

By any standards the mythical or archetypal emphasis in avant garde drama, with its ideal of authentic participatory experience, its return to ritual and pre-social roots, and its aim of creating cathartic spiritual change, which is also reflected in the designation of the performer as the 'holy actor' (Grotowski) or 'shaman' (Schechner, the Living Theatre), corresponds closely to this primary concept of tragedy. Not the rational and heroic neo-classical version of tragedy, nor academic definitions that concentrate on plot formulations, the nature of the protagonist or the thematic role of gods and fate; but the Dionysian. In conventional terms tragedy may be alien to contemporary vision, and the argument that the 'death of tragedy' has followed the 'death of God' and the substitution of scientific explanations for a 'horizon ringed by myth' (George Steiner, Nietzsche) is convincing. The common man has proved unable to carry the weight of symbolism that made the classical hero a paradigmatic tragic focus, and (despite Arthur Miller) economic or political pressures lack the compelling imaginative force of arbitrary and malign divinities. But the avant garde has reintroduced archetypal figures and the spiritual dimension, albeit with varying success, while the recurrent theme from the expressionists to the Living Theatre, implicit in Artaud's scenarios and epitomised in a production like Grotowski's *Constant Prince*, is that of transcendence – the transformation of physical suffering into spiritual ecstasy, 'transfiguration' or 'translumination'. At its rare best this succeeds in exciting pity with admiration and therefore terror, the authentic tragic response that has eluded more conventional dramas, like *Mourning Becomes Electra* or *A View from the Bridge*, despite their authors' attempts to rival Aeschylus.

Appendix

The intellectual context

What we have followed is an avant garde movement that, seen as a whole, shows a perhaps surprising focus on myth, ritual and what might be called the spiritual side of human nature – the subconscious, instinctive and irrational. By itself this might seem atavistic, a retreat from contemporary issues in a way that must isolate avant garde directors and dramatists, condemning their work to irrelevance once their technical innovations have become generally accepted. But seen in the wider philosophical and theatrical context, it is precisely these qualities that link them to the mainstream of modern thought. Most of those mental attitudes we customarily accept as representing what is specifically contemporary about our intellectual climate – materialism, scientific empiricism, agnosticism, rationalism – are in fact carry-overs from the nineteenth century. The premises and interests of psychology and social anthropology, both founded around the turn of the century, are far more typical of our age, and it is these that prepared the public and provided the material for the avant garde primitivism. In particular the search for quasi-mystical 'roots' reflects a really significant revaluation of the 'primitive mentality', through which these new sciences have given fresh relevance to myth and mythopoeic qualities.

For Frazer and the nineteenth-century rationalists, however imaginatively fascinating, myths were merely mistaken explanations about the natural world. They were considered to show deductive thought, comparable to the empirical scientific attitude but reaching false conclusions because based on ignorance. Alternatively for Cornford or Lévy-Bruhl they were the products of imagistic, random mental associations, which were superseded by scientific logic as civilisation developed. In either case 'mythical' meant inferior, synonymous with 'false'. This was partly due to the influential position of Greek mythology, which later anthropologists like Eliade realised was unique as the single body of myth to be preserved in literature and divorced from its ritual context. As such it existed only in a 'demys tified' form to which the Greeks themselves had attached allegorical and rationalising interpretations.[1] But around the turn of the century this negative judgement was reversed by philosophers like Cassirer, picking up on the romantic idealisation of the primitive mentality to postulate a qualitative distinction between scientific, rational abstractions and mythical thought – a pre-logical apprehension of experience embodied in concrete images. 'Primitive' became a positive value, and this was given an additional dimension by the work of Freud, Rank and above all Jung, for whom myth gave a symbolic picture of the internal world of dream and the subconscious. Such a revaluation provided the framework for the expressionists and surrealists, suggesting an alternative to the rational impersonality associated with modern society that seemed characterised by a disproportion of mechanism over spontaneity, matter over spirit.

More recently myth has also been approached from a linguistic viewpoint – again with results that had considerable relevance to the development of avant garde theatre. Roland Barthes, for instance, has analysed myth as a 'mode of signification', a form of language qualitatively different from discursive language, where the relationship between an object and the word signifying it is arbitrary, being determined by convention and usage. In myth, on the other hand, the relationship is 'motivated', since the level of reality referred to is not the world of objects but imagination, and has already passed through the prism of language. What is signified, being in the realm of concepts, has already been given prior significance, so the materials of myth inherently carry a high emotional charge since their point of reference is subjective. As an additional value for art the characteristic of a myth is 'to transform a meaning into a form'.[2] To this should be added Ernst Cassirer's theories stressing the dynamic, expressive and creative aspects of mythmaking. This process is seen as intuitive, occurring involuntarily when the mind is confronted by phenomena it cannot cope with logically. Thus 'the mythic mind never perceives passively, never merely contemplates things; all its observations spring from some act of emotion and will', so that 'the spirit consciously confronts the force of the "impression" with an active force of "expression"', transforming objective reality into dynamic projections of emotion and generic emotion at that: not personal but rather universal in rising spontaneously from the subconscious.[3]

The apparent opposition between the primitive and the rational mind has since been revealed as untenable.[4] But the wide-spread belief in it was artistically productive, as was the concept that the essential quality of a myth lies in the mythopoeic mode of thought, rather than in its supernatural content which is no longer credible. In particular the distinction of 'mythos' (communication in actions, images, physical signs) versus 'logos' (the analytic use of verbal language), and the direct nature of mythopoeic representation as well as its immediacy, together with the conclusion that generic emotion is the supreme creative force, are precisely the principles that formed the basis of expressionist theatre. At the same time the points on which these anthropological theories can be attacked are also where the expressionists and their followers are vulnerable. Take Cassirer's description of how the 'mythic mind' communicates as an example. Symbols are supposedly used in such a way that they are not susceptible to logical analysis because they become 'images charged with meaning, but the meanings remain implicit, so that the emotions they command seem to be centred on the image rather than on anything it merely conveys; in the image... many meanings may be concentrated, many ideas telescoped and interfused, and incompatible emotions simultaneously expressed'.[5] This undervalues the logically associative way the meaning of a symbol is defined by prior connotations that in turn are conditioned by the specific context in which they are used; and although a symbol (in Ezra Pound's phrase) is a nexus of meanings, containing multiple associations, these are all interrelated. An image cannot embrace an infinite or self-contradictory range of content. In fact this seems so obvious that it diverts our attention from what is being stated to the reasons for making such a statement – to the emphasis on purely subjective comprehension and pre-verbal emotional communication, to the merging of stimulant and response, expression and impression. These were indeed the qualities sought by expressionist theatre; and as we saw the effect of such subjectivity was to make the thematic intention of many expressionist works unclear except on the most general (and therefore platitudinous level), while instead of being a transparent conductor that transfers the artist's vision directly to the spectator's mind, the techniques of presentation became obtrusive. The means overshadowed the meaning, and consequently the style has dated badly because it seems artificial.

Another productive area of cross-fertilisation between anthropology and the avant garde, which is in some ways responsible for the return to the 'roots' of theatre, came from the investigation of the origins of drama in religious ritual by the Cambridge School: Cornford, Gilbert Murray and Jane Harrison. If myth and ritual are now seen as almost synonymous, it is because anthropology has provided the data on almost all the mythical material outside the Greek tradition, and since anthropology is the study of behaviour, it tends to deduce the imaginative content of a myth from its re-enaction in a ceremony. As a result, from the Cambridge School on, the predominant view has been that ritual precedes myth, which becomes constructed as an explanation or justification for performing the rites.[6]

Obviously actual myths were of limited value to the theatre, because their conceptual content was alien to the audience and not 'lived experience' as in their native context, and although there have been various attempts to create new mythologies (notably by Brook and the Living Theatre) the avant garde have usually drawn on archetypes from the Christian tradition. But as a hieratic mode of expression, ritual created symbolic resonances precisely because it was strange and its actual signification obscure. So it is hardly surprising to find not only ritualistic stylisation in gesture and movement, but the overall structure of rites appearing in performance, in particular 'rites of passage' (analysed by Van Gennep as early as 1908). Thus the sources of the mythic movement in modern theatre are to be found in the 'new sciences' – not only Jungian psychology but social anthropology – which exactly mirrors the avant garde connection between 'theatre laboratories' and archaism.

Notes

As there is no bibliography, bibliographical details are given in the notes.

Where adequate translations are available, these have been used for quotation, and in all such cases references are to the English texts, not to the originals. Where references are to foreign language works, the translations in the text are my own.

1. The politics of primitivism

1 Renato Poggioli, *The Theory of the Avant-Garde*, Cambridge, Mass. 1968, p. 224.

2 For example there are striking similarities between Artaud and Grotowski, even though Grotowski knew nothing of the 'theatre of cruelty' at the time when he developed his concept of 'poor theatre', while, as Anthony Swerling has pointed out, 'there is hardly an element, theme, fact or condition of *Godot* and *Fin de Parti* which is not to be found or paralleled in Strindberg's theatre' (*Strindberg's Impact in France 1920–1960*, Cambridge 1971, p. 111). Swerling puts down these detailed correspondences to direct borrowing, but since Beckett has categorically denied any influence, it would seem more accurate to take this overlap as a sign that both writers belong to the same movement, though separated by half a century.

3 Artaud and Vitrac named their theatre after Jarry, Ionesco is a member of the Collège du Pataphysique and includes the figure of Jarry in one play, while Jarry's *Ubu* plays have been performed by Peter Brook, Jean-Louis Barrault, Joe Chaikin and the Becks. 'Theatre Laboratories', following Grotowski's in Poland, have been established in Belgium, Denmark, Japan and America, and the term recurs in variations like Brook's 'Centre for International Theatre Research'. Artaud worked both with Blin, who directed the major productions of Genet and Beckett, and with Barrault, who was responsible for establishing Brook's research centre in Paris; it was specifically his influence that led Brook to branch out from the traditional theatre, and it is hardly coincidental that the movement represented by Ionesco, Beckett, Genet and Adamov developed in the theatre about five years after *The Theatre And Its Double* was republished. Grotowski, Brook and Chaikin have cooperated on projects, as have Brook and Marowitz; Barba was trained by Grotowski and Chaikin by the Becks, while Grotowski has held international seminars and 'research universities'. Such cross-indexing could go on endlessly, linking dada and surrealism (through Breton), expressionism and the absurd (through the influence of Strindberg), etc.

4 See Mircea Eliade, *Myths, Rites, Symbols,* New York 1976, vol. i, p. 88.
5 Peter Brook (following Grotowski) in the Programme to the *Tempest* exercise, Centre for International Theatre Research, 1968.
6 W. B. Yeats, *W. B. Yeats and T. Sturge Moore: Their Correspondence, 1910–1937,* New York 1953, p. 156, Yeats, *Essays and Introductions,* London 1961, p. 333.
7 Yeats, note to *A Vision,* cit. in Richard Ellmann, *The Identity of Yeats,* New York 1964, p. 166, and see *Essays and Introductions,* pp. 224ff.
8 Jean Cocteau, Preface to *Les Mariés de la Tour Eiffel* (1922), in *Modern French Theatre,* pp. 95 and 99, 98, 96–7.
9 As he himself later admitted. See Cocteau, *Oeuvre,* 11 October 1938: 'I was the first to proclaim that a text was only a pretext for creating tableaux... *Antigone, Roméo, Orphée* and *La Machine infernale* were designed for... the pictorial framework, in short, for everything which now seems to me to be irrelevant.'
10 Leopold Jessner, cit. in D. Calandra, *Theatre Quarterly,* vi, no. 2 (1976), p. 52.
11 Charles Marowitz, in *Mobiler Spielraum–Theater der Zukunft,* ed. Karlheinz Braun, Maurice Kagel, Frankfurt 1970, p. 127. Ionesco made exactly the same point in his argument against Tynan's criticisms: see *Notes and Counter Notes,* New York 1964, pp. 101ff.
12 Eugenio Barba, *TDR (The Drama Review/Tulane Drama Review),* 19, no. 4, p. 53, and Richard Schechner, *Theatre Quarterly,* i, no. 2 (1971), p. 62. See also Judith Malina and Julian Beck, *Paradise Now,* New York 1971, p. 7. The dubious premise that ritual is efficacious is derived from anthropologists like Eliade: 'Rituals are symbols acted in reality; they function to make concrete and experiential the mythic values of a society... Hence rituals *act,* they perform, modulate, transform' (*Myths, Rites, Symbols,* vol. i, p. 164).
13 Eliade, *Myths, Rites, Symbols,* vol. i, p. 164.
14 Antonin Artaud, *The Theatre And Its Double* (trans. Mary Richards), New York 1958, pp. 57–8.
15 *Ibid.,* pp. 53–4.
16 See Beryl de Zoete, *Dance and Drama in Bali,* London 1938.
17 Artaud, *The Theatre And Its Double,* p. 54.
18 The codification is in some ways similar to western ballet, which is perhaps why anthropologists have classified Balinese theatre under dance rather than drama.
19 A. F. Ansimov, in *Studies in Siberian Shamanism,* ed. Henry N. Michael, Toronto 1963, pp. 101–2.

2. Dreams, archetypes and the irrational

1 For instance Pierre Quillard's *La Fille au mains coupées,* or Lugné-Poe's production of *Les Aveugles* at the Théâtre d'Art on 19 March and 11 December 1891.
2 Maurice Maeterlinck, *Théâtre II,* Paris 1904, p. 56.
3 Artaud, *The Theatre And Its Double,* pp. 37 and 80–1.

4 Preface to Amiel, *Le Voyageur*, Paris 1925, p. 11. Compare Harold Pinter, Programme Note for *The Room* and *The Dumb Waiter*, Royal Court Theatre 1960: 'The desire for verification is understandable but cannot always be satisfied . . . A character on the stage who can present no convincing argument or information as to his past experience, his present behaviour or his aspirations, nor give a comprehensive account for his motives, is as legitimate and as worthy of attention as one who, alarmingly, can do all these things. The more acute the experience the less articulate the expression.'

5 *L'Ermitage*, 1893, vol. II, p. 120, and *La Plume*, 1892, vol. IV, no. 82, p. 395.

6 Paul Margueritte, *Le Petit Théâtre* (*Théâtre de Marionettes*), Paris 1889, pp. 7–8.

7 *The Autobiographies of W. B. Yeats*, New York 1958, pp. 233–4.

8 According to Lugné-Poe, 'Gémier . . . imposed silence by a wild and startling jig which he danced without a break until he collapsed into the prompter's box with his legs quivering in the air' (*Acrobaties*, Paris 1931, p. 177); while Yeats recorded that 'the audience shake their fists at one another' and that 'the most spirited party' were those who 'shouted for the play' (*Autobiographies*, pp. 233–4).

9 Programme Note for *Ubu roi, Selected Works of Alfred Jarry*, London 1969, p. 80.

10 See George Wellwarth, who analyses Jarry as 'rebelling not only against the outmoded conventions of the current drama . . . but against absolutely everything' (*The Theatre of Protest and Paradox*, New York 1964, p. 3).

11 Guillaume Apollinaire, *Il y a*, Paris 1949, p. 176.

12 *Selected Works of Alfred Jarry*, pp. 192–3.

13 *Ibid.*, pp. 77–9.

14 See *Gestes et opinions du docteur Faustroll, Pataphysicien*, reprinted in *Evergreen Review*, vol. 4, no. 13 (1960), pp. 134ff.

15 Alfred Jarry, *The Ubu Plays*, London 1968, p. 106.

16 *Selected Works of Alfred Jarry*, pp. 83, 86, 72–3.

17 G. de Pawlowski, in *Nouvelles Littéraires*, 3 September 1912.

18 André Therive, In *Revue Critique*, vol. XXIV, no. 197, February 1922.

19 *Six Plays of Strindberg*, New York 1955, pp. 65ff.

20 12 November 1887. *Brev*, vol. VII, p. 218 (also cited in Meyer, *The Plays of Strindberg*, vol. I, New York 1964, pp. 21–2.)

21 See *Strindberg: The Plays* (trans. Michael Meyer), London 1975, vol. II, pp. 82, 85 and 88.

22 *Ibid.*, p. 58.

23 *Ibid.*, pp. 258 and 259.

24 *Ibid.*, p. 94. In *To Damascus* this symbolic pattern is varied. Within the street scene 'frame' there are indeed seven scenes leading to the Golgotha of the asylum, but since another seven follows to repeat the structural pattern in reverse, the Unknown could be said to go through the full fourteen Stations of the Cross.

25 *Strindberg: The Plays*, p. 150.

26 *Ibid.*, p. 621.

27 *Ibid.*, p. 564.

28 *Ibid.*, p. 563.

29 See Martin Heidegger, *Sein und Zeit* (1927). For an analysis of the relation-ship between Heidegger and the German expressionists, see Walter Sokel, *The Writer in Extremis*, Stanford, California 1959, pp. 52ff.

30 *Strindberg: The Plays*, vol. II, pp. 628ff, and letter to Carl Larsson, 2 November 1901, cit. *ibid.*, p. 547.

31 *Myths, Rites, Symbols*, vol. I, pp. 2–3.

32 What is relevant here is not the validity of this idea but its vogue. It was also accepted by Freud who defined myths as 'the distorted vestiges of the wish phantasies of whole nations – the age-long dreams of young human-ity' (*Collected Papers*, vol. IV, London 1925, p. 182), even though it is based on dubious assumptions: that a 'people' has a collective mind, and that a race passes through the same sort of mental development as an indi-vidual, growing from infancy to adulthood.

33 Strindberg, *Open Letters to the Intimate Theatre*, Washington 1966, p. 294.

34 *Ibid.*, pp. 76, 21.

35 Lugné-Poe, *Nouvelles Littéraires*, 3 February 1923.

36 Abbé Louis Bethléhem, *Les Pièces de théâtre*, Paris 1935 (third edition), p. 397.

37 Artaud, cit. in *Paris-Midi*, 5 June 1928.

38 'Das Theater von Morgen: I. Vom Geist des Theaters . . . II. Die Förderung einer geistigen Bühne . . . III. Entstehung', *Die Schaubühne*, 11, 18, 25 May 1916, pp. 453ff, 474ff, 499ff. As a term for describing painting, of course, 'expressionism' antedates Hasenclever's essays, and is usually attributed to Julien-Auguste Hervé in 1901.

39 Hasenclever, *Humanity*, in *An Anthology of German Expressionist Drama*, ed. Walter Sokel, New York 1963, p. 179.

40 *Ibid.*, pp. 196 and 186.

41 *Seven Plays by Ernst Toller*, New York 1936, p. 105.

42 *Humanity*, pp. 199–201.

43 *Ibid.*, p. 172, and Fritz von Unruh, *Ein Geschlecht*, Leipzig 1918, p. 8.

44 *Seven Plays by Ernst Toller*, pp. 57 and 115ff.

45 *Humanity*, p. 189.

46 Reinhard Sorge, *Der Bettler*, Berlin 1912, p. 156.

47 This was one of the first complaints. See Julius Bab's attack on ex-pressionism as 'a kind of *horror vacui*, a vertigo in the face of the void, of this abstract space where only the ghosts of emotive exclamation marks move about'. *Die Weltbühne*, 22 August 1918, p. 176. Significantly the terms in which Kenneth Tynan attacked Ionesco (*The Observer*, 22 June 1958) are precisely the same, which indicates how comparable the absurd and ex-pressionism actually are.

48 Paul Kornfeld, epilogue appended to *Die Verführung*, reprinted in Sokel, ed., *An Anthology of German Expressionist Drama*, p. 7.

49 Kasimir Edschmid, *Über Lyrischen Expressionismus*, Berlin 1917, pp. 59–60.

50 Edschmid, *Über den Expressionismus in der Literatur und die neue Dichtung*, Berlin 1919, p. 57.

51 Erwin Kalser, Programme Note to *Von Morgens bis Mitternacht*, Les-singtheater 1916.

52 See Strindberg, *Open Letters to the Intimate Theatre*, p. 23, and Felix Emmel, *Das ecstatische Theater*, Prien 1924, pp. 35 and 37, where Friedrich Kays-

sler's acting notes are cited. These subjective feelings could hardly be transferred to the audience without loss of intensity. Indeed it is arguable that the more self-preoccupied an actor is, the less he communicates; but the general response does seem to have been qualitatively different from that evoked by the conventional theatre, at least according to critics at the time, even though there are (naturally) no 'transfigured' audiences on record. See Günther Rühle, *Theater für die Republik*, Frankfurt 1967.

53 'Das neue Pathos', in *Das Neue Pathos* I, 1913, vol. I, pp. 1ff.
54 Georg Kaiser, *From Morn to Midnight*, New York 1922, p. 154.
55 *The Theatre And Its Double*, p. 82, and Artaud's lecture on 'Post war theatre in Paris' (1936), in *Cahiers Renaud-Barrault*, vol. 71 (1970), p. 7.
56 Mary Wigman, cit. in André Levinson, 'The modern dance in Germany', *Theatre Arts*, February 1929, p. 151.
57 See *The Arts*, July 1923, p. 45; *Modern Music*, VIII, no. 2 (January–February 1931), p. 20; *Theatre Arts*, December 1931, p. 966 and February 1929, p. 144.
58 Jacob Levy Moreno, *Das Stegreiftheater*, Potsdam 1924, cit. in Paul Pörtner, *Theater Heute*, September 1967, pp. 11 and 12.
59 *Ibid.*
60 See Charles Dullin, *Souvenirs et notes de travail d'un acteur*, Paris 1946, p. 60.
61 See Artaud, *The Theatre And Its Double*, pp. 95–7 and 57.
62 *Ibid.*, p. 108.

3. Antonin Artaud and the Theatre of Cruelty

1 Artaud, 'Post war theatre in Paris', in *Cahiers Renaud-Barrault*, vol. 71 (1970), pp. 6 and 17. It should be stressed again that Artaud's statements about Balinese theatre were based on fundamental misconceptions, since the only performance he saw was out of context, and therefore lacked the cultural and religious significance that would have allowed a proper estimate of its qualities.
2 Artaud, *The Theatre And Its Double*, New York 1958, pp. 82 and 86.
3 *Ibid.*, pp. 15 and 23.
4 See Jacques Derrida, 'Le Théâtre de la Cruauté et la clôture de la représentation', *Critique*, 230 (July 1966), pp. 609ff; Bernard Dort, *Théâtre public*, Paris 1967, p. 245; George Hangher, 'When is a play not a play?', *TDR*, 5, no. 2, pp. 54ff; and Paul Arnold, 'The Artaud experiment', *TDR*, 8, no. 2, pp. 15ff.
5 See André Franck, commentary to *Lettres d'Antonin Artaud à Jean-Louis Barrault*, Paris 1952; Ross Chambers, '"La Magie du réel": Antonin Artaud and the experience of theatre', *Australian Journal of French Studies*, vol. 3, no. 1 (January–April, 1966), pp. 51ff; and Eric Sellin, *The Dramatic Concepts of Antonin Artaud*, Chicago 1968, *passim*.
6 Artaud, *The Theatre And Its Double*, p. 42.
7 Cit. in Sellin, *Dramatic Concepts... Artaud*, p. 101.
8 Romain Weingarten, 'La force d'un peu plus vivre', *Cahiers Renaud-Barrault*, vol. 22, no. 3 (May 1958), p. 149; Paul Arnold, preface to *Lettres ... à Jean-Louis Barrault*, pp. 45–6; and Alain Virmaux, *Antonin Artaud et le théâtre*, Paris 1970, pp. 30, 47–8, 168, 171 and 172. The common currency

of this latter idea can be indicated by the way it is reiterated in V. Novarina, *Antonin Artaud, théoricien du théâtre*, Paris 1964, pp. 8ff, and J. L. Barrault, *Cahiers Renaud-Barrault*, vol. 69 (1969), p. 18.

9 Artaud, *The Theatre And Its Double*, p. 12.
10 Letter to Jean Paulhan, 25 January 1936, *Oeuvres complètes* (hereafter *OC*), Paris 1961–74, vol. v, pp. 272–3.
11 Marginal note to a letter dated 17 June 1936, *Lettres... à Jean-Louis Barrault*, p. 105.
12 *To Have Done With the Judgement of God*, TDR, 9, no. 3, pp. 81–2.
13 '*Marat/Sade* Forum', TDR, 10, no. 4, p. 226. See also Michael Kustow, 'Sur les traces d'Artaud', *Esprit*, May 1965, pp. 958ff; and Charles Marowitz, 'Notes on the Theatre of Cruelty', TDR, 11, no. 2, pp. 161ff.
14 16 October 1934, *OC*, vol. iii, p. 308.
15 'Théâtre Alfred Jarry... saison 1926–7', *OC*, vol. ii, p. 15.
16 *The Theatre And Its Double*, p. 111, and letter to Louis Jouvet, 29 April 1931, *OC*, vol. iii, p. 206.
17 Raymond Rouleau, Letter on Artaud's *Dream Play* production, in A. Swerling, *Strindberg's Impact in France 1920–1960*, Cambridge 1971, p. 175. See also Tania Balachova, in *From Script to Stage*, ed. R. Goodman, San Francisco 1971, p. 150.
18 In the possession of Roger Blin. Act I, sc. iii has been published in *Cahiers Renaud-Barrault*, vol. 51, November 1965.
19 Artaud, *The Theatre And Its Double*, pp. 58 and 55.
20 *OC*, vol. ii, p. 27.
21 'Théâtre Alfred Jarry... saison 1928', *OC*, vol. ii, p. 29.
22 1st Manifesto of the Théâtre Alfred Jarry, *OC*, vol. ii, pp. 12–13.
23 *OC*, vol. ii, p. 13. My italics.
24 See *Artaud Anthology*, ed. Jack Hirschman, San Francisco 1965, pp. 111, 171 and 82; also *The Theatre And Its Double*, pp. 102–3.
25 *The Cenci* (trans. S. Watson Taylor), London 1969, p. 8; and *OC*, vol. v, p. 303.
26. *The Cenci*, pp. 38, 47–8, and *The Theatre And Its Double*, p. 102.
27 *The Theatre And Its Double*, p. 130.
28 'Après *Les Cenci*', *OC*, vol. v, pp. 58–9.
29 See the letter of 16 November 1932, reprinted in *The Theatre And Its Double*, p. 103, and 'Les Cenci', *La Bête Noire*, no. 2 (1 May 1935), reprinted in *The Cenci*, p. 7.
30 *OC*, vol. v, p. 303.
31 'Théâtre Alfred Jarry... 1929', *OC*, vol. ii, p. 34.
32 Ross Chambers '"La Magie du réel": Antonin Artaud...' p. 58, and *Lettres... à Jean-Louis Barrault*, p. 90.
33 *OC*, vol. ii, p. 38.
34 *Revue des Deux Mondes*, 1 November 1893.
35 *Lettres... à Jean-Louis Barrault*, p. 96.
36 *OC*, vol. ii, p. 38.
37 Letter to Roger Vitrac (undated), cit. in Henri Béhar, *Roger Vitrac*, Paris 1966, p. 290. In the same letter Artaud defines his approach as 'the point of view of a stage director... theatre is essentially everything that relates to staging'. For a fuller treatment of Artaud's relationship with the surrealists, see J. H. Matthews, *Theatre of Dada and Surrealism*, Syracuse 1974.

38 *OC*, vol. II, p. 16.

39 'A la grande nuit', *OC*, vol. I, p. 281.

40 Roger Vitrac, *Victor, ou les enfants au pouvoir*, in *Théâtre*, Paris 1946, p. 63.

41 Artaud, letter to *Paris Soir*, 12 December 1928, reprinted in the programme to *Victor*.

42 *Comœdia*, 27 January 1938.

43 Vitrac, *Poison*, in *Théâtre III*, Paris 1964, p. 54.

44 Tristan Tzara (1918), in *The Dada Painters and Poets*, ed. Robert Motherwell, New York 1951, p. 81. For the links between the Parisian dadaists and surrealists see Barrault, *Memories for Tomorrow*, New York 1974, p. 77; and for the ideological implications of the Berlin dadaists see my book on *Erwin Piscator's Political Theatre*, Cambridge 1972, pp. 13ff.

45 Tzara, cit. in René Lacôte, *Tristan Tzara*, Paris 1952, p. 68; and his introduction to Georges Huguet, *L'Aventure Dada*, Paris 1975, p. 7.

46 Maxim Jacob, letter to Robert Maguire, published in Virmaux, *Antonin Artaud et le théâtre*, p. 320.

47 *OC*, vol. II, pp. 78–9.

48 *Six Plays of Strindberg*, New York 1955, p. 293.

49 Artaud, Lecture on 'Post war theatre in Paris', *Cahiers Renaud-Barrault*, vol. 71, p. 17; and pp. 10–11.

50 *OC*, vol. II, pp. 117, 124 and 121.

51 *The Cenci*, pp. 45 and 55.

52 Pierre Jean Jouvé, *Nouvelle Revue Française*, vol. 23, no. 281 (June 1935), p. 94.

53 Interview, 6 June 1935, cit. in Jean-Pierre Faye, 'Artaud vu par Blin', *Lettres Françaises*, 21 January 1965, p. 4; *Comœdia* and *Le Journal*.

54 *Il n'y a plus de firmament*, *OC*, vol. II, p. 92.

55 *OC*, vol. II, pp. 131–4.

56 *OC*, vol. II, pp. 185–6. My italics.

57 André Bellessort, *Le Gaulois*, cit. in Artaud, 'Théâtre Alfred Jarry ... saison 1929', *OC*, vol. II, p. 262.

58 Virmaux comments that 'the two media [film and theatre] appear more like twins than opposites in Artaud's mind', but limits his illustration to a brief consideration of the relationship between words and images in *La Révolte du boucher* and *Le Jet de sang* ('Artaud and film', *TDR*, 11, no. 1, pp. 164–5). Bounoure and Caradec simply state 'it was precisely [Artaud's] long frequentation of the cinema which led to those scenic concepts ...', but do not elaborate ('Antonin Artaud et le cinéma', *K Revue de la Poèsie*, no. 1–2 (June 1948), p. 49. Hayman includes a chapter on 'Film actor and surrealist' in *Artaud and After* (Oxford 1977), but disappointingly it refers to Artaud's film acting hardly at all and makes no mention whatsoever of any possible film influence on his stage work.

59 See Letters to Yvonne Allendy, 21 and 26 March 1929, *OC*, vol. III, pp. 150ff. Bounoure and Caradec even go so far as to claim that 'it was the introduction of talking-films which determined [Artaud] to drive the theatre into a new road' (*K Revue de la Poèsie*, no. 1–2, p. 53).

60 Herbert Jhering, *Drama von Reinhardt bis Brecht*, vol. I, Reinbeck 1967, pp. 374–5. See also Artaud, 'Sorcellerie et cinéma' and the draft of a letter to Steve Passeur, 12 December 1921, *OC*, vol. III, pp. 81 and 240.

61 See *OC*, vol. III, p. 74; 'La Coquille et le clergyman', *Cahiers de Belgique*, no. 8, October 1928; and *OC*, vol. II, p. 34.

62 *OC*, vol. II, p. 91.

63 *OC*, vol. III, p. 47.

64 *Cinémagazine*, 9 September 1927.

65 Valentin Hugo, 'La Passion de Jeanne d'Arc', *Ciné-Miroir*, 11 November 1927. Falconetti played Joan.

66 Artaud, *The Theatre And Its Double*, pp. 116, 79 and 123.

67 Interview for *Cinémonde*, reprinted in *K Revue de la Poèsie*, no. 1–2 (June 1948), p. 59.

68 See Artaud, *The Theatre And Its Double*, pp. 87 and 94.

69 André Breton, *Anthologie de l'humour noir*, Paris 1966, p. 347.

70 C. G. Jung and K. Kerényi, *Essays on a Science of Mythology*, Princeton 1973, p. 73, and Ernst Cassirer, *The Philosophy of Symbolic Forms*, New Haven 1955, p. 38.

71 Letters to André Gide, 10 February 1935, *OC*, vol. V, p. 241, and to Germaine Dulac, 25 September 1927, cit. in Virmaux, 'Artaud and film', *TDR*, 11, no. 1, p. 157.

72 Artaud, *The Theatre And Its Double*, pp. 87 and 94–5.

73 *Ibid.*, p. 76, and Letter to Yvonne Allendy, 25 November 1929, *OC*, vol. III, p. 182.

74 Letter to Louis Jouvet, 1 March 1935, *OC*, vol. V, p. 252.

75 *OC*, vol. II, p. 135.

76 *Les Dix-huit secondes*, *OC*, vol. III, pp. 11ff, *La Coquille et la clergyman*, *OC*, vol. III, pp. 25ff, *Les 32*, *OC*, vol. III, pp. 30ff, *La Révolte du boucher*, *OC*, vol. III, p. 50.

77 Martin Esslin, *Artaud*, London 1976, p. 88; Jean-Louis Barrault, cit. in Jean Louis Brau, *Antonin Artaud*, Paris 1971, p. 97; F. Porché, *La Revue de Paris*, 42, no. 10 (May 1935), p. 480.

78 Charles Dullin, 'Lettre à Roger Blin', *K Revue de la Poèsie*, no. 1–2 (June 1948), p. 23.

79 Porché, *La Revue de Paris*, 42, no. 10, May 1935.

80 *OC*, vol. III, p. 285, and vol. V, p. 51.

81 *OC*, vol. II, pp. 37–8.

82 *The Jet of Blood*, in *Modern French Theatre* (trans. George Wellwarth), New York 1966, pp. 223 and 226.

83 Artaud, in *Cahiers Renaud-Barrault*, no. 71, p. 17.

84 *Ibid.*, p. 124.

85 Letter to Yvonne Allendy, 15 April 1929, *OC*, vol. III, p. 160; note (December 1935) to *Vie et mort de Satan le Feu*, Paris 1953, p. 106. See also 'Après *Les Cenci*', *OC*, vol. V, p. 54.

86 See Artaud, *The Theatre And Its Double*, pp. 27, 30, 35, 81; *OC*, vol. II, pp. 186–7 and vol IV, p. 96.

87 See *OC*, vol. V, pp. 54 and 59.

88 Jean Prudhomme, *Le Matin*; Pierre Audiat, *Paris soir*, 7 May 1935; Jouvé, *NRF* (1 June 1935), pp. 914–15.

89 This viewpoint is put forward by Bernard Dort, *Théâtre public*, p. 245, and Jacques Derrida, 'La Parole soufflé', *Tel Quel*, no. 20 (Winter 1965), p. 64, though both make the mistake of assuming that Artaud's theoretic statements about an 'elemental theatre' represent his actual stage aims.

90 See *OC*, vol. II, pp. 42, 38 and 269–70, and Paul Claudel, cit. in Henri Peyre, *Yale French Studies*, 14, p. 95.

91 *OC*, vol. III, pp. 46–7.

92 *OC*, vol. II, p. 39 and vol. v, pp. 358 and 241. In spite of Artaud's insistence that *Les Cenci* was 'an original play . . . not what is called an adaptation' (*OC*, vol. v, p. 248) this central theme is taken straight from Shelley's version of the story.

93 Max Joly, cit. in Robert Maguire, 'Le "Hors-Théâtre"', unpublished Ph.D. thesis, Paris, p. 347; *OC*, vol. v, pp. 326 and 241.

94 Cit. in Maguire, p. 392; *Lettres . . . à Jean-Louis Barrault*, pp. 69–70.

95 Porché, *La Revue de Paris*, 42, no. 10. See also Joly's comment that the first evening of the Théâtre Alfred Jarry 'troubled and disappointed' Artaud because 'the reaction of the audience was not violent' (Maguire, p. 346).

96 *OC*, vol. II, pp. 185 and 187.

97 *OC*, vol. v, p. 50.

98 Arnold argues this point. See 'The Artaud experiment', *TDR*, 8, no. 2, pp. 15ff. So does Sellin, who argues that interest in a theatrical form cannot constitute an 'influence' without practical experience in it (*The Dramatic Concepts of Antonin Artaud*, Chicago 1968, p. 51).

99 *OC*, vol. III, p. 216.

100 *OC*, vol. III, pp. 22–3. (Cf. p. 41 above.)

101 Oskar Kokoschka, *My Life*, London 1974, pp. 26–7.

102 *Ibid.*, p. 28.

103 *Ibid.*, pp. 22–3 and 28.

104 Kokoschka, cit. in Ludwig Goldscheider, *Kokoschka*, London 1963, p. 14.

105 *Neue Freie Presse*, 5 July 1909.

106 Kokoschka, *My Life*, p. 29.

107 Tzara, in *The Dada Painters and Poets*, ed. Robert Motherwell, New York 1951, pp. 237–8.

4. Primitivism, ritual and ceremony

1 Barrault, *Cahiers Renaud-Barrault*, vols. 22–3.

2 Artaud, 'Post war theatre in Paris' (Mexico 1936), *Cahiers Renaud-Barrault*, vol. 71 (1970), p. 18.

3 Jean-Louis Barrault, *Memories for Tomorrow*, New York 1974, p. 74; *Cahiers Renaud-Barrault*, vol. 69, p. 18; and interview in Bettina Knapp, *Off-Stage Voices*, New York 1975, pp. 41–2.

4 Breton, *Anthologie de l'humour noir*, Paris 1966, p. 347; Barrault, *Theatre Quarterly*, 1973, III, no. 10, p. 5.

5 Barrault, *Memories for Tomorrow*, p. 179.

6 *Ibid.*, p. 297; *Télé-Médecine*, 25 October 1975; *Theatre Quarterly*, III, no. 10, p. 3.

7 *Theatre Quarterly*, III, no. 10.

8 Artaud, *The Theatre And Its Double*, p. 145.

9 Cit. in *Cahiers Renaud-Barrault*, vol. 71, p. 22.

10 *Autour d' une mère*, production script in *Cahiers Renaud-Barrault*, vol. 71, pp. 23ff.

11 Barrault, *Memories for Tomorrow*, p. 67.

12 *Ibid.*, p. 101.

13 *Chavari*, June 1935; Gordon Craig, *Arts*, 3 August 1945; Dorothy Knowles, *French Drama of the Inter-War Years 1918–1939*, London 1967, p. 43.
14 Barrault *Memories for Tomorrow*, p. 57.
15 Barrault, *Cahiers Renaud-Barrault*, vol. 69, p. 18, Dullin, *Souvenirs et notes de travail d'un acteur*, p. 60. It is also significant that Claudel's work, which formed the basis of Barrault's 'total theatre', was originally linked to the symbolist movement, *L'Annonce fait à Marie* and *L'Otage* being first performed by Lugné-Poe (1912 and 1914).
16 Blin, in *Off-Stage Voices*, New York 1975, p. 36.
17 Paul Claudel, 'Modern drama and music' (1930), reprinted in *Total Theatre*, ed. E. T. Kirby, New York 1969, pp. 202 and 206. In Barrault's 1953 production of *Christopher Colombus* some approximation to this ideal was achieved by his acting out the whole play to Milhaud 'square by square, and I would hum to him whatever came into my head at the exact places where I "heard" music. He would measure this to the second, and we would then discuss the spirit, the human content required of this piece of music' (*Memories for Tomorrow*, p. 190).
18 See Barrault, *Memories for Tomorrow*, pp. 248 and 243–4.
19 Claudel, *France-Amérique*, 14 July 1946, and in *Total Theatre*, ed. Kirby, pp. 207–8.
20 Barrault 'On the "total theatre" and *Christopher Colombus*' (1965), in *Total Theatre*, p. 209.
21 Artaud, *The Theatre And Its Double*, New York 1958, p. 125; Barrault *Memories for Tomorrow*, p. 191.
22 'L'Acteur: athlète affectif,' *Cahiers Renaud-Barrault*, vol. 29, p. 89.
23 *Memories for Tomorrow*, pp. 248, 208, 89.
24 Barrault, interview in *France Nouvelle*, 28 October 1970, and Preface to *Rabelais* (trans. Robert Baldick), London 1971, pp. 13 and 16.
25 *Memories for Tomorrow*, p. 328.
26 *Rabelais*, pp. 57–8.
27 Barrault, interview in *Combat*, 30/31 October 1970.
28 *Rabelais*, pp. 118–19; 'An actor's eye view . . .' in *Theatre Quarterly*, i, no. 3 (1971), p. 83.
29 *Travail Théâtral*, no. 18–19 (1975) p. 196.
30 See Peter Brook, *The Empty Space*, Harmondsworth 1972, pp. 97–8 and 151; and interview in *Theatre Quarterly*, iii, no. 10 (1973), p. 16.
31 Brook and Charles Marowitz, *Sunday Times*, 12 January 1964; Marowitz, *TDR*, 11, no. 2, p. 156, LAMDA programme note.
32 *The Empty Space*, p. 55; *TDR*, 11, no. 2, p. 155.
33 Brook, *Plays and Players*, February 1964, p. 21.
34 John Kane (Puck in Brook's *Dream* production), *Sunday Times*, 13 June 1971.
35 Marowitz, 'Lear log,' *TDR*, 8, no. 2, p. 103.
36 Brook, *Theater Heute*, no. 2 (1965) p. 9.
37 David Turner, programme note, National Theatre, March 1968; and Director's Notes, National Theatre archives.
38 Marowitz, *TDR*, 11, no. 2, p. 156.
39 Colin Blakely (Creon), *TDR*, 13, no. 3, p. 121.
40 Brook, interview in *TDR* 17, no. 3 (1973), p. 47.

41 *Ibid.*, p. 50.
42 See Brook, *The Empty Space*, Harmondsworth 1972, p. 106.
43 Marowitz, *Plays and Players*, February 1964, pp. 20–2; and *TDR*, 11, no. 2, p. 157.
44 Blakely, *TDR*, 13, no. 2, pp. 120–1.
45 Ted Hughes, interview in *The Times Literary Supplement*, 1 October 1971.
46 *Ibid.*; and A. C. H. Smith, *Orghast at Persepolis*, London 1972, pp. 43–4.
47 See Ilia Zdanévitch, *Ledentu le Phare, poème dramatique en Zaoum*, editions du 41, 1922; Tristan Tzara, *Oeuvres complètes*, vol. I (1912–1924), Paris 1975, p. 77; *Orghast*, cit. in A. C. H. Smith, *Orghast at Persepolis*, p. 50.
48 Claude Lévi-Strauss, *The Raw and the Cooked*, New York 1969, vol. I, p. 12.
49 A. C. H. Smith, *Orghast at Persepolis*, p. 119; Hughes, cit. on p. 97 and Geoffrey Reeves, cit. on p. 181.
50 Bernard Frechtman, Showbill for *The Blacks*, New York 1961.
51 See Norman Mailer, *The Village Voice*, 18 May 1961, p. 14; Lucien Goldmann, *Cahiers Renaud-Barrault*, vol. 57 (1966), pp. 90ff.
52 Jean Genet, *The Balcony* (revised edition), New York 1966, pp. 57, 73–5 and 7; and *The Blacks*, New York 1960, pp. 8, 10.
53 *The Blacks*, pp. 84, 109–10, 99, 38–9.
54 Roger Blin, in *Off-Stage Voices*, New York 1975, p. 27.
55 *The Maids, Two Plays by Jean Genet*, New York 1962, pp. 93 and 86; *The Blacks*, pp. 105 and 20.
56 *The Maids*, p. 86; *The Balcony*, pp. 15 and 19.
57 *The Balcony*, p. 82; *The Maids*, p. 63; *The Blacks*, pp. 24, 106, 107.
58 *Off-Stage Voices*, p. 22, and Genet, *Letters to Roger Blin*, New York 1969, p. 66.
59 Artaud, *The Theatre And Its Double*, p. 103.
60 *The Balcony*, pp. 87–8; Genet, *Miracle de la rose*, Paris 1946, p. 215.
61 Strindberg, *Coram Populo!* (trans. David Scanlan), *TDR*, 6, no. 2, pp. 128ff.
62 Genet, *The Screens*, New York 1962, pp. 75, 96, 198 and 156.
63 *Letters to Roger Blin*, p. 21, and *The Screens*, p. 190.
64 *Letters to Roger Blin*, p. 14, and *Off-Stage Voices*, pp. 38–9.
65 Genet, 1954 preface to *The Maids*, in *TDR*, 7, no. 3, p. 40; Blin in *Off-Stage Voices*, pp. 28–9.
66 *Letters to Roger Blin*, pp. 27, 61, 29 and 13.
67 *TDR*, 7, no. 3, pp. 37–9.
68 See Rose Zimbardo, *Modern Drama*, no. 8 (1965), p. 247; Oreste Pucciani, *TDR*, 7, no. 3, p. 44; Robert Kanters, in *The Theatre of Jean Genet*, ed. Richard Coe, New York 1970, p. 120.
69 *The Balcony*, p. 26.
70 See Frantz Fanon, *The Wretched of the Earth: Black Skins, White Masks* (trans. Charles Markman), New York 1967, p. 31.
71 *The Balcony*, p. 10; *Letters to Roger Blin*, p. 51; *The Screens*, pp. 179 and 190.
72 *The Maids*, pp. 41, 43, 42, 62 and 84.
73 *The Screens*, p. 86.
74 *The Blacks*, p. 12.
75 Blin, in *Off-Stage Voices*, pp. 25–6.
76 1954 preface to *The Maids*, in *TDR*, 7, no. 3, p. 39.

5. Secular religions, communion, myths

1 Paul Gsell, *Gémier, Le Théâtre*, Paris 1925, p. 283.
2 Jerzy Grotowski, *TDR*, 17, no. 2, p. 133.
3 Grotowski, *Towards a Poor Theatre*, New York 1968, p. 19.
4 *Ibid.*, pp. 41, 63; and *TDR*, 14, no. 1, p. 176.
5 Eugenio Barba, in *Towards a Poor Theatre*, p. 84.
6 Grotowski, *Theatre Quarterly*, III, no. 10, p. 24; *Towards a Poor Theatre*, p. 46.
7 *Towards a Poor Theatre*, pp. 131 and 16.
8 See Serge Ouaknine, *Les Voies de la création théâtrale*, Paris 1970, vol. I, p. 115, and Raymonde Temkine, *Grotowski*, New York 1972, p. 60.
9 Eugenio Barba, *TDR*, 9, no. 3, p. 155.
10 *Towards a Poor Theatre*, pp. 119–20; Artaud, *The Theatre And Its Double*, New York 1958, p. 58. Another point of similarity is in Grotowski's use of 'resonators' in different parts of the body, channelling the voice through diaphragm, stomach, back, shoulders and the top of the skull to develop the actor's whole body into an expressive instrument – a concept outlined by Artaud in 'An affective athleticism': 'The important thing is to become aware of the localisation of emotive thought. One means of recognition is effort or tension; and the same points that support physical effort are those which also support the emanation of emotive thought: they serve as a springboard for the emanation of a feeling' (*The Theatre And Its Double*, p. 138).
11 See Emile Copfermann and Michael Kustow, cit. in Temkine, *Grotowski*, pp. 21 and 143.
12 Grotowski, *TDR*, 13, no. 1, pp. 33 and 36.
13 Ludwig Flaszen, in *Towards a Poor Theatre*, p. 75.
14 Barba, Programme Notes to *Dr Faustus*, in *Towards a Poor Theatre*, pp. 79, 86.
15 Grotowski, *Towards a Poor Theatre*, p. 34.
16 Barba, *TDR*, 9, no. 3, p. 154.
17 Flaszen, Programme Note to *Akropolis*, cit. in Temkine, *Grotowski*, p. 65.
18 Grotowski, *Towards a Poor Theatre*, p. 37, and *TDR*, 13, no. 1, p. 44.
19 Barba, *TDR*, 9, no. 3, p. 163; Grotowski, cit. *ibid.*, p. 159.
20 Serge Ouaknine, *The Constant Prince*, text and extended stage directions, *Theater Heute*, no. 8 (1971), pp. 34ff. (The lines are Fernando's speech to Muley in scene 3 of the original.) For a full eyewitness description of the rehearsal process and performance, see Ouaknine, *Les Voies de la création théâtrale*, vol. I.
21 Programme Note, in *Towards a Poor Theatre*, p. 97.
22 Grotowski, *Towards a Poor Theatre*, p. 257.
23 *Ibid.*, p. 22.
24 See Josef Kelera, cit. in *Towards a Poor Theatre*, p. 109; Temkine, *Grotowski*, pp. 27, 31 and 136; Ouaknine, *Theater Heute*, no. 8 (1971), p. 33.
25 Grotowski, *TDR*, 14, no. 1, p. 177.
26 Grotowski, Conference in New York, 12 December 1970, cit. in *TDR*, 17, no. 2, p. 120; and *TDR*, 14, no. 1, p. 177.

27 Grotowski, Press conference in New York, 15 October 1973, cit. in *TDR*, 19, no. 4, p. 61.

28 See Grotowski, *Towards a Poor Theatre*, p. 40.

29 Grotowski, Press conference in New York, 15 October 1973.

30 See Richard Mennen, *TDR*, 19, no. 4, p. 66.

31 Descriptions have been published by Mennen, *ibid.*, p. 68, and Dan Ronen, *TDR*, 22, no. 4, p. 75. Compare Arnold Van Gennep, *The Rites of Passage*, Chicago 1960, pp. 89ff. and Jane Harrison, *Prolegomena to the Study of Greek Religion*, Cambridge 1903, pp. 151ff.

32 Grotowski, *TDR*, 17, no. 2, pp. 133–4, and *TDR*, 22, no. 4, p. 68.

33 See Frédéric Baal, *TDR*, 16, no. 4, p. 102.

34 See Grotowski, *TDR*, 14, no. 1, pp. 173 and 177.

35 See *TDR*, 14, no. 1, p. 54; Barba, p. 56.

36 An outline of the scenario for *Kaspariana* has been published in *TDR*, 13, no. 1, pp. 46ff.

37 Barba, *TDR*, 9, no. 3, p. 164, and 19, no. 4, p. 57.

38 See Richard Schechner *TDR*, 5, no. 4, pp. 124ff.

39 These were three of the subjects that Schechner identified as areas which would be particularly fruitful for the main thrust of avant garde theatre. Others were the analysis of 'performance' in everyday activities (Goffman) and aspects of psychotherapy that emphasise person-to-person interaction and body awareness – both of which relate to his later work. See *TDR*, 17, no. 4, pp. 5ff. This is also reflected in his *Ritual, Play and Performance* (New York, 1976): a collection of essays by anthropologists and sociologists (with the avant garde represented only by Grotowski and himself!), that covers five areas listed as 'Ethology', 'Play', 'Ritual and performance in everyday life', 'Shamanism, trance, meditation' and 'Rites, ceremonies, performances'.

40 See Schechner, *Theatre Quarterly*, 1, no. 20 (1971), pp. 51ff, and *Environmental Theatre*, New York 1973, pp. 176, 55, 101, 82 and 114.

41 See, *The Rites of Passage*, p. 185, and *Environmental Theatre*, p. 253.

42 See *Environmental Theatre*, pp. 44 and 206. See also Julian Beck's comment on the standard of performance in the Living Theatre, p. 199 below.

43 All quotations from the script are taken from The Performance Group, *Dionysus in 69*, New York 1970, unpaginated.

44 *Environmental Theatre*, p. 83.

45 For a more detailed discussion of Peter Stein's work, see my book on *Modern German Drama, A Study in Form*, Cambridge 1979, pp. 145ff.

46 See *Environmental Theatre*, pp. 223, 219, 191, 122. More recently Schechner has developed his 'subjective' theatre in a way that concentrates solely on 'the psychology of perception', producing plays like David Gaard's *The Marilyn Project* in which the action is 'consciously made multivocal and ambivalent', with two sets of actors playing the same scenes simultaneously on a split stage – an extension of the 'mirror exercise' that both he and Peter Brook developed independently to 'raise the consciousness' of the performer and to act as a paradigm of the feed-back between performer and spectator. In Schechner's view this corresponds to the structuralism of Lévi-Strauss.

47 *TDR*, 17, no. 4, p. 4, and *Environmental Theatre*, p. 236.

48 Artaud's theory of 'cruelty' was reinterpreted to correspond to their own preoccupations: 'Artaud believed that if we could only be made to feel, really feel anything, then we might find all this suffering intolerable, the pain too great to bear, we might put an end to it, and then being able to feel we might truly feel the joy, the joy of everything else, of loving, of creating, of being at peace, and of being ourselves' (Julian Beck, introduction to Kenneth H. Brown, *The Brig*, New York 1965). Beck in Aldo Rostagno, ed., *We, The Living Theatre*, New York 1970, p. 81.

49 Judith Malina and Julian Beck, *Paradise Now*, New York 1971, pp. 16 and 77.

50 See *We, The Living Theatre*, pp. 9 and 23–4, *Paradise Now*, p. 20, 'Notes to *Paradise Now*', *TDR*, 13, no. 3, pp. 103 and 97.

51 Beck, cit. in William Glover, *Theatre Arts*, December 1961, and *TDR*, 13, no. 3, pp. 25 and 42.

52 *Paradise Now*, pp. 79–80 and 27. Other examples were the so-called 'revolutionary slogans' in *Mysteries*, 'Abolish money, Abolish police, Change the world, Fuck for peace . . .', *We, the Living Theatre*, p. 80.

53 *The Brig*, pp. 45–6.

54 *Paradise Now*, p. 75.

55 Beck, cit. in Pierre Biner, *The Living Theatre*, New York 1972, p. 89.

56 *Paradise Now*, pp. 3 and 75–6.

57 Cit. in Biner, *The Living Theatre*, p. 48, and cit. in Jan Kott, *TDR*, 14, no. 1, p. 23. However, their production of *The Maids* was an exception, completely conventional in staging.

58 'Notes to *Paradise Now*,' *TDR*, 13, no. 3, p. 91.

59 *Paradise Now*, p. 105, and Beck, cit. in Biner, *The Living Theatre*, p. 93. See also *TDR*, 13, no. 3, p. 43, where Beck proposes the systematic use of psychedelic drugs to 'enable one to begin to associate differently in the head, remember differently, learn time differently'.

60 Beck, introduction to *The Brig*, p. 31.

61 *TDR*, 13, no. 3, p. 41.

62 *Paradise Now*, p. 15.

63 See Malina, cit. in Biner, *The Living Theatre*, p. 181; Van Gennep, *Rites of Passage*, p. 170.

64 *Paradise Now*, pp. 27, 61, 65, 95–6, 125–7 and 140.

65 Eliade (citing material collected by Negelein, Frazer and Frobenius) *Myths, Rites, Symbols*, vol. I, pp. 234ff, 242–3 and 240.

66 *Paradise Now*, pp. 63–4 and 111.

67 *Ibid.*, p. 8, and Malina, *TDR*, 13, no. 3, pp. 30–1. (In the opening scene of *Frankenstein* the actors seriously attempted to make one of their number levitate, though in fact the whole play was predicated on the failure of this mystical attempt to defy physical laws.)

68 *Paradise Now*, pp. 23, 44, 125.

69 Beck and Malina, interview in Biner, *The Living Theatre*, pp. 92–4, and *TDR*, 13, no. 3, p. 42.

70 For a discussion of early agitprop drama, see my book on *Erwin Piscator's Political Theatre*, pp. 23ff.

71 Scripts of these productions and comments by Beck and Malina have been published in *TDR*, 19, no. 3, pp. 80ff and 94ff.

6. Mythic dimensions and modern classics

1 See Martin Esslin, *The Theatre of the Absurd*, Harmondsworth 1968, pp. 153ff, George Wellwarth, *The Theatre of Protest and Paradox*, New York 1967, pp. 54ff.
2 Eugène Ionesco, in *Cahiers Renaud-Barrault*, vol. 69 (1969), pp. 27 and 22–3.
3 Ionesco, *Notes and Counter Notes*, New York 1964, p. 199. See also Ionesco, *Present Past Past Present; A Personal Memoir*, New York 1971, pp. 77ff.
4 *The Chairs*, in Ionesco, *Plays 1*, London 1963, pp. 45 and 84.
5 Ionesco, cit. in Esslin, *The Theatre of the Absurd*, p. 149; *Notes and Counter Notes*, pp. 192 and 215; *Present Past Past Present*, pp. 157, 150–1 and 154.
6 Ionesco, *Notes and Counter Notes*, pp. 164–5. Compare Strindberg's very similar psychological state: 'It seems as if I'm walking in my sleep, as if fiction and life were jumbled . . . My life has become a shadowy existence. I imagine myself no longer on earth but floating weightlessly in an atmosphere, not of air but of darkness. Whenever light falls on this darkness, I crumple, shattered' (letter to Axel Lunegård, cit. in Martin Lamm, *August Strindberg*, New York 1971, p. 207).
7 *Notes and Counter Notes*, pp. 257 and 131; *Present Past Past Present*, pp. 54–5.
8 *Victims of Duty*, in Ionesco, *Plays II*, London 1958, pp. 119 and 157–8.
9 Ionesco, 'ein Paar Bemerkungen zur Inszenierung', *Theater Heute*, November 1968, pp. 8–9.
10 *Ibid.*, see also *Notes and Counter Notes*, p. 264.
11 *Notes and Counter Notes*, pp. 219–20, 92, 16, and 229.
12 *Improvisation*, in Ionesco, *Plays III*, London 1960, p. 150.
13 *Notes and Counter Notes*, pp. 159, 187.
14 Samuel Beckett, *Waiting for Godot*, New York 1954, p. 27B. See Jean Anouilh, *Arts*, 27 January 1953, and Harold Hobson, *The Sunday Times*, 7 August 1955 (reprinted in *Casebook on Waiting for Godot*, ed. Ruby Cohn, New York 1967, pp. 12 and 27).
15 Holograph, printed in programme to Toronto performance, Hart House Theatre 1971.
16 *Waiting for Godot*, p. 57B.
17 Alternatively, perhaps the fact that Blin was obviously prepared to produce unpopular work was what attracted Beckett (there was almost nobody in the audience), although equally his attendance argues a strong interest in Strindberg – and a detailed analysis of the correspondences between Beckett's and Strindberg's plays can be found in Anthony Swerling, *Strindberg's Influence in France 1920–1960*, pp. 111ff, though Swerling grossly overstates his case in claiming that 'there is hardly an element, theme, fact or condition of *Godot* and *Fin de Partie* which is not to be found or paralleled in Strindberg's theatre', and consequently that Beckett's work lacks originality.
18 Beckett, cit. in Jessica Tandy, interview in *Modern Drama*, 18, no. 1, p. 50.

19 *Waiting for Godot*, pp. 14B, 22, 8 and 13B; see Jack MacGowran, interview in *Theatre Quarterly*, III, no. 2, p. 17; James Joyce, *Finnegan's Wake*, New York 1947, p. 256.

20 Beckett, *Endgame*, New York 1958, pp. 8, 11, 62–3, 79, 78.

21 Beckett, cit. in *Materialen zu Becketts 'Endspiel'*, Frankfurt 1968, p. 83.

22 *Ibid.*, pp. 38, 49, 65, 90–1.

23 Fernando Arrabal, interview in Swerling, *Strindberg's influence in France*, p. 167; Arthur Adamov, *August Strindberg*, Paris 1955, p. 8.

24 Arthur Adamov, production note, *Théâtre I*, Paris 1953, p. 102.

25 Adamov, *L'Aveu*, Paris 1946, pp. 106, 45 and 110.

26 *Ibid.*, p. 58.

27 Adamov, *Théâtre II*, Paris 1955, p. 12.

28 *Ibid.*, p. 237. See John McCann, *The Theater of Arthur Adamov*, Chapel Hill, North Carolina 1975, p. 38, and Esslin, *The Theatre of the Absurd*, p. 104.

29 Adamov, *Théâtre II*, p. 14.

30 Arrabal, in *Off-Stage Voices*, pp. 85 and 93.

31 Arrabal, 'Auto-Interview' in *TDR*, 13, no. 1, pp. 74–5, and 'Dialogue with Arrabal', *Evergreen Review*, no. 15 (November/December 1960), p. 71.

32 *The Architect and the Emperor of Assyria*, in *Arrabal: Plays III*, London 1970, pp. 24, 88, 92.

33 *Ibid*, see pp. 71 and 30.

34 Jacques Lemarchand, *Figaro Littéraire*, see *Off-Stage Voices*, p. 87; *The Grand Ceremonial*, in *Arrabal: Plays III*, pp. 104–5.

35 Peter Weiss, *Die Ermittlung*, Frankfurt 1965, p. 89. For a fuller analysis of documentary drama and Weiss' contribution to the genre, see my book *Modern German Drama: A Study in Form*, chapter VII.

36 Erwin Piscator, *Blätter der Freien Volksbühne*, 1965, no. 6.

37 Weiss, *Rapport I*, Frankfurt 1971, p. 142.

38 Weiss, *Discourse on Vietnam*, London 1970, pp. 70 and 172.

39 See Ruby Cohn, *Modern Shakespearean Offshoots*, Princeton, New Jersey 1976, p. 7.

40 Edward Bond, interview in *Gambit*, no. 17, p. 24. See also Shaw's preface to *Caesar and Cleopatra*: 'Better than Shakespear?' or Brecht's rationale for adapting Marlowe: 'We wanted a production that would break with the Shakespeare tradition of the German theatre – that plaster-monument style so dear to the bourgeoisie' (*Gesamte Werke*, XVII, p. 951).

41 Marowitz, *Theatre Quarterly*, I, no. 3 (1971), pp. 48–9; Schechner, *Makbeth*, New York 1978, pp. xvi, xiv.

42 Marowitz, *Theatre Quarterly*, I, no. 3 (1971), p. 49, *A Macbeth*, London 1971, p. 15, and *TDR*, 11, no. 2, p. 156.

43 Schechner, Paul Epstein, Brooks McNamara, *Makbeth*, pp. vii, xii, 25 and xxii.

44 Ionesco, *Macbett*, London 1973, pp. 91, 102, 21–2 and 23, 103ff.

45 Ionesco, interview, *New York Times*, 18 January 1972.

46 Heiner Müller, *Theater der Zeit*, no. 8 (1975), pp. 58 and 59; interview in *Theater Heute*, Sonderheft 1975, p. 120.

47 Müller, *Macbeth*, in *Theater Heute*, June 1972, pp. 40, 45, 46 and 47.

48 Ann Jellicoe, Preface, *The Sport of My Mad Mother*, London 1964, p. 5.

49 *The Sport of My Mad Mother*, pp. 21–2.

50 Jellicoe, *Some Unconscious Influences in the Theatre,* Cambridge 1967, pp. 13 and 17–18; p. 21.
51 *The Sport of My Mad Mother,* pp. 86–7, and Jellicoe, Programme Notes, Royal Court Theatre 1958.
52 Lindsay Kemp, interview with the author, Toronto 1978.
53 *Ibid.*
54 Peter Shaffer, Author's Notes to *The Royal Hunt of the Sun,* London 1964, p. viii.
55 Shaffer, *The Royal Hunt of the Sun,* p. 79.
56 Shaffer, *Equus and Shrivings,* New York 1975, p. 9. Compare with pp. 161–2 above.
57 Shaffer, interview in *The Sunday Times,* 29 July 1973.
58 *Ibid.*

7. The avant garde today

1 John Juliani, cit. in *Theatre Quarterly,* v, no. 20 (1975), p. 160.
2 The one and only performance of *The Sky is Falling* was documented with excerpts from the scenario by Schechner in *Theatre Quarterly,* I, no. 2, pp. 59ff.
3 A descriptive commentary on the performance by its author was published in *TDR,* 14, no. 4, pp. 53ff.
4 Robert Wilson, interview in *TDR,* 20, no. 1, p. 109.
5 Wilson, interview in *The New York Times,* 16 March 1975.
6 Excerpts from the text for *KA MOUNTAIN AND GUARDenia Terrace* were printed as part of the 1972 Shiraz festival programme.
7 Jean Vauthier and Jorge Lavelli, interviews in *Off-Stage Voices,* pp. 127 and 58–9.
8 Meredith Monk, interview in *Chicago Reader,* 13 May 1977.
9 Programme Note, *Tour 4: Lounge,* Alfred University (New York), 19 November 1969.
10 Some of the information on the productions of *Quarry* and *Vessel* comes from Sally Banes, 'The art of Meredith Monk', *Performing Arts Journal,* Spring/Summer 1978, where these lines are quoted, p. 8.
11 Monk, interview in *TDR,* 20, no. 3, pp. 53 and 56.
12 Ann Halprin, cit. in *Dance Magazine,* October 1965, p. 74.
13 Halprin, cit. in *TDR,* 17, no. 3, pp. 65, 76 and 79.
14 Brook, interview in *TDR,* 17, no. 3, pp. 48–9.

Appendix

1 Greek mythology had been analysed allegorically by Thales (as the personification of cosmic forces) and Zeno (as the embodiment of moral principles), translated as hyperbolic distortions of prehistorical figures (Euhemerus), and dismissed as unauthenticated fable (Thucydides). Such interpretations were to some extent built into the way writers like Sophocles or Euripides had recorded the myths, and determined the way they were analysed from the Renaissance to the nineteenth century.

2 Roland Barthes, *Mythologies*, London 1972. See pp. 109–31. Barthes' distinction between discursive and symbolic language on the basis of a one-to-one ratio between object and sign versus a multiple sign (the myth) seems to break down at the point where everyday language is used to refer to concepts rather than objects, or for formal rhetorical or poetic purposes. But it does seem generally true that myth in his sense is not concerned with the utilitarian manipulation of ideas.

3 Ernst Cassirer, *The Philosophy of Symbolic Forms*, pp. 69 and 38. See also Cassirer, *Language and Myth*, New York 1946, p. 33.

4 See Claude Lévi-Strauss, *The Savage Mind*, Chicago 1966, where evidence is not only presented 'to dispose of those theories making use of the concepts of "archetypes" or a "collective unconscious"' to explain myths (p. 65), but primitive habits of thought are demonstrated to be as logical as modern science, though based on a different framework of assumptions, using equally complex correlations and subtle discriminations based on close observation of empirical data.

5 Susanne Langer, *The Philosophy of Ernst Cassirer*, Evanston 1949, pp. 388 and 395.

6 This has subsequently been questioned, but as Lévi-Strauss has put it: 'Regardless of whether the myth or the ritual is the original, they replicate each other; the myth exists on the conceptual level and the ritual on the level of action' (*Structural Anthropology*, New York 1963, p. 232).

Index

Note: capital letters indicate artistic movements or traditions

Abdy, Iya, 91, 95
Abelman, Paul, 131
Adamov, Arthur, 10, 60, **215–17**, 218, 222
Adding Machine, the (Rice, Elmer), 189
Aeschylus, 121, 139, 141, 142
Afore Night Come (Rudkin, David), 231
Akropolis (Wyspianski, Stanislaw), 110, 160, 163–5, 167–8
All God's Chillun Got Wings (O'Neill, Eugene), 101
Amédée (*Amédée, or How to Get Rid of It –* Ionesco, Eugène), 208
Amiel, Denys, 20
Ancestors (Mickiewicz, A.), 160, 164
Animal Ritual (Halprin, Ann), 251
Anouilh, Jean, 5, 6
Antheil, George, 1
Antigone (Anouilh, Jean), 6
Antigone (Brecht, Bertolt), 187, 190–2, 194–5
Apocalypsis cum Figuris (Polish Laboratory Theatre), 162, 163, 166–7, 168, 175–6
Apollinaire, Guillaume, 25
Appia, Adolphe, 102, 118
Aragon, Louis, 72, 75, 244
Architect and the Emperor of Assyria, the (*Architecte et l'Empereur D'Assyrie, l' –* Arrabal, Fernando), 220–1
Arden, John, 131
Aristotle, 253
Arp, Hans, 180
Arrabal, Fernando, 215, 217, **218–22**, 242
Ars Longa Vita Brevis (Arden, John), 131
Artaud, Antonin, 3, 8, 10, 12, 14, 15, 16, 19, 25, 29, 33, 38, 45, 50, 57, **58–102**, 103–6, 108, 109–10, 111, 112, 113, 114, 117–18, 124, 128–9, 131, 132, 135, 144, 150, 151, 153–4, 159, 163, 164, 175, 178, 187, 200, 203, 215, 222, 231, 233, 243, 246, 254
As I Lay Dying (*Autour d'une mère –* Faulkner/Barrault), 111, 113, 114–18, 122, 124, 127

As You Like It (Shakespeare, William), 185
Athanasiou, Genica, 79, 114
Automobile Graveyard, the (*Cimetière des voitures, le, –* Arrabal, Fernando), 218, 220
Avant-Garde, l', 2, 9

Baal, Georges, 178
Bacchae, the (Euripides), 181
Bakunin, Mikhail Aleksandrovich, 1–2, 9, 196
Balcony, the (*Balcon, le –* Genet, Jean), 144–6, 148–9, 151, 153, 154, 155
Bald Primadonna, the (*Cantatrice chauve, la –* Ionesco, Eugène), 202–4, 206
BALI, 3, 10, **12–16**, 58, 64, 101, 104, 182
Balthus (Rola, Balthazar K. de), 114
Barba, Eugenio, 128, 163, **178–80**, 186
Barrault, Jean-Louis, 20, 57, 61, 75, 91, 110, **111–19**, 121, **122–8**, 129, 137, 144, 159, 177, 194, 197, **241**
Barthes, Roland, 256
Battle of Trafalgar, the (*Coup de Trafalgar, le –* Vitrac, Roger), 82, 84, 90, 96
Baudelaire, Charles, 203
BAUHAUS, THE, 102
Beardsley, Aubrey, 236
Becher, Johannes Robert, 199
Beck, Julian, 62, 64, 125, 187, 194, 197–8
Beckett, Samuel, 20, 113, 180, **209–14**, 215, 241
Before Sunrise (*Vor Sonnenaufgang –* Hauptmann, Gerhart), 77
Beggar, the (*Der Bettler –* Sorge, Reinhard), 43, 45
Béjart, Maurice, 4
Bentley, Eric, 33
Berg, Alban, 39
Bernard, Jean-Jacques, 20
Bernauer, Rudolph, 33
Blacks, the (*Nègres, les –* Genet, Jean), 98, 146–8, 149, 151–2, 155, 157, 194
Blin, Roger, 64, 68, 95, 114, 125, 147, 153–4, 157, 211, 215
Bliss Apocalypse (Floating Lotus Co.), 243

277